AGGERS' ASHES

JONATHAN AGNEW

AGGERS' ASHES

The Inside Story of England's 2011 Ashes Triumph

blue door

First published in Great Britain in 2011 by
Blue Door
An imprint of HarperCollinsPublishers
77-85 Fulham Palace Road,
Hammersmith, London W6 8JB

1

A catalogue record for this book is available from the British Library

ISBN 978-0-00-734312-6

Typset in Adobe Garamond Pro by PDQ Digital Media Solutions Limited,
Bungay, Suffolk

Book design by Marcus Nichols

Printed and bound in Great Britain by Clays Ltd, St Ives plc

Picture Credits
The Publishers acknowledge the trademarks of Cricket Australia in these pages
and where used note that they have been reproduced with the approval of Cricket
Australia. All pictures are courtesy of Philip Brown with the exception of the
following referenced by page number and picture number from left to right, top
to bottom: page 5 picture no 2 AP Photo/Rob Griffith; page 7 picture no 2 Getty
Images; page 8 pictures nos 3 and 4 BBC/Adam Mountford; page 9 picture 2
Gareth Copley/PA Wire; page 10 picture no 3 AP Photo/Rob Griffith; page 19
picture no 3 Gareth Copley/PA Wire; page 23 picture no 2 Getty Images; page 24
picture no 3 Getty Images

Find and more about Harper Collins and the environment at
www.harpercollins.co.uk/green

This book is dedicated to England's Ashes heroes
past and present

ALSO BY JONATHAN AGNEW

Thanks, Johnners (Blue Door, 2009)

BY BEN DIRS AND TOM FORDYCE

We Could Be Heroes (Macmillan, 2009)
Karma Chameleons (Macmillan, 2010)

CONTENTS

FOREWORD

by Jim Maxwell

Two performances stood out as England completed a comprehensive Ashes victory just before high noon on Friday, 7 January 2011 at the Sydney Cricket Ground.

Throughout the series the Barmy Army chorused every moment of play. They should have been given free entry because they were so entertaining, rapturously encouraging the dreaded Poms, and alternately mocking the Aussies. Mitchell Johnson was a favourite target.

Johnson found his mojo in Perth with some surprising swing bowling, but like his accomplices, Hilfenhaus and whoever passed as a spinner, the bowling was mediocre, chasing the game that Australia's batsmen had lost.

While England celebrated with a traditional victory lap and acknowledgement of their supporters, the BBC correspondent Jonathan Agnew conducted the post-match interviews as he had done so thoroughly in 2005 and 2009 when England regained the Ashes at The Oval. Formalities completed Aggers broke off into a weird gyration, twisting like a Hills Hoist clothes line (for our English readers, a Hills Hoist is a height-adjustable rotary clothes line invented just after the War in Adelaide), or a giraffe on speed, he thus began a nervous performance of the Sprinkler Dance. Having watched England cop Down-Under hidings for twenty years and endured Australian co-commentator Kerry O'Keeffe's jibes about the Poms going for silver and not for gold, Aggers cut loose.

Like the Barmy Army he had earned the right to celebrate, because Andrew Strauss's team played better cricket than any England team in Australia for at least 56 if not 78 years.

Alastair Cook's expedition was the most significant *tour de force* by a Cook since Captain James's visit in 1770, and his polishing skills made the Kookaburra laugh at Australia's batsmen, helping Jimmy Anderson to swing through the top order.

Andrew Strauss's composure and maturity formed a strong partnership alongside Andy Flower, whose hard-nosed managerial skills rivalled Sir Alex Ferguson's at Old Trafford. When will Andrew and Andy get their gongs?

Cook's remorselessly efficient batting was complemented by Jonathan Trott's hungry accumulation. Aussies expected them to be nicking catches to slip or getting whacked on the pads in front. Instead, they settled in for a banquet.

In the *TMS* box 'Sir' Geoffrey Boycott was in full flight at Australia's batting ineptitude, with just a hint of *schadenfreude* when wickets were tumbling. There was a moment when England were on top and, as you can on radio, I digressed to Australia's rugby league connection with Yorkshire. I'm ready to continue that reminiscence in 2013 if Geoffrey appears to be gloating again!

Michael Vaughan showed his versatility by tweeting as frequently as Shane Warne, extolling England's virtues; Vic Marks sagely scrutinised the contest and wondered where James Hildreth might fit in; while scorer Andrew Samson answered every ridiculous question from the ABC commentator as calmly and accurately as a quiz mastermind.

Shuttling between the *TMS* and the ABC commentary boxes, Aggers had been preparing, anticipating England's historic moment. Happily for him that moment coincided with Christmas in Melbourne in the company of wife Emma and stepson Tom. I look forward to seeing them again in England when our friendship is rekindled and the Ashes are regained.

ACKNOWLEDGEMENTS

Every time I have toured with England, the broadcasting technology has improved, as have the means by which people back at home, in the depths of winter and often through the night, can follow the cricket. This Ashes tour broke all manner of new ground in the way we were able to establish a surprisingly close level of contact and rapport with our listeners. Email and text messages seem old hat now when compared to Twitter, which has taken the cricket world by storm. Players tweet, journalists tweet and so do the fans – in their tens of thousands.

This was undoubtedly the 'Twitter Tour', featuring Ashley Kerekes, a 21-year-old nanny from Massachusetts, whose boyfriend had unwittingly supplied her with the username *@theashes*. It says a lot about the modern world of social networking and its appeal to commercialism that, following an extraordinary week in which Ashley's followers soared from a couple of hundred to more than ten thousand – as cricket fans demanded scores and Ashes gossip from an initially bewildered Ashley – that both she and her boyfriend picked up a free trip to Sydney to watch the final Test. It had all started as a big joke, but certainly she had the last laugh.

Another Twitter star was EllaW638. A Chelsea football fanatic and, coincidentally, another children's nanny, this time from the Home Counties, Ella stayed up all night – almost every night – to tweet scores and updates after every over. All from her mobile phone to another 4,000 insomniacs. Then she went off to work.

The BBC website carried blogs from just about everyone, it seemed. Tom Fordyce was with us on the tour and wrote colourfully every day. Some of his excellent contributions are reprinted in this diary, and I am very grateful to him for allowing me to do so. I'd also like to thank Ben Dirs, Oliver Brett and everyone at the BBC online team who, with Lewis Wiltshire, have all played a part in producing the additional and wonderful material that sits alongside my entries.

None of this would have been possible without the help of Adam Mountford, the BBC cricket producer and all my colleagues on *Test Match Special*. Many of the humorous comments and pithy observations of Geoff Boycott, Michael Vaughan, Michael Slater, Ian Chappell and Justin Langer are also included here. And I must thank the England coach Andy Flower for overcoming his early misgivings and allowing the injured Stuart Broad to work with us on *Test Match Special* for the Perth Test. Of course I must also mention my old friend Vic Marks for providing the live radio commentary of my unique version of the Sprinkler Dance when England won the series in Sydney.

When the Ashes were finally won on Australian soil, I fulfilled my life-long broadcasting ambition to be on-air to report the moment. I am forever grateful to my ABC broadcasting colleague and friend Jim Maxwell for generously ceding the microphone at the critical moment and for writing the foreword to the book. It is a measure of the man that shortly after the Melbourne victory was secured, Jim joined Michael Vaughan and myself at our celebratory lunch.

This was also a series of records broken and outstanding personal achievements – on an almost unprecedented scale. Andrew Samson, a South African statistician with a formidable reputation, had expressed his desire to watch an Ashes series from a neutral perspective. I bet he is glad he chose this one, and I am very grateful for his immaculate presentation of the scorecards, averages and statistical milestones you will find throughout the book.

This book has been a team effort and I am particularly grateful to Michael Doggart and Jonathan Hayden for keeping the ship afloat and on schedule, and Stephanie Beltrame of Cricket Australia for her help in clearing the pictures.

Finally I must thank my wife Emma for her support and encouragement over the years. She came with me on to the outfield at the Melbourne Cricket Ground when England secured the Ashes and she is next to me in the photograph as I am about to interview the two captains after England had retained the Ashes. It must be incredibly difficult being a cricket widow at times, and I am so thrilled that we were together to share one of the highlights of my life.

PREFACE

For an England cricket correspondent, an Ashes tour of Australia should be as good as it gets – the pinnacle of one's career. It is a wonderful country with plenty to keep you occupied and, despite the traditional semi-serious Pom-bashing by the media, a genuinely warm welcome is guaranteed. Comfortable hotels and easy travel make it difficult to argue against this being the best job in the world. But, and it is a big but, for the past twenty years the cricket has been anything but competitive, inevitably robbing each of my last five tours of the continent of its key ingredient. I have witnessed England winning only 3 of the 25 Tests they played in Australia during that time, and losing, sometimes quite badly, 18 of them.

It has not always been easy reporting on those disastrous campaigns. My emotions would typically range from initial disbelief – how can England be this bad again? – through anger at the team's continuing ineptitude to ultimate despair. It has been impossible for me to be entirely impartial as I am sure many *TMS* listeners will understand. Commentating on the local Australian Broadcasting Corporation [ABC] – something I have always loved doing, incidentally – had become embarrassing, as time and time again I would invariably have to sign off with an apology to the Australian listeners for the gulf between the two teams, a gulf that created such one-sided Test matches.

But buoyed by England winning the Ashes in 2009, and having watched Australia struggle against Pakistan the following summer, the Ashes tour of 2010/11 from the outset felt altogether different. Without players of Australia's golden age of the 1990s like Shane Warne, Glenn McGrath and Adam Gilchrist, I was not alone in feeling genuinely optimistic about England's prospects this time around. So much so, that when pressed for a prediction before the players left home, I put my neck on the block and forecast that England would return 3-1 winners. And so it proved.

Jonathan Agnew, February 2011

ONE

THE PHONEY WAR

"Cook is hanging on to his place by the skin of his teeth."
RICKY PONTING

DAY 1 **3 November 2010**

It is one of those 'where am I?' moments when I am awoken by bright Australian sun beaming through the curtains of a yet another unfamiliar bedroom. The digital display on the television tells me that it is six o'clock in the morning. How is it possible, having gone to bed at two o'clock after a sixteen-hour sleepless flight, that I have managed to kip for only four hours, and yet feel as fresh as a daisy? It won't last of course.

It was dark when I arrived last night at Perth Airport, Western Australia and by the time I had found a taxi and reached the hotel, my brain was thoroughly befuddled. I know I started to unpack after checking in and had made sure my phone worked by speaking to Emma to report my safe arrival. I also checked that there was a decent Internet connection in the room, so vital for work (and listening to music) while on tour these days. The Internet has transformed the way in which we send interviews and reports back to London. Not so long ago a set of screwdrivers to dismantle telephone connectors was an absolutely essential piece of kit to be lugged around. Now it all transmits magically from the laptop straight to BBC Television Centre, while an iPhone and a Napster account means I no longer need to pack a selection of carefully chosen compact discs. The hotel's price for the Internet connection strikes me as expensive though – £18 per day. In fact, by the end of the tour I will have clocked up over £2,000 in Internet charges!

Apart from being the first day of the hugely anticipated Ashes tour, it is also the first day of my new and sure-to-be rigorous training regime. I am determined to lose a stone by the time Emma arrives in Australia, and to try to live a more healthy on-tour lifestyle. That is not as easy as it sounds: the job means that as commentators and pundits most of the day we are sat down in front of the microphone, while long evenings away from home inevitably draw you to the bar to meet with colleagues who are equally lonely and at an end-of-play loose end. A few too many drinks are followed, usually far too late into the evening, by something to eat. Given that journalists by their very nature are an outspoken, opinionated bunch, these evenings can often be very argumentative. They also become a dangerously routine part of being on tour. So a sensible alcohol intake and daily exercise will be the way forward this time although, physically, I am going to pace myself. No doubt Emma will say I am going to be far too easy on myself, and because I take absolutely no pleasure in jogging whatsoever, she is probably right. But nonetheless I am determined to get fit.

Langley Park, Perth lies directly between my hotel and the Swan River and is ideal for my purpose. A stroll at a brisk pace around its rectangular form takes about 25 minutes. Apart from the swarms of infuriatingly persistent flies and a temperature already well on its way to the predicted 37 degrees celsius, it is all very pleasant. Swatting the flies is surprisingly tiring. I walk one lap and then jog the long sides of the park to complete the second. Forty minutes in the beautifully clear and fresh air. That'll do for a start.

On my return to the hotel I encounter a typically cheerful Graeme Swann in the lobby, while Irish-born Eoin Morgan, shy and quiet in public at least, gives me a nod as he emerges from the lift. Kevin Pietersen shouts "Hello Bud!" from the breakfast room. His form and general demeanour will be greatly scrutinised by the media over the coming fortnight.

The England team have already had a couple of days in the nets at the WACA. Today they have opted for a centre-wicket practice at Richardson Park, which is a ten-minute taxi ride from the hotel. My Bangladeshi driver is amazed when we arrive at the ground that absolutely nobody is watching. "If the England cricket team practised in the middle of Dhaka," he exclaims, "thousands of people would be there."

Frankly, it would have helped a great deal if the dozen or so gathered journalists had been briefed in advance about how this practice session was going to be organised. Pairs of batsmen come and go – apparently after six overs have been bowled at them, and there are some strange fields set, including one that features a large blue bucket standing at short-leg. Chris Tremlett bowls a succession of attempted bouncers to Ian Bell. In the blistering heat these are not in the least bit threatening and end up being flogged through mid-wicket. Bruce French, England's wicketkeeping coach and an old county cricket colleague of mine, belatedly explains that each 'spell' is in fact a game plan: early innings, mid-innings and this particular phase is designed to rough up the batsmen. I fear Tremlett's confidence, which is already known to be suspect, will have taken rather a battering today.

James Anderson, who broke his rib while boxing during England's unusual and clearly controversial pre-tour boot camp in Germany, manages a couple of overs. Pietersen is caught at slip for 2 off Stephen Finn, who is comfortably the pick of the quick bowlers, only for Bell and Andrew Strauss to stress in their interviews afterwards how well KP is striking the ball in the nets. He would do everyone a favour by scoring a hundred against Western Australia this weekend, putting a stop to the constant talk about his form.

This evening I enjoy one of those rare, wonderful, insightful on tour social occasions when I spend it with the England coach Andy Flower. Sadly, much of what we discuss over a number of drinks has to remain 'off the record', but I feel very privileged that such an ice cool and deliberate individual, who is always meticulously careful when speaking in public, feels that he can chat with me about a number of issues concerning the England team and English cricket in general.

Keen to give his side of the Anderson injury saga [Anderson suffered a broken rib while boxing during England's bonding trip to Germany], Flower is certain that the boot camp was a great success. He argues that it challenged every member of the squad, and the management set-up too. He seems genuinely surprised by my optimism about the forthcoming tour, but his reserved pragmatism about what might follow may be simply an example of his naturally guarded character. I am sure he will not mind me repeating his answer to my question about the 'Gabba factor': how is he preparing the team to overcome England's dreadful record there [England have not won a Test Match at the Gabba since November 1986] and on the first day in particular? Do they talk about it or completely ignore it? He tells me that they discuss it every day, quite deliberately, so England's recent record at the ground is not thought of as anything sinister or, more importantly, insurmountable.

First evening of the tour, and I have already broken my vow not to drink too much. Worth it though.

DAY 2 4 November 2010

This morning I wander down to the WACA to install the broadcasting equipment for tomorrow's game. These technical duties are rather easier these days – just a case of plugging in a box and the line immediately goes through to London. On my return to the hotel I discover there is great excitement about comments made in Sydney about Michael Clarke's suitability to succeed Ricky Ponting as captain of Australia. This follows Sri Lanka's remarkable one-day international win against Australia in Melbourne yesterday, in which the Sri Lanka ninth-wicket pair added a record 132 and in so doing prolonged Australia's losing run. Inevitably the bulk of the criticism has focussed on Clarke's contribution as captain, and there are suggestions of a rift in the camp. Marcus North, who faces England tomorrow for Western Australia in the opening tour match, is being openly talked about as a more suitable candidate than Clarke. It is remarkable really, and must be destabilising the Australian team. Ponting's leadership is effectively being spoken about in the past tense.

I have dinner with Peter Baxter – former producer of *Test Match Special* and a close friend. Sensibly, following an unhappy experience last winter in South Africa, the BBC has decided that site visits to overseas cricket grounds prior to the team's arrival are now an essential part of the broadcaster's preparation. (As an example, we commentated throughout the Durban Test from a concrete step, sitting on pillows taken from our hotel rooms and entirely open to the elements). Now married to an Australian lass, Peter spends half his time in Brisbane these days, and was the ideal person to fly around Australia making sure that the BBC's sizeable investment in the form of broadcast rights fees includes basics like commentary boxes.

DAY 3 **5 November 2010**

England's first day of cricket on the tour coincides with another Australian ODI defeat by Sri Lanka at the SCG giving Sri Lanka their first series win on Australian soil. Problems are certainly mounting in the Aussie camp, although realistically these are more about team morale than anything else. Their build-up to the Ashes is not nearly as organised as England's, and Ricky Ponting has been despatched to Hobart to make his first appearance for Tasmania in the Sheffield Shield for three years, rather than play for Australia in the last ODI against Sri Lanka. I am looking forward to reading the newspapers tomorrow.

Meanwhile England have had a reasonable opening day against Western Australia, spoiled only by the dismissal of Alastair Cook for 5 just before the end of play. It is very refreshing to watch three-day cricket for a change rather than the four-day variety used in England's county game, because it requires much more innovation and imagination by the captains. Western Australia declare on 242 for 8 to leave the England's openers six awkward overs to face, a declaration no captain would ever make in the four-day game. Cook, who is in desperate need of runs after a poor summer, manages to deflect the ball on to his wicket attempting a pull shot. Bearing in mind that Cook only saved his selectorial skin with a hundred during the Oval Test against Pakistan, it won't take many more failures for his place in the team to come under the spotlight again. The trouble is that there aren't many other options – Jonathan Trott or Ian Bell would have to be promoted up the order.

Happily, James Anderson is passed fit to play, putting a stop to the endless talk of his boxing injury. To begin with he looked rather ring rusty and tentative, but improves as the day goes on. Stephen Finn is thoroughly out of sorts and can never have bowled so many full tosses. Finn's falling flat requires some explaining to my colleagues in the

ABC box who have been looking forward to seeing the new English fast bowling find in action. They can't help but be disappointed by what they have seen so far. Stuart Broad is comfortably the pick of the bowlers, taking two wickets in his first over. He also dismisses Marcus North – the only Test batsman in a weak batting line up – and is successful by pitching the ball up. I am still concerned that England will want him to be more aggressive and bowl too short in the absence of any genuine pace in the attack, but he is not that type of bowler. Hopefully, having taken three wickets early on, England will resist the temptation and encourage him – and Finn – to follow Glenn McGrath's methodical and metronomic example.

With the day done, a lively session in the hotel bar includes a discussion with a young lad from the bush who is getting married the next day and me issuing an invitation through Twitter to the people of Perth to accompany me on my early morning run. I don't suppose anyone will turn up. Tomorrow will be a KP story, whatever happens.

DAY 4 **6 November 2010**

At 7.30 a.m I anxiously approach the park behind the hotel to find a very athletic chap, neatly turned out in full training kit waiting for me. He introduces himself as Brett, my running partner for the morning. I feel I have to explain to him that I am gently feeling my way back into training and cannot be described, by any measure, as being at the absolute peak of fitness. Off we go at quite a rate over the Causeway and on to Heirisson Island. Thankfully I am able to make the most of photographing some amiable kangaroos who happen to be hopping by and, catching enough breath, stagger back to the hotel. Lesson learned – but I should mention that Brett's father Brian was a leading administrator employed by Kerry Packer to run World Series Cricket. Consequently it was a very interesting chat indeed, even if I ache for the rest of the day.

At least it is a KP day for all the right reasons. He scores a half-century in what was overall a poor batting performance by England despite a true if rather sluggish pitch. England are 159/8 before Broad and Swann fling the bat and put on 64 with Pietersen's 58 from 90 balls the highlight. He is dropped at slip on 25 and has several rushes of blood, but KP also plays some fine strokes until a loose drive ends his innings. Pietersen can be an awkward customer to interview sometimes, offering up very short answers to keep you on your toes; today he certainly plays down the significance of scoring runs early on the tour even though I press him. I'll bet privately he is very relieved indeed.

Of the others, Trott looks comfortable for his 24, Collingwood scores 4, Bell 21 and Prior a duck – all responsible for their own dismissals, which, given the importance of these three practice matches, is very disappointing. Broad's confidence is sky high at present, and he launches himself at the Western Australian bowling to hit 53 from 48 balls, while Swann's 37 comes off only 25 deliveries. With England 19 runs behind, Strauss declares in order to move the game along and increase the chance of his batsmen having a second innings, some of whom need to redeem themselves. Having seen Broad and Swann tuck into their bowling, Western Australia start their second innings at a tremendous rate, getting stuck into Finn again, although he eventually traps Liam Davis lbw. At the close, Western Australia lead by 128 with 9 wickets in hand – thus setting up the prospect of a run chase on the final afternoon.

Later I see Andy Flower and batting coach Graham Gooch locked in conversation in the bar for an hour. They certainly have a lot to talk about. The West Australian newspaper causes a bit of a stir by printing all over its back page a photograph of Ricky Ponting, diving full length to his left where – just out of reach of his outstretched fingers – is a superimposed Ashes urn. The headline reads: 'Out of Reach'. A poll of the newspaper's readers reveals that the majority believe England will win the Ashes this time.

Coincidentally, this is the second day of a strike by BBC journalists who belong to the National Union of Journalists in a dispute over pensions. General programming is affected, but neither being a member of the BBC staff nor part of its pension scheme, or a member of the NUJ come to that, I continue to report from the WACA, contributing to the much-reduced sports desks throughout the night. As I see it, my duty is to work for those who are paying for me to be here – the license payers. Unfortunately I, and others in a similar position, have now become the focus of a rather nasty campaign in the course of which I have been publicly labelled, on the Internet, as a scab. Not only is this inaccurate, but it is offensive. For those wishing to criticise my stance it demonstrates a careless lack of research on their part because, although I have not said so publicly, the Agnew household budget will be affected as much as anyone else's at the BBC. Emma's pension will be cut under the current plan. More strikes are scheduled for next week and while those who are planning to walk out again are perfectly entitled to do so, I hope they leave me alone this time. Twitter, when used properly, is a wonderful modern communications tool, but it also gives people an opportunity to be most unpleasant when they choose to be.

DAY 5 **7 November 2010**

England win their opening match pretty comfortably in the end. In the morning the bowlers demonstrate an improved performance and this is followed by a spirited run chase, which is led by Strauss. Finn's first two balls of the day are hit for 4 – a bit of a worry – but he fights back splendidly, confirming that he is a young man of great heart and discipline. Marcus North fails a second time when Eoin Morgan, popping up as substitute fielder, runs him out from square leg. Swann, although he takes a little more tap than he will have liked, is soon wearing his familiar chirpy smile, finishing with figures of 4 for 101. Western Australia lose 9 wickets for 114, setting England 243 to win in 52 overs.

Cook strikes two firm fours, but is then comprehensively bowled for 9. Inevitably this gets everyone talking because England have brought only two full-time opening batsmen and the loss of form of Strauss or Cook will necessitate Trott moving up to open the batting, Bell to number three and reintroduce Morgan at number six. That is quite an upheaval which is why, when others might be given a rest, Cook will be given every opportunity to get runs between now and Brisbane.

Pietersen again plays some firm and fine shots in his innings of 35 before perishing lbw by way of a reverse sweep to the left-arm spinner Beer. It takes an eternity for KP to drag himself away from the crease. As my commentary position is behind him, and with no TV replays, I cannot tell whether it is a poor decision or not. But it underlines again the importance of England's batsmen not giving their wickets away on this tour. Racking up a large first innings total will be vital and while I accept that this was a run chase, the unvarnished truth is that Pietersen has managed to get himself out twice in this match.

Strauss's century was a lovely knock. It is always important for the captain to start a tour well so that his form is not an issue before the main event. During the course of his innings Strauss has once again demonstrated the advances he has made as a one-day batsman.

Meanwhile, someone called Ella has contacted me on Twitter. I say 'someone' because there is absolutely no way of knowing on these social networking sites if anyone really is who they claim to be. Ella's avatar – her profile picture – does not contain a photo, only a cartoon character, but whoever he or she is, is following the cricket all night – presumably from England.

In a Twitter exchange, I agree with Ella if she is still up and listening at 3:00 a.m GMT, I will follow him/her. In the Twitter world this is seen as a sign of friendship, just as 'unfollowing' somebody is viewed as a major insult. I am very choosy about the number of people I follow because, quite simply, the more you follow, the more messages you have to scroll through on your phone. Sure enough a message – or Tweet – duly pops up at 3:00 a.m. I click the button, which signs me up as one of Ella's 150 or so followers. Now every one of her (I am still not sure she is indeed a she) tweets now lands on my laptop. I am amazed that this unknown individual is providing a brilliant score update service, with full bowling figures, the lot, all crammed into the strict Twitter allocation of only 140 characters. Even more than that, there are a number of highly comical asides couched in, at times, decidedly colourful language. The whole magnificent effort seems entirely wasted on so few people. So, during the course of the day, I encourage my loyal followers, who by now are waking up and expecting a full scores service on England's bid for victory, to follow @EllaW638 instead. It is brilliant. By the end of the match Ella has more than two thousand people following her updates, which are apparently being typed out on an iPhone – not even anything as comfortable as a computer keyboard. It is a fantastic performance, which is hugely appreciated by everyone – not least me because I can now concentrate on my radio work and leave Twitter to her.

Some hours later Ella puts up a picture: she is indeed a young woman of about 20 years of age, although my guess at her age is made difficult by the blue Chelsea FC woolly hat she is wearing. Apparently she is a children's nanny. Isn't it great that someone of her age should be so fanatically and enthusiastically interested in cricket? A breath of fresh air, and it absolutely makes my day. *(Incidentally, she keeps going throughout the whole series, providing an invaluable and colourful service to ultimately more than four thousand followers).*

DAY 6 **8 November 2010**

It is our first travelling day and I am reminded of just how vast this country is. I snatch breakfast at Perth airport at 6:20 a.m at a table beside two men already drinking pints of lager before our three-hour flight to the City of Churches.

Adelaide is one of my favourite locations on the international cricket circuit and I especially love the city's cricket ground – the Oval. Set in a large park on the bank of the River Torrens, it is a truly beautiful ground overlooked by St Peter's Cathedral. The entire western side of the ground has been redeveloped since I was last here, at enormous cost and at the risk, in my eyes, of damaging the heritage of this great cricket venue. Cricket grounds must modernise of course, but there is always the danger that the identity and character of an historically-laden ground will be compromised, and it would be a terrible shame if this proves to be the case at the Adelaide Oval, which, after Lord's, is my second favourite venue in the world. We fly in to Adelaide directly over the ground and from my left-hand window seat I have a first glimpse of the white shell-shaped roof of the new stand shining brightly in the morning sunshine. Actually, it looks lovely. This afternoon I take a stroll along the riverbank to the ground. Pelicans and black swans paddle about while overhead red and green parrots flash past against a now brilliant blue sky. It is all absolutely stunning – and later, from ground level, I get a chance to examine the new stand: it gets a big thumbs up from me.

Late in the day comes the first news of the mysterious disappearing act by the Pakistan wicketkeeper Zulqarnain Haider. Rather than travelling with his team for their fifth one-day international against South Africa in Dubai, Haider has apparently abandoned the tour and boarded a flight to London. He had played a key role in Pakistan's narrow one-wicket win in the previous match, including hitting the winning run, and his brother is reported as saying that Haider claims to have received serious personal threats.

Clearly Pakistan cricket is in a dreadful mess at the moment: the ICC cases, following the allegations of spot fixing in England last summer, against Salman Butt, Mohammad Asif and Mohammad Amir is still being examined. Frankly, it is difficult to know what to believe at the moment. I do remember Haider being quite a character during his single appearance in the Test series against England. He top scored at Edgbaston, hitting a rather spiky 88, during which Stuart Broad over-reacted by throwing the ball at, and managing to hit, him. Haider returned home after the game, a little mysteriously as I recall, when he was suddenly diagnosed with a fractured finger. This enabled Kamran Akmal to return as wicketkeeper. This will be another strand of the Pakistan story we need to keep our eyes on, but it won't be easy from twelve thousand miles away.

DAY 7 **9 November 2010**

Overnight comes the confirmation that Haider has, indeed, arrived in London and has been given a visa to stay for a month. There are conflicting reports about the background to his leaving the tour, but he has now announced his retirement from international cricket. He confirms that he was threatened in Dubai, but did not tell the Pakistan team management because, it seems, he did not trust them. Pakistan's sports minister says that his country's government does not support the player. It is the main topic of conversation here, where it is a day off for the England team, the majority of whom head for the golf course. Andy Flower faces the press and confirms that there is an option for England to split the squad following the upcoming match against South Australia, sending the likely Test bowling attack straight to Brisbane rather than take them to Hobart for the four-day game against Australia A.

It is an interesting thought. Certainly the bracing, probably chilly late spring conditions in Tasmania will be nothing like the tropical heat and humidity of the Gabba. Let's not forget that Tasmania is nearly a three-hour flight south of Brisbane, with a climate not unlike England's, and seasonally this is the equivalent of early May at home. There is a lot to be said for Anderson, Broad and Finn having an extra week in which to acclimatise to the conditions they will have to bowl in during the Brisbane Test – but absolutely only if they are in good form. I don't see an issue in splitting up the team, and there is enough cover in the bowling department to fill the gaps, but the game against Australia A is a high profile match, which is to be televised throughout Australia and on Sky television at home. If England field Bresnan, Tremlett, Shahzad and Panesar – none of whom have bowled a ball in anger so far – will England be properly competitive? Is there a danger of England having a poor match chasing leather and, should they lose, suffering a psychological blow before the opening Test? Strauss has repeatedly emphasised his determination to win all of the warm-up matches and not simply use them for practice. The England management would also do well to remember that Cricket Australia have agreed to this excellent tour preparation at England's request; is there a danger – if the match is downgraded by England effectively fielding a second string eleven – that they won't be so co-operative next time around?

Flower reiterates that splitting the squad is only an option under consideration – but the proverbial cat is out of the bag. If the first-choice bowlers do go to Hobart, will it suggest that the coach is not happy with their progress? And what about the captain and coach's oft-repeated assertion that it is important to win every game? It certainly makes easy copy for we hacks and is just what we need – something to write about on an otherwise blank day. Opinion in the media is camp is split, to be fair.

Training is going well. I walk along the river for half an hour and then run back to the hotel. I am almost enjoying it, but in this fabulous place it would be hard not to. It is still delightfully quiet without the full Ashes 'circus' of reporters, television crews, photographers and so on who are yet to arrive and, of course, I am operating entirely by myself for the BBC. The lack of feeling of being under the microscope means that the players are much more accessible and friendly too. This is what cricket touring is all about, but it won't last.

DAY 8 **10 November 2010**

A vital round of Sheffield Shield matches gets underway with off spinner Nathan Hauritz very much under the spotlight. He had a poor tour of India, but simply put, there does not appear to be any other serious contender within Australia. It must be very awkward for Hauritz, carrying the expectations of being the latest to follow in Shane Warne's footsteps, and clearly there is no comparison to be made between them. Arguably, this is Australia's weak link. Playing against Victoria, Hauritz goes for five runs per over and is wicketless. Ponting, meanwhile, scores 32 in Tasmania's first innings against Queensland.

England have nets at the Adelaide Oval, but do not name their team. I presume it will have to be their Test X1 again, so the decision can be taken about the bowling attack. It is also an open media day giving the press from both sides an opportunity to interview a number of players in a large conference room that has been set aside in the basement of the team hotel. It is also the moment when all of the players are filmed by Australia's Channel 9, folding their arms and smiling rather self-consciously at the camera. These brief clips will be shown during the Test coverage as the players walk out to bat. I can hear much guffawing and leg-pulling coming from the room next door.

James Avery is the excellent ECB media manager who tours with the team, and with whom I have a brilliant working relationship. I am not saying that he gives me what I want in the way of interviews all the time, but he is always very cooperative; particularly when I am out on the ground itself immediately at the end of a Test, live on air, and in desperate need of players to talk to. Today I opt first for Stephen Finn. He is on his first tour of Australia, and did not bowl at anything like his best during the opening match, so it will be interesting to find out how he feels he is getting on.

Unfortunately, the quietest place I can find to chat with him is outside the hotel toilets. Not exactly glamorous. Finn is a delightfully laid back 21-year-old and seems like a really nice young man. Feet on the ground and all that. He laughs when I tell him that I compare him to Angus Fraser, but without the tantrums. Graeme Swann is next. Graeme is the very definition of a 'character', and gives you so much in an interview including, this time, pointing out that behind me James Anderson has dropped his trousers and is mooning at the pair of us! The Swann/Anderson double act will be an amusing feature of the tour with their ECB videos.

Dinner at the Verco family home. Tom and Lucy Verco have been friends of mine for years, and it is so nice to get out of the hotel and into a family environment for an evening. I know everyone believes that hotel life is one long holiday, but it soon becomes very claustrophobic. It is also easy to settle into a very dull routine unless you really make an effort to get out in the evenings.

DAY 9 11 November 2010

As we anticipated, England name the same team. This confirms two things – that this is their favoured line-up for the First Test, and that if the bowlers fare well here, they will almost certainly miss the match against Australia A. This is still a confusing issue for me. Why give the reserve players the hardest and most challenging practice match of the three? I would have played a reserve player or two here – like Morgan and Bresnan or Tremlett – then gone into the Hobart match with most of my Test players. By naming this team, it would seem England certainly intend to send the first-choice bowlers to Brisbane when the Hobart team is announced next Wednesday. That would give them an extra four days of acclimatisation.

The overriding priority today is for Alastair Cook to get some runs. Traditionally the Adelaide Oval is a batsman's paradise, but this morning it is dull and overcast, and the South Australian pace bowlers – Peter George in particular – are quite a handful. Strauss perishes unluckily for 4 to a catch down the leg side and walks off swishing his bat in frustration. He knows he is in good form at the moment and a leg-side nick to the 'keeper is always an infuriating way to get out. It gives us a chance to study Trott at the crease, particularly his unusual and obsessive marking of the crease. This begins with him asking the umpire for his guard, which he marks with three deliberate and long rakes of his boot. He then runs his bat along the groove before asking the umpire for his guard again. This happens at the start of every over at least, and sometimes more often than that. He has received warnings in the past from umpires for time wasting – the batsman should be ready to receive the next ball when the bowler is at the end of his run-up – and it seems certain that the Australians will do everything they can to put him off. I can't believe that Shane Warne, if he were still playing, would allow Trott to hold him up. I suspect Warne would have adopted the Norman Gifford approach. I have seen the wily 'Giff' sneak up undetected behind the umpire many times in his Warwickshire and Worcestershire days, to clean bowl a young batsman before he was ready. With Trott, his crease-scratching antics are a touchy subject. Last summer I took a deep breath and asked him live on the radio at Lord's if he was worried that the Aussies would have a go at him using the time-wasting complaint to distract him. Trott muttered something unintelligible and walked off.

It was interesting watching some of the tennis stars at Wimbledon last summer, going through their various routines before every point. Maria Sharapova pulls at the strings of her racquet with her back to her opponent and then taps her left thigh twice when she is about to receive serve. Rafa Nadal seems to take superstition – for that is surely what it is – even further. Emma and I sat almost directly behind the umpire at ground level for the men's singles final so were only a few feet from Nadal's chair. It was astonishing to witness the tortured lengths this great sportsman goes to in order to make sure that he sips exactly the same amount of liquid from the two drinks bottles he has under his seat Then, when replacing the bottles, obsessively making sure they were perfectly lined up. As the psychiatrist in Fawlty Towers says, "Enough for a whole conference there". One can't help wondering whether Trott's excessive fiddling about is really necessary. And I know there are members of England's camp who think that it is bordering on the idiotic and makes Trott look unnecessarily vulnerable.

Trott does seem to have made an effort so far to get a bit of a move on, but after being dropped at slip on 11, he mis-pulls George and is caught and bowled for 12. Cook battles away, occasionally lapsing into the poor footwork around off stump that has caused his technical problems, before playing a desperate firm-footed flash at a wide ball from George, edging it to the wicketkeeper for 32 from 91 balls. It is not a convincing innings and as he troops off, Cook knows that questions about his form and place at the top of the order will continue to be raised in the media. At least he still has three more innings before the Gabba in which to get some runs.

Just as he had at Perth, Pietersen plays some good shots before getting out – this time to a catch on the deep square-leg boundary to a hook shot for 33. It is frustrating that he has not gone on to make a really big score. He is in good touch but cameos won't win the Ashes. It is left to Collingwood to make the one substantial score of the day. The first 30 or so of his 94 runs are rather scratchy, in my opinion, and I suggest that to him when I interview him after play. "Oh," he replies rather defensively, "I thought I played rather well." As an interviewer there is nowhere to go after that other than trying to persuade a top-class sportsman that, in your opinion, he has not played very well after all. That does little to foster good relations and it is best to move on.

Bell makes a typically pretty 61, but manages to miss a gun-barrel straight half-volley that hits his off stump. Again, it is the sort of lapse that he can arguably get away with here, but is precisely the sort of misjudgement that can cost his side a Test match. Strauss declares on 288/8 and, with 8 overs left in the day, is hopeful of taking a South Australian wicket or two, but they breeze to 26 for no wicket at the close of play.

I am thankful to read that the second proposed strike by BBC journalists has been called off before heading out for dinner with Hugh Morris, managing director of England Cricket, at a delightful restaurant almost under the bridge over the River Torrens. Last time I was here Geoffrey Boycott was at an adjoining table; it is altogether quieter this evening.

DAY 10 **12 November 2010**

I wake up to a brilliant interview on the BBC website by errant Pakistani cricketer Zulqarnain Haider who has been speaking to BBC sports editor David Bond. Haider describes in much more detail the threat he received in Dubai and, tellingly, that he had not felt confident enough in the integrity of the tour management to inform them of what had happened, or what he proposed to do. He says he is making a stand – and we must applaud his bravery. What will he be able to tell the ICC Anti-Corruption Unit I wonder? If he can give them names and facts, he will be doing cricket a massive service.

This is an important day for England's bowlers as we in the media continue to debate their dispersal or otherwise ahead of the First Test. Here at the ground, it is cold and dark enough for the floodlights to be switched on. From where I am sitting they make an infuriating and quite intrusive buzz. I suppose when the ground is full you can't hear it. Disappointingly, despite the conditions, the ball does not swing much. Getting the ball to swing is such an important part of England's armoury – Anderson's ability to swing the ball in particular is going to play a huge part in the Ashes campaign. But the Kookaburra ball, with its flatter, wider seam, does not have the same rudder-like properties that make the Duke ball we use at home so much more swing-friendly.

I remember asking Anderson at Trent Bridge last summer, after he had destroyed Pakistan, what would happen in Australia if the ball didn't swing. Is there a plan B? He told me that his plan B is the ball not swinging and that he would have to depend on accuracy and some reverse swing instead. Reverse swing is usually achieved when the pitch and outfield are dry and abrasive and is a skill that has developed quickly in recent years. Anderson can have his awful days when he is terribly expensive and frustratingly he hadn't, until the series against Pakistan last summer, made the jump up to someone who was utterly dependable, but on this tour, when the ball won't always swing, he should still bowl accurately, probing away, changing pace waiting for the ball to reverse swing when he will come back into his own again. Of course someone like him has got it made, swinging the new ball in the orthodox manner then going away and fielding in the outfield for a while, then coming back when the ball starts to reverse; so he's got two weapons.

Largely because the art of reverse swing bowling is still something of an enigma and it is thought can be assisted by illegally scratching the ball, there is often a good deal of suspicion about the whole subject. But it is such an asset when there is nothing else to help a bowler on an unresponsive pitch that reverse swing has become a vital asset. Ironically, England's best tutor was the Australian coach, Troy Cooley, who has now returned to the Australian set-up. England's coach on this tour is another Aussie David Saker, who will undoubtedly be keen to put one over his still better known predecessor – even if they are both Australians. There is so much freedom of movement for coaches these days that patriotism really doesn't come into it. Indeed, it is rare to find a national coach who originates from the country he is now employed by. I must say, I can't see any problem with it at all.

Today Anderson was bowling the line of last summer and it is too straight here, so he is picked off through the leg side. It will be something for him and Saker to work on. Broad didn't bowl much and I think the pick of the lot was again Finn. He ran in well and combined hostility with his usual accuracy. He only picked up two wickets to Anderson's three and Swann's four, but deserved better than that.

Callum Ferguson is a name we might encounter later in the Ashes if Australia need to replace their old guard. He certainly plays some shots, but gave his wicket away on 35 when he tried to pull Finn and was caught at mid-on. We will see him again in Hobart.

With the floodlights doing their best to illuminate the gloom, wickets tumble and South Australia are bundled out for 221, giving England a lead of 67. It is a good effort, but leaves under-scrutiny Cook exposed; he faces the prospect of a no-win innings in tricky conditions. With Strauss in glorious form at the other end, Cook carefully claws his way to 37 not out, and with it the opportunity to go on and enjoy the final morning.

Meanwhile, word reaches me of trouble at home. My dog Bracken (a Springer spaniel) has raided the chicken run, not, it must be said, for the first time, and Emma is terribly distressed by what was waiting for her when she returned home. Somehow it is entirely my fault – as I knew it would be. Since I am 12,000 miles away, I hadn't actually contrived to leave the gate open, but I am guilty of employing the man who had put the gate up in the first place. It will be the boiler next – I know it.

DAY 11 13 November 2010

It is another chilly and overcast morning, meaning the floodlights are buzzing away again, and will be for most of the day; in fact the day's play will be curtailed by bad light. Although it is disappointing that the prospect of an exciting run chase is ruined, England have every reason to celebrate because Cook makes a century. It is a battling effort in stark contrast to Strauss who hits four sixes in his 102 before deliberately giving his wicket away. It is such an important innings as far as Cook's confidence is concerned and that of the whole team. I suspect Cook would have opened at Brisbane even had he not made a decent score in the warm-up matches, but it would have been an inescapable talking point. The only realistic option would be for Trott to open, Bell to move to number three and Morgan to come into the team at number six; quite an upheaval and certainly something England could do without.

Cook is not one of the most graceful left-handers, the majority of whom seem to have an elegance all of their own. I'm not sure why, it would seem to be purely a matter of aesthetics. Cook's bat is often crooked, with the blade turned to the leg side and he plants his front foot on the line of off stump and plays around it, which helps to explain his low scores. But he is a fighter. South Australia's attack buckles under the weight of the onslaught from Strauss, and 156 runs are added before the captain declares, setting the home team 308 to win in 65 overs. A long break for rain ruins that, and after Trott and Collingwood take outstanding catches off Anderson, the umpires decide the light has deteriorated sufficiently to bring proceedings to an early close.

Has it been enough of a run out for the bowlers to take the Brisbane option? Broad and Swann certainly look as if they could be trusted in a Test match tomorrow. Finn is coming on but not yet one hundred per cent, while I reckon Anderson is at about eighty per cent. Given the team that has been chosen here, everything is geared to playing the back-up attack in Hobart.

A final run along the riverbank and I watch as a Singapore Airlines flight comes in over the ground. It is the flight that will bring Emma here in five weeks' time. It seems an age away. I haven't been here a fortnight yet, but already a lot seems to have happened in this phoney war. All, that is, except shedding the pounds. How depressing.

DAY 12 **14 November 2010**

A frustrating travel day. There are no direct flights between Adelaide and Hobart, so we all scatter to the four winds. There are at least three different travel agencies handling the media travel on this tour and I am essentially doing my own thing, which gives one a certain independence. We are very welcome to travel on the same flight as the players, but I have learned that it is generally a mistake to do so because of the chaos created by the massive amount of baggage that accompanies them. This often results in long waits at the luggage carousel at the other end while everything is sorted out behind the scenes and increases the possibility of your bags not getting on to the flight. In the Caribbean the odds on this occurring shorten to a dead cert.

On this occasion the team's logistics planners have done a great job and, despite leaving some time after me, and flying via Sydney – which looks uphill on the map – the players arrive in Hobart an hour before I do. Three hours is a long time to kill in Melbourne Airport and, door-to-door, my journey has taken eight-and-a-half hours. It is cold and drizzling in Hobart where, once again, I am with the players in a hotel that has a lovely view of the harbour. Or it would if you could see through the mist.

DAY 13 **15 November 2010**

It is without doubt the busiest day of the tour so far. It begins with the Australian selectors naming a squad for the First Test of seventeen players. Seventeen! That is bigger than England's Ashes touring squad. To be fair to the selectors, the marketing men at Cricket Australia, who want a big launch of the Ashes in Sydney at an iconic venue, have determined that the announcement should be made today while there is a full round of Sheffield Shield matches still to go. This could give rise to injuries, so it seems that the selectors have had little choice but to cover all bases. "Sod 'em!" was the view of one selector, apparently, but it has thrown up some intriguing scenarios. The launch, by the way, is a thoroughly windswept, bleak and damp affair (the rain is incessant) to which no one comes.

The out-of-form batsmen Michael Hussey and Marcus North now have Callum Ferguson and Usman Khawaja breathing down their necks. The latter two have been named in the squad, and they will play for Australia A against England. What happens should either Hussey or North fail in their Shield match for Western Australia against Victoria (the Retrovision Warriors vs the DEC Bushrangers. Ugh!) and one of the youngsters makes runs against England? Surely in the interests of maintaining the integrity of the selection process Ferguson or Khawaja would have to be picked, while the feeling is that if their hands had not been forced, the selectors would, rightly or wrongly, go for experience, choosing North and Hussey for the Test. Likewise in the spin department. Xavier Doherty is a mostly unknown left-arm spinner from Tasmania, but he is in the party and will have a 'bowl off' with Nathan Hauritz when he plays against New South Wales on Wednesday. Again, if Doherty takes more wickets, won't he have to be picked? It will certainly make the Sheffield Shield matches competitive, but this really is an extraordinary situation. You have to go back to the late 1970s, when Australian cricket was torn apart by the Packer revolution of World Series Cricket, to find the last time the Australian camp was so divided before an Ashes series had even started.

Therefore, it is with perfect timing that England announce what we all suspected would be the case: England's main attack of Anderson, Broad, Finn and Swann will fly to Brisbane on Wednesday evening. Quite frankly, the weather in Hobart has been so foul – windy and wet – that it is difficult to argue against the decision. I conclude my thoughts on the matter by saying that in an ideal world, a touring team would field its best players in the toughest warm-up match before the Test, and had this game been played anywhere in Australia other than in Hobart, they probably would have done so. Flower makes the announcement at the training ground and tells me that he has been surprised by the level of press interest in this particular topic. I disagree. It has been a fascinating early tour story to air and debate; usually at this preliminary stage of the campaign, we get little more than groin strains suffered in the nets to report on.

The highlight of the day is an invitation extended to the media to take part in a very special training and skills session with the England team. Organised by England's sponsor Brit Insurance, it has to be held indoors because of the weather. With complete wholeheartedness, the England team and back room staff set about giving the travelling press pack a thorough insight into the sort of skills and training an international cricketer takes for granted. All that is apart from your BBC correspondent, whose wonky fingers after seven operations to correct Dupuytrens contracture, simply cannot take it. Flower addresses the group at the start and makes it clear that the event is to be taken seriously by everybody. It is exactly the right approach and the result is that the players buy into it immediately and, I think, genuinely enjoy it.

There are bowling clinics, batting classes and fielding drills during which the players give catches to members of the press. Can you imagine this happening in football? We really are incredibly fortunate to be involved in this wonderful sport. The highlight for me is the bowling clinic. Coach David Saker produces a framework model of a batsman featuring a helmet, a metal plate over where his ribs would be, a marker indicating the height of the bails and, by his feet, a bar two feet above the ground under which the ball must pass if it is to be deemed a perfect yorker.

The clinic starts and round one requires the bowler to aim a bouncer at the helmet. Unsurprisingly, virtually every ball delivered by the press boys ends up in the side netting. Saker calls up Anderson, who hits the helmet with his first ball. It's the same with his next two balls – the first aimed at the 'ribs', and the second a perfect, bail-high ball. His yorker inevitably flies under the bar. It is mightily impressive.

Less impressive is the *Sun's* John Etheridge, whose repeated attempts to catch balls spat out by one of the training machines are at the hopeless end of the scale: he manages to drops five out of five. Poor Tim Abrahams of Sky News, who is a magnificently fit athlete, takes his first wicketkeeping catch from Matt Prior straight in the unmentionables and ends up in a crumpled moaning heap on the floor.

Graham Gooch conducts a batting drill that will guarantee some of my senior colleagues won't be able to walk for a week. Fully padded up they repeatedly advance down the pitch as if they are attacking a spinner and then have to pick up a ball from one of three coloured cones that Gooch designates in his curiously squeaky voice. He then produces something I have never seen before: I am not sure where he has got the idea from but Graham uses a very whippy plastic slinger – the sort I use to launch tennis balls in a field for Bracken, my Springer Spaniel. These slings can fire a tennis ball twice the distance you can normally throw it. I don't know how he does it, but Graham has mastered the art and timing of an over-arm release of the ball, like a bowler, with the thing sending the ball down the wicket with pinpoint accuracy. So we watch as he slings the ball at 90 mph with seemingly no effort at a bunch of hapless pressmen, many of whom have never faced a cricket ball in their lives. One well-known tour photographer is cringing and ducking, having an absolute nightmare, as the ball brushes his nose and then thumps in to his foot. It is a fantastic example of the innovative skills of the England coaching staff, and a great demonstration of what the day is all about.

The whole afternoon passes off extremely well. Because we are in a cricketing environment, rather than simply making small talk around the hotel, I find myself having several fascinating chats with members of the England set up – firstly about bowling with Stuart Broad, during which we compare our respective generations' styles and approaches, and then with Alastair Cook on the subject of three-day cricket. I think the two matches so far have been much more entertaining than most tourist games we see because they have been shorter and the captains have looked to play positively. Cook's point about four-day matches being better preparation for Test cricket is correct, but we must not forget the spectator.

It is while chatting to Broad that Graeme Swann appears with his video camera, clearly in recording mode. "Go on Broady," he urges, "do your Sprinkler." Broad seems to be rather embarrassed, but performs a strange movement involving an outstretched right arm, then rotating the top half of his body taking the arm with him. It is most peculiar and appears to be a new dance move. Swann finds the whole thing very amusing and moves on.

DAY 14 16 November 2010

My first potentially dangerous invitation of the tour arrives by text message: 'See you in the bar at 7. IC'. Ian Chappell and the rest of his colleagues from Channel 9 have flown in for tomorrow's match. At the appointed hour, I enjoy a drink with former Australian Test players Mark Taylor, Ian Healy, Michael Slater and Ian Chappell (Michael and Ian Chappell will both be working on *Test Match Special* during the series). I get the feeling that all four are genuinely fascinated by the build up to the Ashes and Australia's current woes in particular. We have a robust conversation about the spot-fixing allegations surrounding members of Pakistan's team. There is very little sympathy around our particular table. Eventually Ian and I move next door to the appropriately named Drunken Admiral. Chappell is the most enthusiastic storyteller – about any topic – I have ever met; to be frank he never stops! His tales inevitably involve getting into scrapes with Rodney Marsh, Dennis Lillee and his team-mates from the time when I was just getting into cricket, so I am always fascinated and amused by his anecdotes. Mind you, if you cut out the swear words, they could be told in half the time. But then that's Ian.

CAN SWANN PROVIDE THE KRYPTONITE?

Ben Dirs | 16 November 2010

You sometimes hear the argument that visiting finger spinners simply aren't a deciding factor in Ashes series in Australia, an argument that, when scrutinised, appears to be buttressed largely by cherry-picked evidence. Ashley Giles, it is true, was wholly ineffective on the last, disastrous trip Down Under and while his replacement Monty Panesar took a five-for on his Ashes debut in Perth, he was tamed in Melbourne and Sydney.

Yorkshire's Richard Dawson toiled for scant reward in 2002-03, and even though Phil Tufnell had his successes – including 5/61 in Sydney in 1990-91 – they were few and far between. Yet John Emburey and Phil Edmonds collected 33 wickets between them the last time England won the Ashes in the old enemy's backyard while Fred Titmus bagged 21 wickets at 29 in 1962-63. While Raymond Illingworth and Tony Greig are among the more illustrious England twirlers to have found the going much tougher in Australian conditions (although it should be remembered Greig also bowled seam), there are two other significant names whose figures do pass muster: Derek Underwood (50 wickets in 14 Tests at 31.48) and Jim Laker (15 in four at 21.2).

Those figures will be of some comfort to England fans who believe Andrew Strauss's party contains the country's best off-spinner since Laker and best spinner of any kind since Underwood, a certain Graeme Peter Swann. "They say finger spinners don't have an impact in Australia," says Tufnell, who garnered 19 wickets in eight Tests Down Under, "but if you're a good enough bowler you will take wickets, it's as simple as that. He's the player the Aussies will fear most, he's had a phenomenal couple of years in Test cricket."

"Graeme Swann will be the key," adds Emburey, who took 35 wickets in 10 Tests in Australia. "He'll relish the extra bounce and if the pitches do turn, the ball will turn quicker because the pitches are harder. And if it's not spinning he gets a lot of drift, so if he's not beating the inside edge he's beating the outside edge instead."

Swann is the fastest England spinner to 100 wickets since Kent's Colin Blythe in 1910, and like Laker and Underwood in their time, he can claim to be the best slow bowler in world cricket. He is currently ranked second overall in Test cricket behind South African quick Dale Steyn, and it is not often an England spinner has been able to say that. His elevated status will make him a target, with batsmen looking to attack him. But Tufnell believes that will only play into the Nottinghamshire man's hands, especially when he is bowling into the footmarks created by Australia's left-arm seamers Mitchell Johnson and Doug Bollinger.

"The Australians like to put spinners off their game but that could be good for England," says Tufnell, who toured South Africa with Swann in 1999-2000. "They'll make mistakes, try to hit balls that aren't there. It's a form of flattery, because they know if they just hang around he's a good enough bowler to get them out. It won't faze him at all if the Aussies decide to get stuck into him, he's that type of character. Whether it's the first day and the wicket's flat or it's a green seamer, you throw him the ball and he believes he can get people out."

'Character' is a word you will find cropping up a lot where Swann is concerned, in part because it's a quality that has been in such short supply on recent trips Down Under. Swann, in contrast to the stereotype of the buttoned-up, risk-averse England spinner, is confrontational, attack-minded and possesses that 'unfathomable something'. And it is this 'unfathomable something', as much as the guile and the drift and the tremendous 'revs' Swann puts on the ball, which is kryptonite to many batsmen.

"If he can stay fit, he's going to be a massive part in us winning the Ashes," says Giles, who took eight wickets in three Tests Down Under. "He's a phenomenal bowler at the moment. Every time he comes on, you think something's going to happen." When Giles says 'you', he means opposition batsmen, too. It is this 'unfathomable something' that makes batsmen play the man rather than the ball, convinces them the bowler is trying something on when he is doing nothing of the sort. Ian Botham had it in spades, especially later in his career when the waistline had expanded and the run-up was little more than a saunter; and Shane Warne had it, too, even when a creaking body had pared down his many variations.

Moving from the abstract to the practical, both Tufnell and Emburey concede a finger spinner's lot is made more difficult by the Kookaburra ball used in Australia, with its flatter, perishable seam that disintegrates into little more than dots. However, both Tufnell and Emburey are quick to point out that, for all his chutzpah, Swann is essentially a team man, able to lock down his ego for the greater good.

"When Phil Edmonds and myself weren't getting wickets at least we bowled long spells and controlled the game," says former Middlesex stalwart Emburey.

"That's the key with Swanny, if he's not taking wickets he's good enough to keep it tight." Tufnell adds: "England will be looking for him to be a major wicket-taker, but with a four-man attack he's also going to be the guy who's going to look to dry up one end while the seam bowlers rotate at the other."

A few weeks back, when England's Lee Westwood became golf's world number one, his coach Peter Cowen said his pupil had got to where he was because he remained "very comfortable in uncomfortable situations". It doesn't get more uncomfortable for an English cricketer than an Ashes tour Down Under, yet you get the feeling it is going to take more than a bit of bullying from the Aussie batsmen and a dumpling of a ball to knock Swann out of his groove.

DAY 15 **17 November 2010**

England spring a surprise by fielding their Test batsmen, so the one reserve, Morgan, will have had no cricket before the First Test. There is an element of risk to this, but Flower and Strauss clearly want to give the first-choice players every opportunity to find form and, hopefully, play long and meaningful innings against Australia A's decent-looking pace attack. The pitch is very green indeed. Strauss wins the toss and no one is surprised when he puts the home team in to bat against his reserve attack.

With Anderson, Broad and Finn looking on before they leave to catch their flight to Brisbane, the support seamers have something of a field day. Conditions are perfect for Tremlett, Shahzad and Bresnan, but it is no surprise that they are all rather ring rusty, well short of match practice. Australia A slip to 118 for 6 from which point England's frontline bowlers would have ruthlessly finished them off. But fighting half centuries by Steve Smith and Stephen O'Keefe combined with England's bowlers' lack of puff, enables Australia to reach 230. It shows that it doesn't matter how many miles you run or weights you lift, only through bowling in match conditions can you really get fit for cricket.

I hope we get a little closer to understanding and appreciating Chris Tremlett on this tour. He is tall, has a great action and enough pace to hurt you, but his reputation of being rather soft continues to haunt him. Those who watch him play for his second county, Surrey, believe he has hardened up and become more aggressive and self-confident. I hope so because now aged 29, it really is make or break time for him.

Understandably, he starts his spell somewhat rustily, but produces a really good ball to the Australian dashing opener, Phillip Hughes, which the left-hander edges straight to Strauss at first slip. Tremlett bowls Cameron White, and then has Tim Paine and O'Keefe caught at the wicket – although there is an element of good fortune about both of these dismissals – and his figures of 4 for 54 are the best of the day. But he still seems to lack a 'presence' on the field. He runs up and bowls then immediately turns and walks back to his mark. I'm not suggesting he should indulge in sledging or silly things like that, but the odd moment of eye contact with the batsman or any show of emotion will help convince the spectator he really means it. Tremlett's approach contrasts sharply with that of Shahzad who scurries in, glares at the batsmen and bristles with aggression. For my money, with 3 for 57, he is the bowler of the day, and because of his confidence would also be my first reserve if a pace bowler suddenly needs to be drafted in.

Bresnan dismisses test-hopeful Ferguson with a beauty, which is edged to Prior and then watches in stunned amazement as Monty Panesar flings himself full length to his right to pull off an astonishing reflex catch at mid-wicket. Wide-eyed and jumping about in celebration, Monty seems as surprised as everyone else that he has held on to it. Further credit to the skill and fielding drills devised by Richard Halsall (as experienced by the press pack on Monday). It is not long before the catch is available on YouTube and my delighted listeners are soon logging on for a look. Later, in the hotel lobby, I tell Monty that he is trending on Twitter and receive a delighted high five in return. Monty Rhodes!

Meanwhile we are all keeping an eye on the Australian squad players who are appearing in the first day of the latest round of Sheffield Shield matches – and it has been a disaster. Hussey 0. Watson 6. Katich 1. Ponting 7. North 17. Bollinger 0. Haddin 10. Hauritz 0. Only Mitchell Johnson, who is 81 not out overnight, has made a score at all and without him, the tally is 41/8. In reality, scores in Sheffield Shield matches should be largely irrelevant, but it does underline the problems the Aussies have going into the First Test.

DAY 16 **18 November 2010**

I arrive at the ground to discover that Swann's latest video diary on the ECB website is the talk of the town and that the Sprinkler is clearly the team dance. The video is brilliantly put together and it is hilarious to watch every member of the team – even Mushtaq Ahmed, the heavily bearded ('black and grey stripes, so sponsored by Adidas') spin bowling guru, performing the 'Sprinkler'. The tabloids are onto it and Twitter has gone into meltdown. A new craze has been created by, it later turns out, Paul Collingwood.

On the face of it this appears to have been a really good day for the batsmen. England are already 105 runs in the lead at the close, with Bell having hit the most stylish hundred I have seen by an Englishman for a very long time. But look below the surface at the close of play scoreline, and you see the problem: England were 137 for 5 until the stand of 198 between Bell and Collingwood salvaged the situation and, on closer inspection still, every one of the four batsmen that perished today (Strauss was caught in the gully yesterday) got themselves out. This is precisely the sort of casual batting that has to be eliminated if England really are to win the Ashes here for the first time in 25 years, and while the team PR machine prefers to dwell on the strength of the recovery from England's poor position, England should not have got into such a mess in the first place. It is all about discipline and there has not been enough of that in the approach of England's batsmen in recent years. Dashing half-centuries are not what is required. The batsmen have to play the long game.

Even Monty, the nightwatchman, is out hooking. Cook and Trott then add 87, but Cook hoists a catch to mid-on off the left-arm spinner O'Keefe for 60, and Trott miscues a pull shot off Mark Cameron so badly that he gives a flat catch to mid-off for 41. Pietersen hits O'Keefe for 4, but then completely misses what appears to be nothing more than a dead straight delivery that rattles his middle stump. From KP's reaction at the time, he seems to think that he is the victim of an unplayable hand grenade and departs the crease slowly as if has been betrayed. In the media centre we watch replay after replay trying to work out how he has made such a misjudgement, and, frankly, it is difficult to make sense of it. Is it that Pietersen really does have an issue playing left-arm spin bowlers, who have now dismissed him fifteen times in Tests?

Bell plays fluently from the outset. He and the bottom-handed Collingwood are an interesting combination and there really are shades of Geoffrey Boycott in the way, in particular, Bell drives: it is the perfectly bent left elbow that does it. He absolutely destroys Smith, the leg spinner, endorsing the majority view that there is no way Smith could play for Australia as the main spinner – he simply is not good enough.

I interview Colly at the end of play and feel I have no choice but to ask him about the Sprinkler. "Wait 'til you see the Lawnmower," is his cryptic reply.

It's dinner with Graham Gooch and Derek Pringle [former England player and now of the *Daily Telegraph*] in a Greek restaurant close to our hotel. Gooch really seems to have found his niche now – he is on call with England as and when Flower wants him and will stay with the tour until the end of the Third Test. He is a hugely respected batting coach, and this role enables him to focus purely on that without having to worry too much about running team affairs. He insists we drink Greek wine to accompany the meal. It is very good but, as usual, Pringle has a damaging impact on the bill by ordering an expensive bottle of Tasmanian red at the end. I'm trying so hard to stick to my beginning-of-the-tour fitness resolution, but discovering that (as Emma would no doubt have forecasted) my willpower really is non-existent.

THE PARADOX OF SHANE WATSON

Oliver Brett | 18 November 2010

How England fans sneered when they saw a familiar blond all-rounder walk out to open the batting for Australia in the Edgbaston Ashes Test of 2009. Here was a man who had produced one solitary fifty in 13 previous Test innings. He apparently had few credentials as an opener, and was more adept, surely, at batting at six or seven and bowling a few overs of fast medium pace. Besides, he seemed to be injured most of the time.

Shane Watson, for he was the man in question, ignored the naysayers, striking 62 and 53 while James Anderson and Graham Onions were swinging the ball sideways. He has played every Test bar one since then, forming a formidable opening partnership with the crab-like Simon Katich, hitting the ball merrily here, there and everywhere with little ceremony spared. Katich has been Australia's top scorer in all Tests since Edgbaston 2009, but only by five runs. Watson has amassed 1,261 runs in that time at an average of 50.44, leaving Ricky Ponting, Michael Clarke and Michael Hussey trailing in his wake. Whatever your allegiance, it is easy to admire Watson's second coming.

He could have been a hero in the 2006-07 Ashes, when England were swept aside 5-0, but unrealised potential is often a recurring characteristic of the Watson story. His was then a career mired in uncertainty, notably because of injuries afflicting every part of an ironically powerful physique, with hamstrings, calves and hips taking a battering. So inevitably he was unfit and missed Australia's glorious summer. Even though he enjoyed the considerable consolation of appearing in the 2007 World Cup-winning side, his Test career appeared in danger of remaining forever unfulfilled.

Now, at 29, he is one of the first names on the Australia team sheet, filling a dual role as Katich's more effusive foil at the top of the order, while also sending down some handy overs as the fourth seamer. He proved particularly effective with the ball in the Tests with Pakistan at Lord's and Headingley in the summer of 2010. The oddity is that many Australian cricket fans find it difficult to admire Watson. There is a view that Watson should not open the batting, despite his success in that role. Former Australian captain Ian Chappell disagrees: "He might have become an opening batsman by accident but he's quite happy opening and I look upon him as a very effective opener." An old-fashioned biffer of the ball, he may lack some of the finesse of others but nevertheless has a sound enough defence. The overall package suits Chappell fine.

"If you have an opener who can score quickly, as Watson does, it's worth gold and makes him very effective," he says. "There are two types of opening batsman, the type that gets a start, makes the most of it and makes a big score, then you have the type who doesn't get out early but doesn't get big scores too often. Watson is in the second category, but if you can't have the first category I'm happy with the second category. The flaw is that he doesn't get a lot of hundreds, but he makes up for that in other ways. So long as he doesn't get out quickly, the guys batting around him are never under pressure to score quickly themselves."

Chappell is not keen to see Watson increase his bowling workload, however, adding: "The more bowling he's got to do the more it means the Australian attack isn't performing as well as you would hope. Watson should be used the way he's been used in the last 12 to 18 months, purely as a change bowler, a few overs here and then he's off. Anything you do with him that takes him away from opening the batting effectively would be counter-productive."

When he picked up the Allan Border Medal in February last year, the annual prize awarded to Australia's top cricketer, Watson fought back tears. His partner Lee Furlong, a TV presenter whom he has since married, beamed in the audience as her man, clad in a designer suit and with his hair perfectly coiffured, thanked a range of people who had helped rebuild his career. Among them was Victor Popov, the Brisbane physiotherapist who transformed Watson's training regime. No more pumping weights in the gym to make those rippling muscles even bigger; instead a gentler schedule of pilates and stretching was ordered. Where there was once an occasional beer or two to unwind, now there was a strict teetotal regime.

To the unreconstructed Australian sports fan, Watson is thus something of an anomaly – and it helps explain the paradox that he does not meet with universal approval in his own country. The Australian blogger Jarrod Kimber really sticks the boot in, writing recently: "It takes real talent to be hated when you are pathetic and just as despised when you are good. Even those who have the talent to get to this level of hatred could never do it as well as Shane Watson. When not in front of the mirror, he seems to be able to move 95% of cricket fans into a frenzy of hate, pure detestation, clear revulsion, and a general uneasy sickness of rage." So he continues, belittling his bowling action by likening it to the movements of "an elderly man getting out of a car".

England's bowlers will have all sorts of strategies lined up for him when the First Test starts at his home ground, the Gabba. Whether they fall into the camp of being admirers or haters of 'Watto' is not strictly relevant. Nevertheless, the renaissance of Watson, and the manner in which it has been received, provides an intriguing backdrop to the opening salvos.

19 November 2010

Finally, after three weeks in the country, the first sledging article appears in the Australian newspapers. And it's a cracker! 'Ten Reasons why the Poms are Duds' is the headline, alongside a full page photograph of Kevin Pietersen who, thanks to his 'Movember' moustache – the month formerly known as November is a moustache growing charity event held each year that raises funds and awareness for men's health – suddenly looks terribly camp, as if he is a member of the 1970s band YMCA. It should be noted that Mitchell Johnson has also grown a particularly fine specimen. The ten 'weaknesses' are 1) Over-rated 2) Pietersen 3) No genuine speedster 4) Over-analysis 5) Passive captain 6) No depth 7) No superstars 8) Chokers 9) Warm-ups 10) Scars. Unfortunately for the writer concerned, he refers to Panesar as an off-spinner which does little for the credibility of the piece, but it is much more like the sort of reception England cricket teams should expect in this part of the world. Some of the points are reasonable enough – England do lack a genuine fast bowler, someone who can turn on three or four overs of real pace like Andrew Flintoff used to do. South Africa were able to score frustrating lower order runs last winter because their tailenders were not intimidated, and that might be an area of concern this time too. However, Australia do not have an out-and-out fast bowler either. Pietersen a weakness? Unpredictable, maybe, but I would never consider KP to be a weakness in the team or a 'pain in the neck' as he was described in the article. And when it comes to lacking depth, I would rather have England's back-up resources than Australia's. But here I am letting this article wind me up, which is entirely the aim of the writer. I should have more experience than that!

On the field, Bell simply carries on where he left off yesterday in the company of Collingwood. Their partnership is worth 240 when Collingwood is caught behind playing a pull shot for 89 – the second time he has missed out on a century in ten days. Here he has batted more smoothly than he did at Adelaide – regardless of what he says! Prior times the ball beautifully, but his dismissal is disappointing and again is a case of impatience. He breezes to 27 from 31 balls but slices a drive to backward point off the leg spinner, Smith. This was Prior's one opportunity and he has given it away.

England pile on the runs with the lead well over 250 when Bell gets out for 192. He drives Smith to extra cover and now seems a likely time for Strauss to declare the innings closed. But he chooses not to and instead gives Bresnan and the lower order the opportunity to plunder some quick runs against a flagging attack – none more so than poor old George who finishes with 0/135. It is an interesting tactic – had Strauss chosen to declare earlier he would have increased the likelihood of England having a second innings and giving Trott and Pietersen another hit. But he had gone on record at the outset, saying he wants to win every match on the tour, and this massive lead of 293 should ensure England win by a big margin.

They take three wickets before the close of play with Australia A still 165 runs behind. It is a change to recent encounters when, I have to say it, Australia's reserves were much stronger than this. It is another sign of the wheel turning down here, but has it turned far enough yet?

I have a rare evening in, during which my Twitter companions introduce me to the talents of young singer Jessie J. Sometimes on tour it is nice just to lock yourself away and have a quiet one.

DAY 18 20 November 2010

It all seems to be going terribly well, doesn't it? England beat Australia A by 10 wickets, needing to knock off just 9 runs. They have completely dominated the game, helped by a good toss to win on the first morning. These matches are usually much more competitive. Panesar gets amongst the wickets today, so every reserve bowler has had a good run out. If there is an injury before the Brisbane Test, I reckon Bresnan would get the nod if it were Anderson in trouble, and Tremlett if either Broad or Finn is ruled out. Cameron White's century is good timing, as there are still rumblings from around the Australian camp that Michael Clarke is struggling with his chronic back complaint, and neither of the reserves, Khawaja (out first ball today) or Ferguson (10) made the most of their opportunities.

That's it, preparations over. Hobart is lovely, but is time to move on to Brisbane.

DAY 19 **21 November 2010**

I interview KP before we all leave Tasmania. I compliment him on his thickening charity moustache and he gives me one of his thoughtful and insightful chats. Sometimes he can be a rather irritable and impatient interviewee, but he is on good form today. I especially like his description of the video analysis of the Australian players that England will now focus on as they build up to the Test. This will include, of course, Xavier Doherty, who KP admits to have never seen bowl a ball. I mention that some people are suggesting that the left arm spinner has been chosen merely to get him out (as mentioned earlier, it has happened fifteen times in Test cricket), Kevin scoffs at the thought. "Right arm seam bowlers have got me out many more times than left arm spinners."

It is a three-hour flight to Brisbane and every member of the travelling media is aboard. This time we are better off than the team, who have to transit in Sydney. Undoubtedly, there is a tremendous sense of anticipation among members of the press pack – even the most experienced, and by definition most cynical, members seem to be genuinely intrigued about what is to unfold. The coming week is why we do this job.

It is a cloudy day when we touch down. My cabbie regales me with stories about how much rain has fallen in these parts over the last few months and how the forecast for the Test is unsettled. It would be too awful if after the huge build up and with so many cricket fans here and back home in a state of massively heightened anticipation the game was a washout. I haven't even considered it as a possibility.

I catch up with Adam Mountford, our *Test Match Special* producer, who arrived in Australia yesterday and is clearly jet lagged, along with Caroline Short, who will be producing Mark Pougatch's output on Radio 5 live. Over dinner I give them both a report on the last couple of weeks and include a quick demo of the Sprinkler. Unfortunately this is spotted by some of the tour photographers who are sitting at a nearby table. I fear it is something that could well come back to haunt me.

DAY 20 · 22 November 2010

It is our first chance to catch up with the Australian side: they are practising at the Allan Border field, a small cricket ground in the Brisbane suburb of Albion that is home to the Australian Cricket Academy. We are then treated to a 'media opportunity'. In reality this means we journalists all stand in a line cordoned off by a rope from the players. Every player walks down the row of queuing journalists, who are given a brief interview of a maximum of two minutes each. I have come hopelessly unprepared, and while waiting 45 minutes for the event to get started, am scorched by the blistering Australian sun, absolutely burned to a crisp. All for two minutes with Ricky Ponting. He is his usual business-like self and, as always, answers my questions honestly and directly. He has a lot on his mind, not least the fitness of Michael Clarke, whose recurrent back problem has struck again. Clarke was not able to practise today and will have to do so tomorrow to have any chance of playing on Thursday. Usman Khawaja is called up as a possible replacement. I ask Ponting if there's a confidence problem within Australian cricket and, naturally enough, he denies it.

Things continue to hot up on the sledging front. Former England coach Duncan Fletcher has riled the Aussies by claiming their Test team has not been in such a muddled state for thirty years. He adds that Australian cricket is in a dark place. Australia's coach Tim Nielsen bites back: "His opinions on most things in Test cricket are irrelevant. Have a look at his record here. His record speaks for itself. He doesn't know what he's talking about, but that's no great surprise. He isn't fit to lace Ricky Ponting's bootstraps."

Meanwhile, Shane Warne, a friend of Pietersen's, claims that England's treatment of Pietersen is responsible for his loss of form. Warne suggests that Pietersen has been made to feel like an 'outcast'. I must admit that is not my impression from what I have seen on the tour, and Andy Flower is forced to reject it during his press conference today.

With a face like a ripe tomato I appear on the Channel 9 evening news and then head off to a delightful party hosted by the Queensland

Tourist Board. Former great Australian fast bowler Jeff Thomson is there, long silver hair flowing, and we all have the chance to be photographed either stroking a gorgeous Koala called Crumpet, or a rather vicious looking Olive Python, wrapped menacingly around the torso of its young female handler. I go for Crumpet. In fact, I think we all do.

THE SECRET OF STRAUSS AS SKIPPER

Tom Fordyce| 22 November 2010

When Andrew Strauss was appointed England captain in the messy aftermath of the Kevin Pietersen and Peter Moores saga, it was almost by default. He was not only a safe pair of hands, he was the only pair. Less than two years later, Strauss leads his country into an Ashes series not only in possession of the coveted urn but more heavily fancied to beat Australia on their home patch than any England skipper in almost a quarter of a century.

If it is a headline-grabber of a transformation, the man himself is almost the polar opposite. From the first moment he arrived at Middlesex, fresh from Durham University and Radley College, Strauss has been personified by the virtues of hard work, steady self-improvement and composure under fire. "Back in the late 1990s, I played with Andrew in the first team at Middlesex and then spent long hours with him as coach," remembers Mike Gatting, the last England captain to secure the Ashes on enemy territory. "You could see the sort of character he was even as a teenager. When he first came into the team, we were more comprehensive schoolboys rather than public school, so we used to chip away at him about that. But he was very good at dealing with it."

While Mike Atherton famously had the initials 'FEC' – 'Future England Captain' – scrawled on his locker, Strauss initially struggled to convince at county level. In his first game in Middlesex colours, a Sunday League match in July 1997, he made only three, bowled by Matthew Fleming. He hit 83 on his first-class debut a year later but his maiden county century did not come for a further two years. "It's always difficult coming in from school cricket as a young up-and-coming hopeful," says Gatting. "It takes a while to settle into the heavier stuff. Andrew worked very hard on technique and playing at that different level. He was prepared to work very hard at it and do what was needed. Importantly, he had a very good grounding at Radley. Their coach, Andy Wagner, did a great job and they gave him a sound understanding of the game. He was always a natural sportsman, too. He was a very good rugby player and had a low golf handicap. From my point of view as coach, it was a pleasure working with someone who had such a good work ethic and who clearly had such a love of cricket."

The young Strauss took particular note of two other men in the dressing-room, skipper Mark Ramprakash and Australian opener Justin Langer. Gatting again: "Justin was the ideal role model, not only as a fellow left-hander who Andrew could work with but as a great example in how to prepare. Langer took his cricket seriously and had a lot of passion for it. There was always that in Andrew. He was always very competitive, never liked coming second. Every time he played, every time he went in, you could see he was striving to become better."

In his early days as full-time England skipper – on the unsuccessful tour of the West Indies, when he appeared loath to make attacking declarations – Strauss was sometimes criticised for being too cautious and unimaginative. At that stage, the aim was to steady the ship, rather than risk steering it back on to the rocks. While he has grown a little more adventurous with time, he remains a study in careful composure. He is both stoical in defeat and calm in victory. Just as there was no panic after the crushing defeat by Australia at Headingley last summer, so there were no wild celebrations after the series-clinching win at The Oval.

"The one key thing about Andrew is that he's very level-headed," explains Gatting. "He always had it very firmly in his mind what he wanted to do, how he was going to do it and how he was going to be as a person. That self-confidence feeds into his displays at the crease. While history has lain heavy on the shoulders of many unsuccessful Ashes skippers, Strauss appears capable of carrying its burden. "It's an integral part of his success," says Gatting. "He knows who he is. He will set his standards and he's not one to then move from that."

During the 2009 Ashes, Strauss scored 474 runs at an average of 52.66, more than any other player in the series. He also hit 161 as England won their first Ashes Test at Lord's in 75 years. His overall average with the bat as skipper is 47.34, compared to 41.04 as a humble foot soldier. This compares favourably with the record of the last England captain to win the Ashes, Michael Vaughan, who averaged a stellar 50.98 as a mere batsman but only 36.02 while in charge of the side.

"We used to have chats about it, about making sure he does enough for himself, being able to relax and focus on his own game as well as the captaincy," says Gatting. "He can be a very selfless player, always thinking about the team, but sometimes you have to focus on yourself. You understand your own game as you get older, and Andrew knows his well enough to know what he has to do. A lot of it is about time management. Work out what you have to do as captain and get there early. Get your own work done and dusted so you can then watch your team. If you need a little more practice, then do it at the end. You have to be calculating."

Strauss has not always found Test cricket easy. Dropped in 2007 for the tour of Sri Lanka, having averaged only 27 over the previous 12 months, the then 30-year-old looked technically troubled. Stuart Clark, the leading wicket-taker in the 2006/07 Ashes, believes the Australian bowlers would target a perceived weakness on the hook and a tendency to put the front foot straight down the pitch rather than following the line of the ball. While his record against the old enemy at home is good – in 2005, Strauss was the only batsman on either side to score two centuries in the series – it is less impressive Down Under. In 2006/07, he scored only 247 runs at an average of 24.7 and a highest score of 50. Should he struggle this time, Australia's task in wrestling back the little urn will be made a lot easier.

What will help him, believes Gatting, is the bond formed with coach Andy Flower. "You've got two people now in charge who are both hard and fair but also passionate about the team doing well. Andrew is a very good communicator. He's very honest with his players and can be hard on them but he'll be fair. But the coach has to remember that when things are going well the captain needs to be patted on the back, too, and told he does well. The skipper will go round and tell his players they've done well but he needs the same from someone above him."

What then are the particular pressures Strauss can expect as an England skipper in Australia? And what is key to successful captaincy Down Under? "The media there will side with the home team and try to make as much of things that happen to the tourists as possible," says Gatting. "Andrew will need to keep the side close-knit and then must make sure they don't take too much notice of what is written or said. He will also know that if you do get on top, the Aussie press will get on top of their own team. You can see it in the reaction to Australia's decision to pick a squad of 17 for the First Test. The Aussie media can turn very quickly."

Gatting points out that England have already made a good start Down Under and thus silenced a lot of the Australian critics. "If England hadn't done so well in the state games, you would have seen a lot more about them in the sports pages. The charge hasn't begun because the guys have started well. The focus has been on what the Aussie selectors are doing." And Gatting has these words of wisdom for Strauss and his men: "When you get even a small chance of getting on top, hit them hard. Capitalise on your chances and never, ever take your foot off their throats."

DAY 21 **23 November 2010**

Today is somewhat over shadowed by a row in the papers. Ian Healy, former Australian wicketkeeper and now cricket commentator, is left 'fuming' by the Poms' apparent snub of a lunchtime event he was hosting along with Sky's Nasser Hussein, producing headlines joshing for position as the most ridiculous seen on the tour so far. The England side are criticised for their single-minded arrogance when they fail to turn up for an 'official' Ashes lunch. "This England side didn't think it was important enough to attend. To me that's bullsh**," blasts Healy. Two things wrong with this as far as I can see: firstly, only half the Australians turn out for the lunch and it is not an 'official Ashes lunch' in any case. England were always scheduled to practise at the Gabba from lunchtime onwards and to the best of my knowledge no one in the England camp actually knew about the lunch.

PONTING UNDER FIRE

Ben Dirs| 23 November 2010

Over the past 15 years Australia has had a great many would-be captains, probably thousands of them – and an awful lot of them have been English. They popped up in pubs and bars and on sofas, throwing their hats into the ring every time an Aussie batsman passed 100 in an Ashes Test, every time an English partnership had seen off the seamers and the ball was then tossed to Shane Warne. You could imagine them muttering under their breath: "Seriously, I could captain this side."

It is, of course, a vacuous statement – but not without a smidgeon of truth.

It can quite easily be argued that Australia had in the team that humiliated England 5-0 in the last Ashes series Down Under more bona fide greats than England has produced in the last 30 or 40 years. When the actual captain Ricky Ponting called it 'arguably the best team in any sport in the world', he was not guilty of hyperbole.

Warne and Adam Gilchrist would be automatic choices for any all-time side, while Ponting and Glenn McGrath would certainly be in the reckoning. Add a legendary opening partnership in Matthew Hayden and Justin Langer, Mike Hussey and Michael Clarke in the middle order and quicks Brett Lee and Stuart Clark, and you have a juggernaut of an outfit. With such weapons at his disposal in his first few years as skipper, Ponting, who replaced Steve Waugh in 2004, was given something of an armchair ride, winning 27 of his first 35 matches in charge. After that, however, Ponting's armchair started losing some of its springs.

In the space of a couple of years Warne, McGrath, Langer, Gilchrist, Hayden and Lee all called it a day, as did lesser lights such as Stuart MacGill and Damien Martyn. And just like that, Ponting went from a skipper in charge of a great team with the best winning percentage in Test history to, well, a skipper with a pretty good record in charge of a pretty good team. "Let's be honest, Ricky's had some wonderful players at his fingertips," says Mike Gatting, the last man to lead England to Ashes glory in Australia, in 1986-87. "A captain can only be as good as his players. If you've got a Warne and a McGrath in your side, you don't have to tell them what to do because they are very good professionals who love winning for their country. You shouldn't have to do too much to get them motivated. The same with Gilchrist, Langer and Hayden."

There are many in Australia – former fast bowlers Geoff Lawson and Jeff Thomson have been merciless in their criticism – who believe Ponting has been unmasked as a poor captain and that he should have been replaced by Clarke following the 2-0 series defeat in India which made it three Test defeats on the spin, something that hadn't happened to Australia since 1988. But former skipper Ian Chappell, who won 50% of his Tests to Ponting's current record of 64%, is not one of them, believing the punchy Tasmanian remains the best man for the job.

"Ricky Ponting is a good captain," says Chappell. "It shouldn't come as any surprise that when you lose Warne and McGrath, Ponting isn't winning as often as he was. But Ponting can point to the fact that he wins 64% of his Tests overall and say it works. I've not seen a day's play with Australia where I've looked out there and felt the team hasn't been pulling as one. I've never seen that happen under Ricky Ponting's captaincy. The day that happens is the day you know you've got a problem and that's when you've got to go."

However, there are many who disagree with Chappell and argue that statistics are not the best way to measure a captain. The same people would argue that former New Zealand skipper Stephen Fleming and former England skipper Michael Vaughan were vastly superior to Ponting, not because of their winning percentages, but because of the manner in which they marshalled inferior sides and got them punching above their weight.

Ponting's frailties were there for all to see during the 2005 Ashes series, when he was knocked out of his groove by an injury to McGrath, the lack of form of some of his key players and the in-your-face aggression of Vaughan's England outfit. One of the biggest mysteries of that series was Ponting's decision not to pick MacGill, a man who finished his career with 208 Test wickets at an average of 29, for the final two Tests when his fellow leg-spinner Warne was scalping England batsmen for fun. Fast bowler Shaun Tait, preferred to MacGill at Trent Bridge and The Oval, was then mysteriously underused.

Roll forward to 2009 in Cardiff, with England nine wickets down in their second innings and Monty Panesar and James Anderson in the middle. Ponting made the truly baffling decision to bring part-timer Marcus North to bowl two of the last four overs, with fellow spinner Nathan Hauritz operating from the other end. Panesar and Anderson held firm, Ponting appeared haunted at not being able to force the win and England went on to reclaim the Ashes.

During the recent Test series in India, Ponting took a lot of flak in Australia's media for negative fields, a lack of faith in his players and a tendency to flinch in the heat of battle, a most un-Australian trait. When Warne criticized Hauritz's field placings during the Second Test in Bangalore, Ponting's reaction of claiming the bowler had chosen them on his own seemed indicative of a lack of leadership skills.

Australian fans declare themselves baffled at why a batsman of such attacking verve and pugnacity and so steeped in the traditions of the game should prove to be so devoid of tactical nous and composure when things get uncomfortable. There won't be too many people putting their hand up to replace Ponting if he becomes the first Australian captain to lose three Ashes series since Billy Murdoch in 1890. But you might hear a lot of people saying: "Seriously, who'd want to captain this side?"

DAY 22 **24 November 2010**

Sod's law: with the First Test starting tomorrow I am struck down by a stomach bug. It is nothing serious, but it is uncomfortable and disabling, and with so much work to do today, rotten timing. My old *TMS* producer and good friend, Peter Baxter, throws a BBQ at his Brisbane home and although I attend I am still feeling pretty crook and can't enjoy it as much as I would have liked. Peter, the lucky so-and-so, spends half the year here, and half back in the UK.

The cabbie who takes me to the Gabba doesn't lift my mood when, having told him where I wanted to go, replies: "Hey! You're Aggers, aren't you?" A little puffed up, I confirm that indeed I am none other, only for my 'fan' to offer up: "My! You're much less handsome than you sound on the radio!" Thanks a lot, mate.

The captains' press conferences are very well attended – the ranks of the English media must have trebled since our arrival in Brisbane, but surprisingly there isn't a reporter present from ABC Radio. This is potentially tricky for me as I need an interview with Ponting, and the usual pre-match form is that I stick my microphone into the ABC interview and send the result on to London. The Cricket Australia people are clearly very agitated that ABC aren't here – they chose to record the television press conference – but kindly agree that I may have a few minutes with Ponting to myself. This takes place in a corridor so dark that I can barely see his face, but he is his usual professional self, and I appreciate his co-operation. This comes only a few minutes after Ponting has fallen for one of the great tabloid stitch ups that always occur on the day before the opening Test of an Ashes series in Australia. Because of the time difference it is a blank day for the writers. John Etheridge of the *Sun* tosses out the usual question about whether the Ashes urn should be held in the country that wins it rather than being permanently housed at Lord's, and Ricky bites: "Why not, that would be good." 'Ponting will Urn Trophy' is the resulting headline in the *Sun*.

Strauss strikes me as being rather tense, which is entirely understandable. After I put down my microphone and he starts to walk away I shout after him: "Andrew. Please make sure you all *enjoy* it. There's nothing better than this!" "Don't worry. We're going to," he calls over his shoulder, before disappearing down the same dark corridor.

Later that evening I make good on a promise and meet up with a group of England supporters – who arrived in Australia only this morning – for a swift question and answer session to get them in the mood. After twenty minutes, loud snoring interrupts my flow. It's all been too much for one old boy in the front row!

AUSTRALIA AWAITS AS ENGLAND EXPECTS

Tom Fordyce| 24 November 2010

There's been talk of little else – a team of English stars, exposed to the toughest challenges Australia can throw at them, battling enormous pressure and a huge weight of expectation back home in Blighty. Still, enough of *I'm a Celebrity*. After months of bellicose build-up and fluctuating form, the Ashes are finally upon us. And for England fans both at home and here in Brisbane, there's an unfamiliar sense of optimism in the humid Queensland air.

It's not normally this way. At this stage of an Ashes ding-dong Down Under, England are usually being ripped apart by a caustic local media and mercilessly taunted by cocksure Aussie fans. It shouldn't even make sense. The hosts haven't lost a Test at the Gabba in over 20 years. England haven't won a series here for almost a quarter of a century. They've only won three of the last 24 Tests on Australian soil.

But this time around, the established order appears to have been turned on its head. Australia are the ones coming into the series with injury problems and ropey form, England are the team with wins under the belt and a settled side. So far the media scorn has been aimed squarely at the Australian selectors. The mood among home fans is positively downbeat. For England supporters reared on a diet of Aussie domination, it's all rather unsettling, almost too good to be true. Even the Brisbane weather and Gabba pitch appear to be on the side of the tourists – grey and sweaty overhead, greenish and a little juicy underfoot.

Whether the track stays that way is another matter. While the forecast for Thursday morning is for clouds and warmth, the pitch may just be a late developer. Queensland might have been skittled for 75 and 96 here by New South Wales earlier this month, but Aussie captain Ricky Ponting thinks groundsman Kevin Mitchell has prepared a classic Gabba wicket – spicy enough to keep the pace bowlers interested, but one which will offer something for the spinners later on and bring full reward for disciplined batting.

"I think it looks particularly good," a chirpy Punter said at the stadium on Wednesday. "It looks exactly like wickets look here the day before a match." Ponting won't be drawn on whether he'll opt to bat if he wins the toss. Nor will Andrew Strauss ("I've got pretty firm ideas of what I want to do, but you've got to be prepared to do both.") After England's chastening experiences on the first day in 2002 and 2006, it should be a no-brainer for the tourists: call correctly, and get the pads on.

Except it's not quite so straightforward. England's bowling attack requires seam-friendly conditions. If there's early swing in the air, goes the argument you increasingly hear in local bars and cafes, might it be better to shove recent history to one side and go hard for the jugular? The stats aren't quite as one-sided as we might imagine. In Ashes Tests at this ground, the team winning the toss has batted first 13 times, and gone on to win on six occasions. In the five matches where a skipper has opted to stick the opposition in, they've won two. In all Tests at the Gabba, 64 per cent of games have been won by the side batting first, 36 per cent by the team batting second. Yet since the end of the 1970s, Australia have opted to bowl on nine of the 15 times they've won the toss.

What isn't in doubt is how spicy the atmosphere will be inside this gold and green concrete bowl come the first ball. The most telling moment of Ponting's ebullient pre-match news conference came when he spoke about forcing his side to watch England celebrate after they had regained the urn last summer. "I made sure it hurt them as much as possible when the Ashes were handed over to Andrew Strauss at The Oval," he said. "There is no doubt that that's been driving us – that empty feeling after walking off the pitch after two unsuccessful Ashes series."

Ponting, combative as always, intends to lead from the front. He has begun the last two Ashes series with a century in the very first innings; while he averages an impressive 66 in Tests at the Gabba, that rises to 100 against the oldest enemy. If he has concerns about Michael Clarke's dicky back, he's keeping them well hidden; if he's worried about giving the unheralded 28-year-old Xavier Doherty (84 first-class wickets in his entire career) his Test debut in the cauldron of an Ashes opener, he wasn't about to admit it to a home media scenting blood.

His England counterpart Strauss has had none of those last-gasp selectoral headaches. He's known his first-choice XI since last summer. After wins in two of the three warm-up games this month, he will also feel his side are coming into form at the ideal time. "We're all very keen to get going," he says. "We're in a good place as a side. At the same time we understand the size of the challenge ahead – not many teams come here and win. But we couldn't be better placed mentally to take on that challenge. I'm fully confident that we've got the players to do that and we thrive on the idea that we could pull off something pretty special."

The mood in the camp has been upbeat and confident from the moment they arrived in Brisbane. Others might worry about Alastair Cook's supposed technical deficiencies, or Kevin Pietersen's Test drought, or the inexperience of the attack in Australian conditions, yet Strauss knows that England will never have a better chance of breaking their dismal run Down Under. Australia have won an intimidating 75 per cent of Tests they've played at home over the past 20 years. But the luminaries who sparked those performances are gone, replaced in most part with players big on honest toil but low on star quality. "The prospect of turning that record around excites us," says Strauss. He knows that for all Marcus North's application he is no Steve Waugh; for all Peter Siddle's snarling aggression, he would rather open against him than Glenn McGrath or Brett Lee.

What England need to do is start well. Graham Gooch, who played in four Ashes series in Australia and is now his country's batting coach, has been telling anyone who'll listen out here how critical the first session of each day will be. Even if a repeat of the Harmison horrors of four years ago is unlikely, the first skirmishes could establish the lines for the battle to follow. "There's no doubt that the first hour here set up the whole campaign for us last time," says Ponting. "We were able to capitalise on some very nervous England players."

Seventy-seven per cent of Tests at the Gabba end in a result. Win here, and England will know the mutterings among locals about Australia's flaws and Ponting's perceived inadequacies as skipper will become a clamour. Already there are signs that the hosts' love affair with cricket might not be as passionate as we always assume. Television viewing figures for the sport are down 24 per cent over the last decade, and while there has been a strong growth in participation among children under the age of 12, there has been a bigger drop-off in the 13-18 age group. Australia needs these Ashes as much as England.

Tourist numbers too are down on last time. The recession back home, allied to a strong Aussie dollar that makes travelling here much more expensive for Brits, means there are fewer England fans visible in the pubs and clubs. The Barmy Army is in position, but its ranks are denuded. For the sport as a whole, the series could not have come at a better moment. At a time when corruption scandals are dominating the headlines, this is one clash you can really believe in.

Has there ever been such a feeling of anticipation before a Test series before? This is my sixth Ashes tour, and I certainly have never felt anything like it. This huge excitement has been generated by the optimism among England supporters who genuinely feel that Andrew Strauss's men have a real chance of defeating Australia. At the same time, there is serious trepidation in the Australian media and the general public that their great run of two decades without a home Ashes series defeat is finally coming to an end.

A great deal has been made of England's preparation for the tour. I've watched it, and it has gone well. I would have liked Kevin Pietersen to make a big score – he, Jonathan Trott and Matt Prior have all looked in nice touch, but got out too early. This series will not be won by breezy half-centuries. The batsmen have to go on and register the big scores that really make the difference in Test cricket. England are also lacking a genuinely fast bowler; someone to come on and bowl a blistering, intimidating spell of four overs in the heat and when the pitch is flat. Someone like Andrew Flintoff. Australia don't have one either, mind you, and both teams have the scope to add annoying lower-order runs as a result.

In many ways, though, the preparation will not count for much come the start of play, when the nerves and adrenalin kick in. We all remember the ghastly opening hour here four years ago when poor Steve Harmison was so wretchedly nervous that he fired the first ball straight to a startled Flintoff at second slip.

Ricky Ponting states that his team knew they would regain the Ashes as early as that first drinks session. True, England's build-up contributed to their downfall, but it is the cricket on the Test field that matters in the end, and England know that they have an awful lot of history to bury, and poor starts at the Gabba to overcome if they are to succeed.

The last time England won here at the Gabba, they won the Ashes. If they do win here, it will be fascinating to see the reaction of the Australian selectors who are already under pressure to bring in new faces in place of Mike Hussey and Marcus North in particular. There is even talk of Ponting's career being in the balance should he lose his third Ashes series. However, should Australia win this opening match, I can see them regaining their confidence – which has taken quite a battering recently – and combined with an inevitable feeling of 'here we go again' from the England perspective, they could become very difficult to beat.

So much depends on this first game. A key battleground for me is Australia's batsmen against Graeme Swann. England will be playing only four frontline bowlers so, particularly in the first innings, Swann will have to play a containing role while the pacemen are rotated at the other end. Will the Australians take the obvious strategy of getting after the spinner to force Strauss to take him off, or will they simply keep him out? Both have risks attached – over-aggression in the first approach while the Decision Review System gives Swann quite an advantage against defensive left-handers in particular.

Predictions always come back to haunt you, but I will repeat mine of some months ago that England will win 3-1.

TWO

BRISBANE TEST

"I couldn't have more faith in the boys. The matches will be close but I'm tipping a 5-0 whitewash."

GLENN MCGRATH

DAY 23 **25 November 2010, First Test – first day**

Even for a seasoned old cricket-broadcasting pro of twenty years experience, this morning really does feel special. I forego my run (not much persuasion required, frankly) in favour of an early interview on ABC radio, for which I will also be working during the series. In the hotel lobby I ask the reporter where her outside broadcast equipment is. She laughs and holds up her iPhone. "We're all cutting edge here in Brisbane, you know," she says. "We can now broadcast in studio quality over this phone." Being something of a gadget geek I am seriously impressed. We take our seat on a bench overlooking the river. A sweating Paul Allott (former England fast bowler and broadcaster) lumbers past – he is also on a health kick – and before I know it we are on the air with me answering questions into her phone. All proceeds perfectly until someone rings her number and knocks us off! Promising, but a work in progress.

Adam Mountford is on duty early in the *TMS* box. There wasn't really the time yesterday to have a full briefing about the broadcasting plans for the lunch and tea intervals for this Test, but today will be easy. We just want to get started.

> "England's preparation has been so good, and the Aussies have had a lot of injuries. But the Aussies will be raring to get at us and it will be very even-stephens, I wouldn't know where to put my money and I suggest you keep your money in your pockets." GEOFFREY BOYCOTT, TMS

Morning session: At lunch – England 86/2, Cook 29*, Pietersen 23*

England win the toss and decide to bat first. Disaster strikes with the third ball of the match when Strauss cuts Hilfenhaus hard to gully where Hussey takes the catch. Strauss immediately clutches his head with his left hand. After all the hard work, preparation and, I'm sure, a sleepless night or two, this is simply horrible. Trott aims an ambitious drive at Watson and is bowled through the gate for 29. England 49/2. Cook is dropped by Doherty at point on 26 but manages to reach lunch on 29 with Pietersen on 23. A nervy start and Australia's morning.

It is lovely to be back with the ABC radio team. Jim Maxwell and I are doubling up with ABC and *TMS* duties, and the vast Gabba, where the commentary boxes are on different floors, will be our greatest test of stamina during the series. ABC's Kerry O'Keeffe is a particular favourite of mine – and being entirely unpredictable, is just the man you want sitting beside you during a long day. He keeps you on your toes by taking the conversation in just about every direction, and has the most infectious laugh in the business – a long crackling, wheezing sort of a laugh, which is very much his trademark. Kerry is a great storyteller who can take a very long time to get to the punch line. In fact during the last tour at the Melbourne Test, he told the story of how he had recently managed to meet Mick Jagger and Jerry Hall – it took the full twenty-minute session to get through it. As a commentator, going from box to box, the fact is you need something to sharpen you up. With Kerry you never know where the conversation is headed, so it keeps you on your toes, thereby avoiding a lazy session.

> *"I am a little concerned – Australia need a wicket. This partnership is going very well and Pietersen especially is a worry. He's getting those twinkle toes going in the way he did a few years ago."* MICHAEL SLATER, TMS

Afternoon session: At tea – England 172/4, Cook 60*, Bell 26*

Cook and Pietersen take the score to 117 with KP his usual mix of edginess and class. Johnson tries to rough him up and KP top edges a four before edging a routine-looking ball from Siddle to Ponting at second slip for 43. Collingwood drives Siddle straight for four but plays the next one away from his body and edges to North at third slip. 125/4. Doherty's opening overs don't look threatening in the least. The Barmy Army give us a taste of what will surely come later in the tour with their first serious singsong of the series to end another absorbing session of cut and thrust.

Evening session: At the close – England 260, Australia 25/0

Siddle rips out the middle order with the first Test hat-trick at the Gabba – on his 26th birthday. Cook is taken at first slip by Watson after a stand of 72 with Bell. Prior plays all around his first ball and is bowled and then Broad, walking out to a deafening roar, is lbw to the perfect inswinger. 197/4 becomes 197/7. Siddle also traps Swann lbw for 10 before Bell – faced with batting with the tail – is caught at deep extra for an excellent 76 to give Doherty his first Test wicket. A collapse of 6 wickets for 63 runs in 11.3 overs is completed when Anderson aims a reverse sweep at Doherty and is bowled for 11.

Australia's openers are barely tested in the final seven overs of the day.

It is an awful journey back from the ground: with Boycott chuntering loudly and pulling his case behind him, Michael Vaughan and I have to walk almost the entire way to the hotel. Vaughan resorts to offering bribes to passing motorists to give us a lift, but unsurprisingly we are assumed to be drunken England supporters. After an hour we fluke a cab just as we are beginning to cross the Story Bridge. As a result it is a rather subdued evening spent at a restaurant overlooking the Brisbane River with Brit Insurance, England's official sponsors. All agree this is not the start we had been hoping for – on all fronts.

> "We're never too sure what a par score is but I think we are probably 100 runs short, considering that Bell played beautifully, Cook batted well and KP got in but none of them got to a hundred. Australia will be saying that one of their guys has to get a hundred and then they will be thinking they are on their way to victory." MICHAEL VAUGHAN, TMS

After so much anticipation, the opening day of the Ashes certainly did not go the way England would have wanted. It was only the first of five days, but Andrew Strauss and his men are already up against it and will be hugely disappointed with the way the First Test has gone so far. They were bowled out cheaply, the ball did not swing for them at the end and Graeme Swann's first two deliveries were smacked for four – it was all a reality check after such a smooth build-up to the series. After looking very comfortable in the warm-up matches, on the first day it actually mattered – bang, it didn't go well.

The man of the day was undoubtedly Peter Siddle, the Victorian who took Australia's 11th Test match hat-trick and produced career-best figures of 6/54, all on his 26th birthday, too. Siddle bowled absolutely brilliantly, just perfect for the conditions – he found the right length, a bit fuller than usual, and got the ball to move away from the bat just enough too. What will frustrate England further is the way the Australian openers breezed on to 25/0 at the end with the ball not swinging. He had a terrific day, no mean feat considering there was controversy about him even playing in the game, with some Australians feeling Doug Bollinger should have been picked, but how he proved the doubters wrong.

Siddle's performance was a model for bowling on this wicket and England must now try to copy it. The hat-trick was hugely impressive – to get a well-set opener caught at slip, bowl Prior and then home the ball in on the stumps to Stuart Broad, a left-hander, for the hat-trick ball was terrific and he deserved all the accolades he received. He was head and shoulders above the rest of an Australian attack that is honest and hard-working but not exceptional and that is where Siddle made all the difference – by producing one devastating spell that rocked England.

This is not normally a high-scoring ground in the first innings of a Test match and if you get 300 you are in with a shout usually, but England fell short of that. They had their moments with Kevin Pietersen, Alastair Cook and Ian Bell all going well and should have got to 320 or 330, but – and I said this during the preparation matches – too many batsmen have been getting in and looking good and getting out and that is not good enough if you want to win an Ashes series.

This is the kind of ground where if you bowl it in the right place on the first morning you will get some assistance, but certainly Pietersen and Jonathan Trott played shots that caused their own downfalls. The pitch is a little slower than we are used to seeing at the Gabba and there is a bit of help in there, and England will also be frustrated by the way the Australian openers breezed to 25/0 at the end. There seemed to be no movement for the attack at all and that is something they will hope changes on Friday, in particular James Anderson, who needs that ball to swing and so far has bowled gun-barrel straight.

Though the England dressing-room will have been a disappointed place at the end of the day, this is only the first of a possible 25 days in the series, and they have the ability to fight back as they have shown before. If they can restrict Australia to 320 or 330 in their first innings, and they will have to work extremely hard to do so, then a positive result will still be possible for England. All is not lost, but they will be looking for an awful lot more from now on.

DAY 24 26 November 2010, First Test – second day

"The pitch looks a bit 'fluffy' but it's still a good pitch and I'd expect one of the Australian batsmen to make a hundred on it." MICHAEL VAUGHAN, TMS

Morning session: At lunch – Australia 96/1, Katich 46*, Ponting 10*

Australia consolidate their position in the morning, losing only one wicket when Watson is caught by Strauss at first slip off Anderson for 36. Katich is given out lbw to Anderson for 27, but umpire Doctrove's decision is successfully overturned by the batsman for being too high. It is a muggy, oppressive day but the ball does not seem to be responding to the heavy cloud cover. The general feeling is that England's pace bowlers haven't got their length right. Swann only bowls the last over before lunch.

Yesterday, I had a rather odd experience in the hotel lift when I bumped into a bizarrely dressed individual who, it transpired, was the horse racing pundit, John McCririck. I introduced myself and, knowing that we're always after people to interview on *TMS* during lunch times, I asked whether he would be prepared to come on. He said he would be delighted to do so.

Normally I spend a lot of time researching my guests for *Views from the Boundary*. With thirty-five minutes of live airtime to fill, you have nowhere else to go if things start to go wrong. Adam reassures me that with this particular guest I will not need to refer to a single note. Sure enough, from the moment he came into the box, McCririck does not draw a breath.

> *"If you are patient enough to put the ball on the right length something will happen. There's still a bit of nibble out there but you have to stick at it and be consistent. You are never in on this wicket – yesterday one wicket brought another, can the same happen again?"* MICHAEL VAUGHAN, TMS

Afternoon session: At tea – Australia 168/5, Hussey 46*, Haddin 9*

England are gifted the prize wicket of Ponting with only the second ball after lunch when he edges Anderson down the leg side to Prior for 10. Ponting departs with a face like thunder. Four runs later Finn takes his first wicket of the series when Katich drives a low return catch and the 6' 7" bowler manages to get down in time. Swann bowls too short to Hussey, but Finn finds excellent rhythm to Clarke who England are convinced is caught behind on 0. Umpire Dar rules not out and on the replay, Hot Spot fails to detect the inside edge which the bowler and slip cordon heard, an edge Snicko confirms minutes later. England are furious at losing a precious review, but Finn has Clarke caught behind for 9 from 50 balls. Next over, North edges Swann to Collingwood at slip and Australia have lost 4/72 in the session. The game is alive.

> *"I thought yesterday was remarkable and now this fightback from England is inspired and something very special. What a start after lunch for England."* MICHAEL SLATER, TMS

Evening session: At the close – Australia 220/5, Hussey 81*, Haddin 22*

Rain and bad light curtail the session, but Hussey and Haddin are already looking in ominous form. Swann persists in bowling too short to Hussey, who ruthlessly pulls him through midwicket for four time and again.

News breaks during the evening that England coach Andy Flower has today had surgery to remove a malignant melanoma from under his right eye. It was spotted by Reg Dickason, the Australian-born security officer employed by the ECB, and if it had remained untreated might have had potentially fatal consequences within months. Andy is a lucky man and it is a sharp reminder to all of us who played cricket in the sun as youngsters without taking precautions that are taken for granted these days. Flower will recuperate tomorrow and hopes to be back on the ground on the fourth day.

END OF DAY REPORT

In Test cricket we always talk about the next stage of the match being crucial, but it is certainly true for England in Brisbane, with the morning session on Saturday now terribly important. With Australia 220/5, England still have a lead of 40 and the new ball is ready to go straight away. Because we lost time on Friday we will have an earlier start, so there might be some moisture around and the ball could nip about a bit.

England must use everything to their advantage because they cannot afford to concede too much of a lead after the first innings – 50 can soon be cleared, but you would not want any more than that. Overall, I thought England bowled really well at Australia. In the first hour of the day they set some strange fields, but once they scrapped all that and got back to basics, they performed effectively as a unit.

They should have taken more than one wicket in the morning but got a bit of luck they deserved straight after lunch when Ricky Ponting was caught down the leg side and James Anderson bowled an absolutely brilliant spell in the afternoon. There is no doubt that after that display, Anderson will have answered a few questions in his own mind about whether he is capable of performing on these Australian pitches, which is something we've all wondered about. He couldn't rely on the ball swinging but found a great line, got a bit of nip off the seam and concentrated on the channel outside off stump, it was great stuff. He beat the bat countless times and was the bristling, aggressive Anderson – I don't mean in the sense of bowling silly bouncers – you want to see. He is the leader of the England attack, so much so that they call him 'bowling captain'.

One of the big question marks about this series was whether Anderson could be effective with this Kookaburra ball in these conditions, and he's shown he has a real role to play. One man who didn't enjoy such a good day was off-spinner Graeme Swann. I think that was the worst I've seen Swann bowl in a very long time, but if I'm honest, I don't think he's bowled at his best on the whole tour so far.

He sent down so many long hops, especially to Michael Hussey, who is very strong off the back foot, and Michael Vaughan made the point that on these harder pitches, if you drop short the ball stands up more to be hit, which makes length even more critical. I don't think it was a case of Australia getting after him, hitting him out of the attack, which we thought might be a possibility, it was just that he didn't bowl well. Looking at his demeanour, Swann was clearly chastising himself for the way he performed, but with Australia set to chase a target in the final innings, he has still got a huge role to play in the Test match.

The same is true of Steven Finn, who produced a great spell, took a brilliant low catch off his own bowling and showed he is here to stay in this series. I've never doubted his talent. For a young man he's very mature, very easy-going, he's got an uncomplicated action and he's a very strong performer. Some of the Australians who doubted him until today were very impressed with him in the afternoon and they now realize he is to be taken seriously in the Ashes.

It's obvious already that the series is going to be desperately close. Both teams are struggling with their batting, though for different reasons. England aren't yet in the habit of putting big scores on the board, while some of the Australian batsmen are struggling with confidence, but it is already making for an enthralling contest.

DAY 25 **27 November 2010, First Test – third day**

My usually quiet breakfast is interrupted several times by disgruntled England supporters complaining about the heavy-handed security guards at the Gabba who are ruining their trip. It seems that if you dare venture to the ground with a bag that has more than one zip, you are sent to the bowels of a stand and forced to hand it over for the entire day. At the end of play, you then have to stand in a long queue to have your bag located and returned. It does seem absolutely ridiculous, but as we know, the dreaded 'elf and safety brigade are even more active in Australia than they are at home. One man had his umbrella confiscated when he arrived at the Gabba, even though it was raining. I promise to relay these various woes on *Test Match Special* later in the day and to warn those coming out later in the tour to bring a bag with only one zip.

"There's no doubt about it but this is the decisive day of the game. By the end of play, unless England change it fairly quickly, Australia will be on top and ready for victory." GEOFFREY BOYCOTT, TMS

Morning session: At lunch – Australia 329/5, Hussey 124*, Haddin 79*

What an outstanding morning's cricket this is. Anderson produces one of the great spells of swing bowling – which yields him absolutely nothing. His figures of 8-2-14-0 are a travesty. Mr Dar gives Hussey out lbw on 82, but the batsman reviews the decision successfully when a replay shows the ball landed fractionally outside leg stump. Anderson then has another apparently plumb appeal against Hussey turned down by Dar, but England have no reviews left in the bank. This time the replay shows the ball pitching in line. England will argue that had they not lost their Clarke review yesterday when Hot Spot failed them, they would still have had one left, and Hussey would have been dispatched on 85. Haddin offers Cook a difficult chance off Collingwood, but by the interval he and Hussey have taken their partnership to 186, and Australia lead by 26.

"We always seem to look at the bowlers but you don't win Test matches scoring 260. We didn't get the runs on the board and that's the problem." MICHAEL VAUGHAN, TMS

Afternoon session: At tea – Australia 436/5, Hussey 176*, Haddin 134*, Australia lead by 176

On and on the Australians go, with England supporters' morale beginning to sag. Even Billy Cooper's trumpet has a plaintive air. When Anderson drops Haddin on 113, I overhear a comment in the ABC commentary box that makes my blood boil: "They're starting to unravel already." It brings back all the painful memories of the dreadful Tests England have played here over the past twenty years, but this team does not deserve to be put in the same category. Things really have not gone their way at all, and events have conspired against them. I am not given to defend England unnecessarily – I am strictly impartial – but I'm becoming seriously wound up. Hussey – who has batted brilliantly on the back foot – and Haddin are still going at tea, having registered the highest ever partnership at the Gabba. Significantly Swann is unable to stop the flow of runs.

> *"What's happened to the great Barmy Army? Has someone stolen their tongues? Very quiet. Mind you what is there to sing about if you're a Pom?"*
> SHANE WARNE TWEET

Evening session: At the close – Australia 481, England 19/0

England finally take their first wicket of the day when Collingwood snares a brilliant catch at slip off Swann to dismiss Haddin for 136, which brings the partnership to an end at 307. Eight runs later, Hussey pulls the persevering Finn to Cook at deep midwicket for 195 from 330 balls, which precipitates a remarkable collapse. Finn routs the tail to take 6 for 125 as Australia's last 5 wickets crumble for 31. I am on air on ABC for the first ball of England's reply to which Strauss plays no shot to an inswinger from Hilfenhaus. From my vantage point, behind the batsman, it looks absolutely stone dead and Strauss seems destined to bag a pair. Umpire Dar confidently gives it not out and, not surprisingly, the Aussies call for a review. The tracker suggests the ball would have passed fractionally over the bails and Strauss escapes what remains for him, a dreadful misjudgement. He and Cook scramble to the close with England still 202 runs behind – and with two days left.

I have seldom felt more depressed – even during the black days of my previous five England tours of Australia because, deep down, I knew England would be beaten. But it feels as if an injustice has been done. I spend the evening in my room with a glass or two of Chardonnay and my Twitter army for company. It is not long before a tweet from someone calling herself @theashes is brought to my attention: "I am not a cricket match. Stop mentioning me and check profiles before you send messages. It's really annoying."

This is repeated to half a dozen would-be correspondents dating back to the first day of the Test. I look up the identity of @theashes and discover that she is a girl called Ashley Kerekes, from Westfield Massachusetts who tweets predominately about knitting and the Glee TV show. An American! Being pestered about cricket! Inevitably this tickles me.

Now it is starting to catch on, with more cricketing tweets aimed at @theashes until she snaps: "I AM NOT A FREAKING CRICKET MATCH!!! That means you @matywilson @zandertrego @thesummats @ atonyboffey and MORE."

I'm afraid all this proves too much of a temptation and I re-tweet her message. That is to say I send it to each of my seventy thousand or so followers on Twitter. An hour later, I check Twittercounter. com and her followers have jumped from a very static 331 to 2,536. Clearly there is some fun to be had with this.

> "I fear that when Hussey gets in the kind of form and rhythm he did today he could have a huge series and be a thorn in England's side like he has been in the past." MICHAEL VAUGHAN, TMS

END OF DAY REPORT

If you woke up this morning and saw Australia's scorecard, you probably assumed England had not played well. Let me tell you that simply was not the case. England could not have done anything more with the ball before lunch. They could have rolled Australia over in the morning session but luck was conspicuously absent for the tourists at the Gabba.

If you look at Australia's innings, the first five wickets went for 143 runs and the last five fell for only 31. But what matters is the 307-run stand between the rejuvenated Mike Hussey and Brad Haddin, a stand which one would think has put Australia in an unbeatable situation. However, the talking point of the day for England fans was once again the Decision Review System.

I know I have repeated this a number of times, but what is the point in having it if it doesn't get decisions right? 'Snicko', the bit of kit used to detect faint edges, is not instantaneous – which means it is not available to the third umpire – and that is why Michael Clarke's original not out decision was upheld when England referred a caught behind appeal on Friday. Snicko showed there had been contact with the bat – but by this time it was way too late, England had wasted their final appeal and were made to pay when Michael Hussey was trapped in front by James Anderson on 85 in the morning session.

I don't blame umpire Aleem Dar. He is probably the best umpire in the world, and has made some superb decisions in this match. But having had a decision overturned by third umpire Tony Hill, when Hussey asked for an lbw decision to be reviewed, it was inevitable that umpire Dar would be more conservative when England went up for an appeal which looked more convincing than the one overturned four overs before. If the system is in place, it has to be used for every single decision and it must be used fully.

That said, England were totally devoid of luck in the morning session, but they beat the bat so many times. James Anderson will never bowl as brilliantly and be as unlucky as he was in the morning. He was outstanding, banishing doubts about whether he could be just as potent with the Kookaburra ball and bowling well in Australian conditions. And to see him drop a catch too – he is one of England's most reliable fielders – he must have done something to upset someone up above.

Watching Anderson tire as the afternoon session wore on, it highlighted the issue of playing four bowlers in the heat and humidity of Australia with only Paul Collingwood for support. The addition of a fifth bowler would have helped considerably, especially with Graeme Swann unusually expensive. The off-spinner bowled five maidens in 45 overs, when that figure would usually be closer to 15. That's not the job he is here to do. He has to create pressure with dot balls and maidens so the seamers can be rotated and rested. If Swann still can't get it right after Adelaide, then playing an additional bowler is something England may have to seriously consider.

There is also an argument that if England drop their sixth batsman and play an additional bowler, it would heap more responsibility on the top five to score vital runs. I'm a big advocate of playing five bowlers but I can't see England moving Matt Prior up to six, even though I think Stuart Broad is good enough to be a number seven in Test cricket. I can only envisage them adopting those tactics in Sydney, the fifth and final Test, if they need nothing else but a win. England's resilience will be tested to the maximum in the next two days if they are to save this Test match.

The best-case scenario is England are 300/4 with an 80-odd run lead on Sunday evening. The worst-case scenario is the Test match is over.

England must bat for at least four sessions to ensure they do not travel to Adelaide 1-0 down.

DAY 26 28 November, First Test – fourth day

"You have to bat time sensibly and not give the opposition an in because you then find two or three wickets go quickly and all of a sudden there's panic in the dressing room." GEOFFREY BOYCOTT, TMS

Morning session: At lunch – England 135/0, Strauss 79*, Cook 51*

England simply have to make a good start to the day if they are to have any chance of saving the Test, but this is almost too much to ask for without being greedy. An early boundary from Cook takes the pair past Jack Hobbs and Herbert Sutcliffe as England's most prolific opening batsmen – the old boys made their partnerships at an average of 87 while these two do so at just over 40. There is a feeling of tension around the ground as the Australians wait for what surely will be the inevitable, while England's many supporters warm to the task of getting behind their side. Ponting is getting frustrated surprisingly early, searching for the breakthrough. Johnson drops Strauss at mid-off on 69 as he aims a drive off Doherty and the pair reach lunch unscathed.

"Every series the Australians say they will target the England captain, saying they want to take him down. Mitchell Johnson said he would flatten him with the short stuff this time. It's significant for Strauss to get a hundred." MICHAEL SLATER, TMS

Afternoon session: At tea – England 238/1, Cook 98*, Trott 23*

It has been a perfect morning, but there's still a long way to go if England are to save the game. The pitch is very slow and flat, offering precious little to Ponting's bowlers. Strauss cuts for four to bring up his hundred, which is celebrated by a roar from the captain. And he was so nearly out first ball. It is his nineteenth Test hundred and he is only the fourth English captain to score a century in the opening Test of an Ashes series. But midway through the afternoon he loses patience, charges down the pitch at Marcus

North and is stumped for 110 from 224 balls. A fine innings, and Strauss has put them on the first rung of the tall ladder to saving the game – but it is rather a waste of a dismissal. Trott looks to be full of determination and is not taking so long with his repetitive raking at the crease. The 50 partnership is posted just before the break, and the deficit is knocked off for only one wicket down.

Evening session: At the close – England 309/1, Cook 132*, Trott 54*, England lead by 88

Australia realise the game is up during the final session and doesn't the Barmy Army know it. The ABC commentary box has noticeably lost its chirp, too. Cook plays a rasping cut off Siddle to bring up his fourteenth Test hundred from 204 deliveries. Trott gives a difficult chance to Clarke at point on 34 as Ponting takes the new ball, but he betrays his instincts by setting overly negative fields. Australia lose their final review after appealing unsuccessfully for lbw against Trott, who brings up England's 300 by clipping another wayward Johnson delivery through the leg side for four. Bad light stops play with English pundits now excitedly talking about getting the Australians in to bat on the final day for a nasty 30 overs or so.

I spend the evening at a question and answer session with some highly relieved England fans, but it is memorable mainly for a faulty microphone. It's all one needs after double stints on the radio all day. Quick check on @theashes before bed: she now has 5,423 followers, but has gone very quiet.

> "This is an example of one of many fightbacks we will see in this series because the sides are evenly matched. It has been a fantastic Test match." MICHAEL SLATER, TMS

> "I hope we can get Australia out there tomorrow and give them a hard time for 30 or 40 overs. Get Swanny on, all the players around the bat and give the Australians a bit of chat in their ears." MICHAEL VAUGHAN, TMS

END OF DAY REPORT

In all my years of covering England, I have seen them roll over in numerous Test matches in a similar situation over the years – but I could never have envisaged the scenario that England find themselves in on Sunday evening.

I wrote yesterday that the best-case scenario would have been England ending about 300/4 with an 80-odd run lead on Sunday evening. Well, they have an 80-run lead – 88 to be precise – but to lose only one wicket is quite phenomenal. It's difficult to describe just what a wonderful batting performance this was by England's top three.

England were adequately compensated with large slices of luck which had deserted them on Saturday as all three batsmen profited from missed chances. But what struck me was how each batsman played quite different innings. Andrew Strauss was the most positive of the three, taking more of a risk with his strokeplay, while Alastair Cook batted with concentration and determination and Trott was equally assured, putting aside his sketchy first-innings display with resolute defence.

There were one or two play-and-misses in the morning session, but that's only natural as the last vestiges of shine and hardness wore off the ball. Seeing Strauss bring up his 100 was my moment of the day, I knew just how distraught he was after his third-ball dismissal in the first innings.

The England captain was absolutely furious when he was eventually dismissed, out stumped for the first time in his Test career, slamming his bat against his pad in frustration after toiling away so admirably.

As for Cook, I can't think of a better innings he has played for England. For someone of his age, he really does have an astonishing record. At just under 26, he has 14 Test hundreds – that's up there with the great Sir Garfield Sobers, which goes to show what august company he is now in. He moved his feet beautifully towards the ball's pitch, playing with authority and confidence on both sides of the wicket. What impressed me about Trott's innings was the way he kept Cook motivated, urging him on and offering encouragement at every opportunity during their 121-run stand.

All three batsmen were abetted by Australia's bowlers, who could not conjure a really testing spell of pressure, offering too many four-balls at the wrong time.

However, a word of caution – only one team can win this match, and that is Australia. It only takes a few quick wickets for panic to set in and England know they have at least a session-and-a-half still to bat before they can start thinking about drawing the match and turning their attention towards Adelaide.

The hosts looked devoid of inspiration throughout most of the day's play, a very, very different picture from the team that won here so convincingly four years ago. If England can accumulate a lead of about 250 to 280 and declare around tea, it would leave Australia an uncomfortable 90 minutes or so in a session that has no real relevance with the draw secured.

A few early wickets can have a significant psychological impact going into the Adelaide Oval next Friday, sending the hosts a real message of intent. Australia's biggest concern is the form of Mitchell Johnson and the composition of their pace attack for Adelaide. As Australia's main strike bowler – remember how Johnson said he was going to target Strauss in the build-up to the series – he has had an awful Test match; no wickets, dropping Strauss on 69 and a first-innings duck. His first spell on Sunday morning was not too bad, bowling with pace and aggression, but he bowled too many four-balls which England gratefully dispatched.

Doug Bollinger is a ready-made replacement, but dropping Johnson on the strength of one Test is a big call. If the Australian selectors take a risk, they could play left-arm seamer Bollinger as part of a five-man bowling attack with Brad Haddin batting at six, but I seriously doubt they would adopt this tactic so early in the series. Ricky Ponting's field placings were conservative too, even when they took the second new ball, which shows his confidence in his main strike bowlers is not as high as it should be.

DAY 27 **29 November 2010, First Test – fifth day**
Morning session: At lunch – England 439/1, Cook 201*, Trott 100*

Once Cook and Trott survive the morning we are safe in the knowledge that this is a drawn match. In front of a crowd made up almost entirely of England supporters, Clarke drops Trott at slip on 75 – an easy chance off Watson – but the sting has long gone from the Australian attack. Johnson fires a ball so wide down the leg side at Trott that it evokes memories of the infamous Harmison ball. Johnson really has had a poor game and looks anything other than a potent spearhead. Cook reaches 200 just before lunch from 361 balls – the highest score at the Gabba by a visiting batsman – and Trott's century comes on the stroke of lunch from 213 deliveries.

> *"Surreal atmosphere round the ground at lunch. Englishmen rubbing their eyes with disbelief – it's like they've entered a parallel, dream-like universe. Wheels haven't just come off the Aussie team – so have the wing-mirrors, the bumpers, the doors..." TOM FORDYCE*

Afternoon session: At tea – England 517/1 declared, Australia 11/1

On and on they go, breaking the record partnership on this ground, which was set by Hussey and Haddin only two days ago. England become only the sixth team in history to reach 500 for the loss of only one wicket, and Strauss seizes the psychological high ground when he declares with 41 overs remaining in the day. Broad, who has had a quiet wicket-less and run-less match so far, nicks out Katich before tea for 4.

> *"England have a great chance to take a few scalps to Adelaide. Could anything else happen? Could they take a few quick wickets and force a win?" MICHAEL VAUGHAN, TMS*

Evening session: At the close – Australia 107/1, match drawn

Ricky Ponting, who has been short of form, plays some fluent strokes for his half-century, but no one is paying much attention. This game is over, and it has been one of *the* great fightbacks. I interview Cook live on the outfield at the end of play and ask him if he realises yet what he has done and whether he is aware of all the records he has broken. He shrugs his shoulders a little bashfully and says that he doesn't – almost as if it isn't important to him. One day, I think as I congratulate and thank him, it will be.

Morale is sky high in the Agnew hotel and it is time to celebrate with a few drinks. Michael Vaughan is quickly developing into a fine summariser on *TMS*. He is also very good (and easy) company with a clear understanding of what it means to be part of a team. Mind you, the bar he assures me will be 'heaving' is deserted. It doesn't matter at all.

@theashes makes her first public utterance since logging on to her computer and discovering her numbers have soared to nearly ten thousand. "Duh? Weird" is the reaction to her new-found popularity but, fair play, she is soon getting in the swing. A campaign to get @theashes to the Ashes is launched and she displays a certain eye for an opportunity by selling T-shirts bearing her famous FREAKIN tweet online for $19.90. It's a crazy world.

> *"In the past England so often lost the First Test and Australia were cock-a-hoop before this match, saying the Gabba is a citadel where they would win. England will have great confidence because they know there's nothing in Australia's bowling and they have batted very well in the second innings."*
> GEOFFREY BOYCOTT, TMS

END OF DAY REPORT

England's performance in saving the first Ashes Test was, quite simply, nothing short of astonishing. From the position they found themselves in at the end of day three, most teams – not just England –would far more often than not have gone on to lose. But England not only rescued the Test, they saved it in such emphatic style that they emerged with a points victory as well. Remarkable.

The final two days were terrific to witness. Superb batting, records falling, the Aussie attack reduced to an utterly innocuous mess. In the future, whenever there is an epic stand or a fabulous innings, this will be the match for correspondents to reference. And the records that tumbled on day five in Brisbane were incredible.

This was the first time England's top three have all made a century since 1924; no Englishmen has ever spent longer at the crease in a Test innings in Australia than Alastair Cook; Cook's score was the highest ever individual Test total at the Gabba, while his stand with Jonathan Trott was a record one; and this was the first time England have passed 500 for the loss of only one wicket. These are not irrelevant, throw-away records. These are serious, serious statistics.

The way Cook and Trott batted was absolutely beautiful. Neither innings was completely flawless – both survived dropped catches – but when you bat for as long and score as many as those two did, it is inevitable you will offer the odd chance.

So there is no doubt that England will come away from this match happier than Australia. I would not say it is quite as big a blow to Australia as the First Test in Cardiff in 2009, when James Anderson and Monty Panesar batted so stoically to earn England a draw against all the odds. But this performance certainly sends a significant message to Australia – that this England team is a completely different proposition to the ones seen Down Under in the past twenty or so years.

Andrew Strauss and his team can fight, can dig deep, are disciplined and have reserves of resolve unlike anything seen from an England side on these shores in recent memory.

It is for those reasons that a number of Australian pundits are backing England to win the Ashes now.

For my part, I have seen nothing in this match to make me change my opinion that England will win this series. I actually had England down to win this match on their way to an overall 3-1 series victory before the start of play. But, even though it ended in a draw, the nature of their performance on the last two days should earn them huge credit.

Going into the Adelaide Test, I expect England to remain unchanged, even though there are questions about their ability to take twenty wickets to win a match. I would always want a five-man bowling attack in any cricket side but England are not going to do that so it is not even worth debating. Ironically, the worry for England right now is off-spinner Graeme Swann. He is just not getting it right at the moment and everything, from his body language to his delivery stride, underlines his lack of form. He has work to do ahead of the Adelaide Test but he is a top-class operator and a key weapon for England.

Australia, on the other hand, have to make changes. They simply cannot afford not to. I just cannot see, for example, how they can pick Mitchell Johnson in the next Test. He was not only awful in this match, he has been off for quite a while now. Not only is he not taking wickets but he is haemorrhaging runs as well. He must be dropped. Ryan Harris and Doug Bollinger, it would appear, will battle it out to replace Johnson and both are decent bowlers. Either would be an improvement on the Johnson we saw in this Test.

Still, I do not think Ricky Ponting is a man under pressure just yet. I thought England's afternoon declaration was absolutely the right thing to do because it sent a wonderful message to Australia, although such a move can backfire if the opposition land a little counter-punch before the end of play.

That is what happened here. Ponting got in and scored a fine half-century that should ease questions about his form.

However, I do not think he captained at all well in this match. I was absolutely astonished by his lack of attack in the first hour on day five – two slips, a gully, an extra cover. It was like a mid-afternoon field rather than one aimed at making the most of any chances that come up. It was poor.

And Ponting will not have been pleased with the chances Australia put down in the field either. I think I counted five chances of varying difficulty that were dropped – and that will hurt the skipper.

Opposite number Strauss, on the other hand, was absolutely thrilled when I interviewed him at the close of play. You cannot help but like Strauss and it was nice to see him so happy. The fact is that he is really rolling on this tour, rattling along.

So it is all square going into the next Test, starting on Thursday, but England's will certainly be the happier camp. What they will want to do is take the discipline, skill and application shown in their second innings here and put it into their first innings. That is the difference between batting big to draw a match and batting big to set up a victory. Take that lesson away from this match and England need not fear this Australia side at all.

AUSTRALIA v ENGLAND

Result: Drawn

1st Test

Played at Brisbane Cricket Ground, Woolloongabba,
Brisbane on 25,26,27,28,29 November 2010

Toss: England
Referee: JJ Crowe

Umpires: Aleem Dar & BR Doctrove (TV: AL Hill)
Debuts: Aus: XJ Doherty. **Man of Match:** AN Cook

Notes: Siddle took a hat-trick in England's 1st innings. His victims were Cook, Prior, Broad. Ponting scored his 50 off 40 balls in Australia's 2nd innings.

ENGLAND	Runs	Mins	Balls	4	6		Runs	Mins	Balls	4	6
*AJ Strauss c Hussey b Hilfenhaus	0	2	3	-	-	st Haddin b North	110	267	224	15	-
AN Cook c Watson b Siddle	67	283	168	6	-	not out	235	625	428	26	-
IJL Trott b Watson	29	62	53	5	-	not out	135	362	266	19	-
KP Pietersen c Ponting b Siddle	43	95	70	6	-						
PD Collingwood c North b Siddle	4	9	8	1	-						
IR Bell c Watson b Doherty	76	183	131	8	-						
†MJ Prior b Siddle	0	1	1	-	-						
SCJ Broad lbw b Siddle	0	1	1	-	-						
GP Swann lbw b Siddle	10	21	9	1	-						
JM Anderson b Doherty	11	38	22	2	-						
ST Finn not out	0	1	0	-	-						
Extras (lb 8, w 7, nb 5)	**20**					**Extras (b 17, lb 4, w 10, nb 6)**	**37**				
TOTAL (76.5 overs)	260					TOTAL (for 1 wkt dec) (152 overs)	517				

AUSTRALIA	Runs	Mins	Balls	4	6		Runs	Mins	Balls	4	6
SR Watson c Strauss b Anderson	36	113	76	6	-	not out	41	119	97	4	-
SM Katich c and b Finn	50	159	106	5	-	c Strauss b Broad	4	22	16	-	-
*RT Ponting c Prior b Anderson	10	34	26	1	-	not out	51	96	43	4	1
MJ Clarke c Prior b Finn	9	76	50	-	-						
MEK Hussey c Cook b Finn	195	462	330	26	1						
MJ North c Collingwood b Swann	1	6	8	-	-						
†J Haddin c Collingwood b Swann	136	374	287	16	1						
MG Johnson b Finn	0	32	19	-	-						
XJ Doherty c Cook b Finn	16	43	30	2	-						
PM Siddle c Swann b Finn	6	7	11	1	-						
BW Hilfenhaus not out	1	16	10	-	-						
Extras (b 4, lb 12, w 4, nb 1)	**21**					**Extras (b 4, lb 1, w 1, p 5)**	**11**				
TOTAL (158.4 overs)	481					TOTAL (for 1 wkt) (26 overs)	107				

Aus	O	M	R	W		O	M	R	W	
Hilfenhaus	19	4	60	1	(2 nb, 2 w)	32	8	82	0	(3 nb, 1 w)
Siddle	16	3	54	6	(2 nb, 2 w)	24	4	90	0	(3 nb, 2 w)
Johnson	15	2	66	0		(4) 27	5	104	0	(1 w)
Watson	12	2	30	1	(1 nb, 3 w)	(6) 15	2	66	0	(2 w)
Doherty	13.5	3	41	2		35	5	107	0	
North	1	0	1	0		(3) 19	3	47	1	

Eng	O	M	R	W		O	M	R	W	
Anderson	37	13	99	2	(1 w)	5	2	15	0	
Broad	33	7	72	0	(1 nb, 1 w)	7	1	18	1	(1 w)
Swann	43	5	128	2		8	0	33	0	
Finn	33.4	1	125	6		4	0	25	0	
Collingwood	12	1	41	0	(2 w)					
Pietersen						(5) 2	0	6	0	

FALL OF WICKETS				
	Eng	Aus	Eng	Aus
1st	0 (1)	78 (1)	188 (1)	5 (2)
2nd	41 (3)	96 (3)	-	-
3rd	117 (4)	100 (2)	-	-
4th	125 (5)	140 (4)	-	-
5th	197 (2)	143 (6)	-	-
6th	197 (7)	450 (7)	-	-
7th	197 (8)	458 (5)	-	-
8th	228 (9)	462 (8)	-	-
9th	254 (6)	472 (10)	-	-
10th	260 (10)	481 (9)	-	-

BRISBANE MILESTONES

Ⓜ **Peter Siddle became the first** player to take a Test hat-trick on his birthday, dismissing Cook, Prior and Broad. It was the fifth hat-trick for Australia against England. The previous four had all been taken at Melbourne.

Bowler	Venue	Season	Victims
FR Spofforth	Melbourne	1878/79	VPFA Royle, FA MacKinnon and T Emmett
H Trumble	Melbourne	1901/02	AO Jones, JR Gunn and SF Barnes
H Trumble	Melbourne	1903/04	BJT Bosanquet, PF Warner and AFA Lilley
SK Warne	Melbourne	1994/95	PAJ DeFreitas, D Gough and DE Malcolm
PM Siddle	Brisbane	2010/11	AN Cook, MJ Prior and SCJ Broad

Ⓜ **It was the second hat-trick** at the Gabba. The first was by Courtney Walsh (split over two innings) for West Indies in 1988/89.

Ⓜ **Matthew Prior took his 100th** dismissal in Test cricket when he caught Michael Clarke off Steve Finn's bowling in Australia's first innings. He was the eighth wicket-keeper to take 100 dismissals for England.

Ⓜ **Michael Hussey's 195 was the third** time that an Australian batsman had been dismissed in the 190s in consecutive Ashes Tests at the Gabba, following Ricky Ponting's 196 in 2006/07 and Matthew Hayden's 197 in 2002/03.

Ⓜ **The partnership of 307** for the sixth wicket between Michael Hussey and Brad Haddin was the third highest for the sixth wicket for Australia in Tests:

Part	Batsmen	Against	Venue	Season
346	JHW Fingleton and DG Bradman	England	Melbourne	1936/37
317	DR Martyn and AC Gilchrist	South Africa	Johannesburg	2001/02
307	MEK Hussey and BJ Haddin	England	Brisbane	2010/11

Ⓜ **Andrew Strauss and Alastair Cook passed** Herbert Sutcliffe and Jack Hobbs' aggregate record for England for first wicket partnerships during the second innings. As at the end of the Test the following were the most prolific opening pairs for England:

Batsmen	Inns	Unb	Runs	Best	Avg	100	50
AJ Strauss/AN Cook	82	2	3415	229	42.68	9	13
H Sutcliffe/JB Hobbs	38	1	3249	283	87.81	15	10
L Hutton/C Washbrook	51	3	2880	359	60.00	8	13
ME Trescothick/AJ Strauss	52	1	2670	273	52.35	8	12
MA Atherton/GA Gooch	44	0	2501	225	56.84	7	12
ME Trescothick/MP Vaughan	54	3	2487	182	48.76	6	15
JB Hobbs/W Rhodes	36	1	2146	323	61.31	8	5

🅜 **Andrew Strauss became only the fourth** England captain to score a century in the first Test of a series against Australia:

Score	Name	Venue	Season
109	AC MacLaren	Sydney	1897/98
116	AC MacLaren	Sydney	1901/02
133	GA Gooch	Manchester	1993
110	AJ Strauss	Brisbane	2010/11

By comparison, the Australian captain has made a century 15 times in the first match of a series against England.

🅜 **Strauss and Cook's opening partnership** of 188 in the second innings was an England record at the Gabba, passing the 114 by Douglas Jardine and Herbert Sutcliffe in 1932/33 and also by Geoff Pullar and David Sheppard in 1962/63.

🅜 **The partnership of 329*** by Cook and Jonathan Trott is the highest for any wicket for England in Australia. The previous best was 323 by Jack Hobbs and Wilfred Rhodes for the first wicket at Melbourne in 1911/12.

🅜 **Alastair Cook's 235* passed Don Bradman's** 226 v South Africa in 1931/32 as the highest Test score at the ground. Only two other double centuries have been scored at the Gabba: 207 by Keith Stackpole for Australia v England in 1970/71 and 201 by Greg Chappell v Pakistan in 1981/82. Cook also joined Michael Hussey in erasing Chittagong from his career best. His previous best was 173 against Bangladesh there in 2009/10. Hussey's previous best was 182 in 2005/06. Cook's innings was the 300th double-century in Test cricket.

🅜 **Jonathan Trott became the second** Englishman to score centuries in each of his first two Ashes Tests, after Herbert Sutcliffe. Trott scored 41 & 119 at The Oval in 2009 and 29 & 135* in this match. Sutcliffe scored 59 & 115 at Sydney and 176 & 127 at Melbourne in 1924/25. Three Australians have scored centuries in each of their first two Ashes Tests: Bill Ponsford, Doug Walters and Greg Blewett.

🅜 **This was only the second** time that the first three batsmen in the order all scored centuries in a Test for England. The other occasion was against South Africa at Lord's in 1924 (Jack Hobbs 211, Herbert Sutcliffe 122 and Frank Woolley 134*).

🅜 **England's 517/1 declared** in the second innings is the highest total for a completed innings with only one wicket down in Test cricket, beating the 442-1 declared made by South Africa against New Zealand at Christchurch in 1998/99. There are only three higher completed totals in all first-class cricket for the loss of only one wicket:

Total	For	Against	Venue	Season
561-1*	Karachi Whites	Quetta	Karachi	1976/77
555-1*	Yorkshire	Essex	Leyton	1932
549-1*	Rhodesia	Orange Free State	Bloemfontein	1967/68

🄼 **England's highest total at the fall** of the second wicket remains 425 v Australia at Melbourne in 1911/12. On that occasion, Jack Hobbs (178) and Wilfred Rhodes (179) added 323 for the first wicket and Rhodes and George Gunn (75) added 102 for the second wicket.

🄼 **Mitchell Johnson** had a wretched match, taking 0/170 in 42 overs, making a 19-ball duck, dropping a catch and missing a run out. Of players who did not score a run, take a wicket or a catch in a Test match, only one bowler has conceded more runs:

Runs	Player	Batting	Bowling	For	Against	Venue	Season
173	PR Adams	0	0-70 & 0-103	South Africa	West Indies	Cape Town	2003/04
170	MG Johnson	0	0-66 & 0-104	Australia	England	Brisbane	2010/11
159	SL Boock	0	0-107 & 0-52	New Zealand	West Indies	Georgetown	1984/85
145	Salim Altaf	0 & 0	0-117 & 0-28	Pakistan	Australia	Melbourne	1976/77
134	Manjural Islam	0 & 0	0-113 & 0-21	Bangladesh	Zimbabwe	Harare	2000/01

🄼 **It was the first time** in his 38-match career that Johnson had gone wicket-less in a Test. Only Fred Trueman (67), Allan Donald (67) and Joel Garner (58) had longer runs of taking at least one wicket in each match from the start of their careers. In Trueman and Garner's case this represented their entire careers.

🄼 **Australia has now played 22 consecutive** Tests at the Gabba without defeat. Their last loss at the ground was to West Indies in 1988/89. They have won 16 and drawn 6 of these Tests. There are only three longer sequences of a team being undefeated at a specific venue:

Tests	Team	Venue	Years	Ended by
34	Pakistan	National Stadium, Karachi	1954/55 to 1999/00	England in 2000/01*
27	West Indies	Kensington Oval, Bridgetown	1947/48 to 1992/93	England in 1993/94
25	England	Old Trafford, Manchester	1905 to 1954	South Africa 1955

* The first 34 Tests at this venue.

THREE

FIRST TEST INTERLUDE

*"Alastair Cook had a phenomenal First Test, but that is
in the past and he starts on nought tomorrow. That said,
I now expect him to go on and beat my tour tally of 633
in 2002-03."*

MICHAEL VAUGHAN

DAY 28 **30 November 2010**

I wake up still feeling utterly elated by England's effort. What a
difference this makes to the tour. I really believe that had England
lost here, Australia's confidence would have come surging back, and
it would have been a massive test of England's character to fight
back from 1-0 down. But now, especially after all the negative press
targeted at the Australian team going into the match, the heat will
be turned up even more. Indeed, the response is exactly as predicted:
'Ashes Humiliation' is plastered over the front page of *The Australian*
newspaper – and that's a broadsheet! *The Brisbane Courier-Mail*
has preferred a direct attack on Ponting's captaincy. 'Clueless' is the
headline over a large photograph of a hapless-looking Ricky. There
will be no escape for Australia's players – the papers are on sale all over
the airport terminal as we make our separate ways to Adelaide.

My aeroplane is packed with England supporters, many of them
bleary-eyed after a big night of celebration – and all in high spirits.
On arrival, I interview Andy Flower in our Adelaide hotel. He has
a large plaster under a yellowing black eye and talks movingly and
seriously about the danger of playing cricket in the sun without
taking proper precautions. Concerning England's performance so far,
he is determined to keep everything in check: "We only got a draw,"

he understates two or three times in the interview. I can see that he is absolutely chuffed though. It is a BBC dinner this evening, and as we stroll down Gouger Street looking for something suitable, we spot the stirringly romantic sight of Mr and Mrs Vic Marks dining *al fresco*. It's marvellous to be teaming up with Vic again for the series; he is one of the most astute summarisers *TMS* possess. In passing, he tells me of the latest Christopher Martin-Jenkins (hereafter referred to as CMJ) mishap – of which there have been many. This one involves Australian squad member Marcus North. At a function the night before the start of the Brisbane Test, Victor during a lengthy conversation with Marcus, who he has known for some time, was joined by CMJ. At some point, Victor headed off to talk to another guest, returning a bit later to find Marcus and CMJ still in earnest conversation about the forthcoming tour. Victor is horrified to hear CMJ politely ask Marcus which paper he actually works for.

DAY 29 | 1 December 2010

With Radio 5 live's Mark Pougatch now on the tour, I am rewarded with a day off. A signing session of *Thanks, Johnners* has been arranged in the local Dymocks bookshop. Back in England, when a publisher obliges me to do a signing session, I usually worry whether anyone will bother to turn up, and am always pleasantly surprised when they do. Because these Australian sessions (there has already been one in Brisbane when two people kindly showed up) haven't been advertised at all, other than by me announcing it on Twitter, I just know I am going to be spending a rather solitary hour. I arrive early and sit outside having a cup of coffee. I am surprised to see quite a queue forming and, feeling rather buoyed up and thinking this is all rather terrific, I march up to the assembled multitude at the appointed hour. "Hi everyone, how are you doing?" I say, only to be met with blank looks and confused stares. It is then I notice the sign announcing the downstairs signing session is for former Prime Minister, John Howard. Utterly deflated, I sneak up the stairs and hide behind a huge pile of books on my desk. Eventually one kind shopper takes pity on me and I sign my copy for the day. Back downstairs I have a chat with John, whom I have interviewed on a couple of occasions.

He knows his cricket and is more than aware that the Australians are up against it this time.

Meanwhile, I have confirmed the appearance on *Test Match Special* of @theashes who now has more than 10,000 followers on Twitter and has been offered a free trip to Australia by Qantas, with accommodation, a car and goodness knows what thrown in. Her life must have gone completely crazy since her 'I'M NOT A FREAKIN'CRICKET MATCH' tweet. I am due to interview Ashley on the telephone during tea on the first day.

Rain ruins England's light practice, after the groundsman apparently left the covers off, resulting in another of KP's Twitter outbursts. He called Damien Hough 'Pathetic!!!!!!!!' which, no doubt, will lead to further calls for England's players to be banned from using the social network, although it makes for good copy.

Tonight, I attend the Glenelg CC charity dinner – once home to the Chappell brothers – with Michael Holding. I saw a lot of Michael in my playing career and he both terrified and inspired me in equal measure. In fact I scored my first Test runs off him – an ugly stab through mid-wicket when he was trying to york me, as I recall. I am more than a little embarrassed to be introduced to the assembled throng, in Michael's company, by a typically understated master of ceremonies as one half of a 'pair of great former fast bowlers'. Michael was a beautiful bowler, a truly great cricketer, and to be even talked about in the same paragraph let alone the same sentence as him in this context is absolutely absurd. Emma loves Michael as well and goes all dippy whenever he appears as part of the Sky commentary team.

It is another one of those evenings when you end up pinching yourself. I shared a taxi with Michael Holding on our way to a dinner where we sat at the same table, spoke to the audience together, and had a really good night – one of those times when I remind myself that my life is, at times, crazy. Also, the night is a healthy reminder of just how strong the feeling is of really *belonging* to a cricket club and what it means over here.

Preview day tomorrow – will Australia be able to name a team, and what will it be?

DAY 30 2 December 2010

Word is out in the Australian press that Mitchell Johnson has been dropped in favour of Doug 'the Rug' Bollinger, the combative left-arm quick bowler. Members of the media spotted Johnson being given the bad news by Greg Chappell in the nets yesterday. Mind you, after the way he bowled at Brisbane, the news hardly comes as a surprise; Australia could not go into the Adelaide Test with the same attack.

Once again in the absence of ABC Radio, Ponting kindly allows me to interview him privately. Radio 5 live need to run interviews in their full length, and it is impossible to achieve this at a typical non-print media press conference with five or six television reporters all jostling for position and shouting questions. Technically-speaking, it is not one of Ponting's many duties on preview day to speak to me, so the effort he makes is much appreciated. First, the main press conference is held in a basement room beneath the new stand, and while waiting for Ricky to finish my eye is drawn to the wonderful polished wooden honours boards that have been fixed to the walls. They go right back to the infamous Bodyline series of 1932/33, which came to an ugly head on this very ground. One D.G. Bradman features rather a lot in the distinctive gold lettering.

Ricky leaves the main press conference, during which he appears to distance himself from Johnson's dropping after being confronted by some pretty hostile questions from the Australian press corps. The two of us find a quiet corner in an adjoining room and I interview him gently (he is doing me a favour after all) for three or four minutes about his disappointment after the Brisbane Test and the rather cruel newspaper headlines that have resulted. He offers up the standard reply of 'never reading the papers', but he does not seem to be his usual, bristling self today.

When we have finished – and I congratulate him on the way he batted in the second innings at the Gabba, which had been largely ignored in the main press conference – I return to the main room and to my amazement find that Johnson has been put up to speak to the press. He has Tim Nielsen, the coach, sitting beside him, and Johnson casts an utterly sorrowful and downcast figure. He answers

The trophy may be small but an Ashes contest is the biggest draw in Test cricket. The talking is about to end as the two captains pose with the little urn before the start of the First Test.

Peter Siddle becomes the fifth Australian to record a hat-trick in Ashes history but the first to record one on his birthday. He leads the Aussies off the field after his six wickets.

After calling correctly and electing to bat, Andrew Strauss is on his way back to the pavilion third ball of the series, caught in the gully off Hilfenhaus.

Stuart Broad is the unfortunate third leg of the hat-trick, following quickly in the footsteps of Cook and Prior.

Steven Finn is England's most successful bowler, taking six wickets on his Ashes debut. He celebrates getting Michael Clarke caught behind for single figures.

Jimmy Anderson bowled some brilliant spells at Brisbane and deserved more than his two wickets. England were wasteful with their reviews and this cost them dearly on at least one occasion as Australia's innings progressed.

England's three happy centurions – Trott, Cook and Strauss – save a match that looked absolutely nailed on for Australia after their 221-run first innings lead.

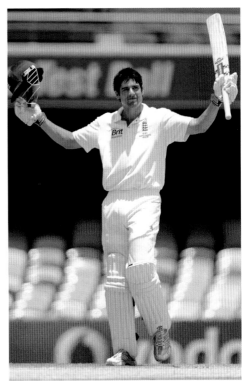

Ultimately, Brisbane was all about two record-breaking partnerships. The first between Mike Hussey, here celebrating his century, and Brad Haddin who put on 307 for the sixth wicket.

The second was between Alastair Cook and Jonathan Trott, who eclipsed the earlier record by scoring an unbeaten 329 for the second wicket. Cook batted for over 15 hours in the match.

A draw that felt like a win for England. The two captains shake hands at the Gabba

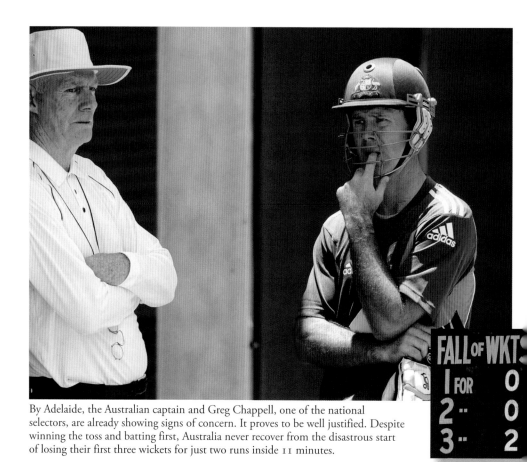

By Adelaide, the Australian captain and Greg Chappell, one of the national selectors, are already showing signs of concern. It proves to be well justified. Despite winning the toss and batting first, Australia never recover from the disastrous start of losing their first three wickets for just two runs inside 11 minutes.

After Jonathan Trott runs out opener Simon Katich before he has even faced a ball, Ricky Ponting departs for a golden duck, caught by Graeme Swann in the slips off the bowling of Anderson. It is not a happy 150th Test cap for the Australian captain.

This was the big innings that Kevin Pietersen had promised for some time. It was his first Test century since March 2009 and he revels in the moment as he turns the ball through the leg side.

For good measure, he adds another, and in the process records his highest Test score of 227.

Alastair Cook scores his second hundred of the series, helping Pietersen put on 175 for the third wicket. By the time he is out, the Essex opener had batted for 1,053 minutes since he was last dismissed in the first innings in Brisbane.

The last ball of the fourth day – and Pietersen turns the game again, this time by dismissing Michael Clarke, caught at backward short leg by Alastair Cook, for 80.

Clarke is reluctant to go but the England players all know that he will soon be on his way back to the pavilion and Australia have a mountain to climb with only six wickets left going into the final day.

Graeme Swann came back to form in Adelaide with five Australian second innings wickets. He finishes off the match before lunch by bowling Peter Siddle through the gate.

In the end, England had only a couple of hours in hand as a huge electrical storm swept in after lunch, turning the outfield into a lake as England celebrated their innings victory.

Stuart Broad cuts a forlorn figure on the balcony at Adelaide as a side strain rules him out for the rest of the series. But he was back in Perth, swapping his whites for a testing debut in the *TMS* commentary box alongside Geoffrey Boycott.

Perhaps it would have been less intimidating if Geoffrey had been wearing his Harry Potter shirt.

Or Michael Vaughan had brought along his personal masseuse.

every question about his future and his career quietly and politely and when the media is done, hurries away. I am all for having access to the players, but nonetheless feel very sorry for Johnson. He really seems to have been hung out to dry.

I meet Strauss on the outfield and interview him in front of a large and excitable gathering of England supporters. He plays the usual game of declining to name his team until the toss, but it is pretty clear that England will be unchanged.

EVE OF MATCH THOUGHTS

While everyone connected with English cricket was both buoyed and mightily impressed with the fighting draw at Brisbane, the message from the management to the players has been to keep their feet firmly on the ground. Andrew Strauss was quick to make that point again this afternoon, repeating Andy Flower's observation that the match was no more than drawn, and the scoreline remains 0-0.

Strauss confirmed that everyone in the squad is fit and from that we can conclude that England will probably be unchanged, but there are areas that have room for improvement. The first is the frustrating business of England's first innings scores. There has to be much more focus on batting with the same discipline and commitment shown by Strauss, Alastair Cook and Jonathan Trott in the second innings at the Gabba, but when it really matters in the first innings. It can be easier second time around, when there is a definite target to aim for be it a score to beat, or a specific number of sessions to survive. Batting first has no such obvious focal point other than the aim to score as many runs as possible, and the top six batsmen really need to knuckle down and bat Australia out of the match if they possibly can.

The other area of concern – albeit mild at the moment – is Graeme Swann's form. Strauss strongly defended him today, as you would expect, but the off-spinner was well below his best at Brisbane. Pulled far too often by Michael Hussey in the first innings, he was then driven down the ground by Ricky Ponting and Shane Watson in the second, suggesting that he is still searching for the right length here. Things might have been different had Paul Collingwood taken a routine slip catch: it did rather sum up Swann's match.

Ponting always likes to name his team in advance if he can, and I reckon this is the first time against England he has been unable to do so. The decision to drop Mitchell Johnson was entirely the right one, even though Ponting seemed to load the blame, as it were, on to the four selectors. Australia had to do something with the bowling attack and I fully expect Doug Bollinger to play, but dare they drop Ben Hilfenhaus as well and replace him with Ryan Harris? Hilfenhaus bowled pretty well on that flat pitch, and Harris and Bollinger are both returning after injuries. With doubts about Michael Clarke's decision to declare himself fit for Brisbane, and then bat as if he was seriously discomforted, Australia can't afford to take a chance that one of their bowlers could break down again.

There is a little more grass on the pitch than usual, but with hot weather forecast for the first two days at least, this is a definite bat first pitch if you win the toss. Then we can see if either team has the firepower to bowl the other out twice.

FOUR

ADELAIDE TEST

"England believes Australia's aura has gone, it is not just a war of words – all eleven of the Poms are believers."

SHANE WARNE

DAY 31 3 December 2010, Second Test – first day

Morning session: At lunch – Australia 94/3, Watson 50*, Hussey 36*

Ponting wins the toss on a hot morning, bats first and in the third over Australia are 2 for 3. It is the most dramatic start to a Test I have seen, and it is a rare privilege to commentate on a passage of play such as this, simply thrilling. Katich is run out off the fourth ball of the day when he responds slowly to Watson's call for a leg bye. Trott swoops, running to his right from mid-wicket and hits the stumps at the batsman's end with a direct and arrow-like throw. Trott is the least mobile and least athletic man in the team, and this magnificent effort, like Panesar's catch at Hobart [in the Australian A warm-up match], is testimony to the work of Richard Halsall. Next ball, Ponting edges Anderson low to second slip where Swann takes a brilliant catch. Unbelievably it is 0/2 in the first over; the next man in, Michael Clarke, is forced to dash from the nets behind the new stand next to the pavilion, and then take his earlier-than-anticipated walk to the middle. It is hardly the proper preparation for a Test innings, and in Anderson's next over he is neatly caught by Swann for 2. Hussey is dropped by Anderson, low to his left off his own bowling, for 3. And Australia stagger like a drunken man to lunch at 94/3.

"More wickets than FIFA votes already. Took us just 15 minutes." MICHAEL VAUGHAN, TMS

Afternoon session: At tea – Australia 159/5, Hussey 71* Haddin 2*

England tighten their grip on the match on a pitch that is helping the seam bowlers more than traditional Adelaide tracks. Shane Watson aims to drive Anderson in the second over after the break, and is well caught by a jubilant Pietersen in the gully for 51. It is yet another example of Watson getting in, making 50, and then getting himself out. North, whose place in the team is under intense scrutiny, adds 60 with Hussey before edging Finn to Prior on the stroke of tea for 26.

During the tea break I catch up on the telephone with Ashley Kerekes, better known to my listeners as @theashes. She is still in Massachusetts and has clearly done the rounds with interviews so is very comfortable on the air. She confirms that she will be coming out for at least one Test in this series, which will ensure that this bizarre story runs and runs. Her original count of 301 followers has now swelled to 12,025 in a week.

> "England's fielding has been exceptional, they have saved 20 or 30 runs today. They have been really good in that ring." MICHAEL VAUGHAN, TMS

Evening session: At the close – Australia 245, England 1/0

Having reached 207/5, with Hussey on 93, Australia lose their last 5 wickets for 38 runs, Hussey becoming Swann's first victim to a ball that spun and found the edge, which Collingwood takes at slip. Next ball Ryan Harris, who has replaced Hilfenhaus, is lbw to Swann off a delivery that the batsman appeared to edge into his pad. However, not for the first time, the review fails to show this. The tail crumbles; Anderson finishes with 4/51 and England have to face just six balls.

The high-octane opening day ends, and with his team very much in the driving seat, Strauss leaves the field with Haddin and Ponting launching verbal assaults at the England captain. The flare-up is later described as 'inconsequential' by the England camp, but it is an unedifying spectacle, which demonstrates Ponting's short temper and highlights the pressure he is feeling.

A quiet evening is spent with the Boycott family. Rachael, Geoffrey's wife is, as usual, immaculately turned out, pink lipstick, perfectly manicured nails, not a hair out of place – and not someone you would naturally associate with swinging a golf club. But there is Geoffrey chuntering away about losing the latest round in the epic Boycott family golf tournament. It began in New Zealand before the First Test, and Geoffrey is currently in fourth place out of four! Rachael routinely beats Geoffrey, under the handicap system of course: she dobs the ball 50 yards down the fairway every shot, and naturally Geoffrey hasn't got that sort of control. Geoffrey, being the competitive animal he is, is thoroughly riled. We make a date for dinner on Monday evening.

"England have got under the skin of Ponting. More good signs that he is ruffled. Fantastic day." MICHAEL VAUGHAN, TMS

END OF DAY REPORT

By bowling Australia out on a hot, sunshine-filled day, England have enjoyed a near-perfect start to the first day at the Adelaide Test, from the first ball to the last.

There was one tiny blemish, when Mike Hussey, who went on to make 93, was dropped by the otherwise immaculate James Anderson on just 3. But we cannot attach any blame to Anderson, who took four wickets in the day, and it was one of those tough ones off your own bowling which most people would not have got close to.

To see Ricky Ponting remonstrating with Andrew Strauss about something at the end illustrated the emotions of an Australian captain, who is a rattled man. It started off when wicketkeeper Brad Haddin said something just after the last ball had been bowled. We don't know what happened but Ponting waded in and his actions were those of a man whose team are in crisis.

This is not a typical Adelaide wicket. There is more bounce in it than usual, and the bounce is a bit variable. The ball swung for Anderson again, and he picked up the wickets he had deserved at Brisbane with Ricky Ponting and Michael Clarke swiftly sent packing.

What ignited Anderson and England was that wicket in the first over when Jonathan Trott pulled off the run-out of Simon Katich with a measured aim and direct hit. It was just a brilliant start, Ponting had to come in and got a lovely ball first up, there was a sharp catch by Graeme Swann in the slips and England were away.

Just six days in, the series is turning out pretty much according to my predictions. It was vital that Brisbane was not lost, and now we see real problems in the Australian camp. We have batsmen playing for their place, two changes already to the pace attack – a virtually unheard-of move after one match – and to see the Australians underperforming and people starting to seriously worry about it, plus the captain losing his rag, just plays into England's hands.

England still need to do well on Saturday with the bat, make as big a stride as they can but be careful and disciplined and make sure they bat for five sessions or so for a 200-run lead.

Australia are still in the game, thanks largely to Hussey, who made that big century at Brisbane and seemed set for another in Adelaide. He appears to be emerging as the Aussies' most important batsman, which is extraordinary when you consider the doubts surrounding his participation.

He probably needed that century in the Sheffield Shield for Western Australia to guarantee his place after poor form. It was fingernails on the blackboard stuff at the time, and fair play, he looked a fine player today. He knows Swann well from their Northants days, and went down the pitch to him on a regular basis very aggressively. Swann got him out today, tossing one up, getting it to spin, but not before some lovely leg-side shots by Hussey hit against the spin.

Steven Finn looked a bit tired at times and did not bowl his best. It's new territory for him – this is high-octane cricket in front of big crowds and it's exhausting just walking out there to play.

It was a little bit worrying seeing Paul Collingwood bowling with Australia five wickets down and attempting a counter-attack. I thought our bowlers might be exposed, but England do plan to rotate their bowlers during the series – which they need to if they pick just four per match – and remember they have 10 days off after this Test.

It was pleasing that our bowlers were able to wrap up Australia's tail cheaply despite the absence of a strike bowler, but I feel there are runs in this wicket for lower-order batsmen like Swann and Stuart Broad – and those runs could make a big difference. Broad, incidentally, has bowled much better both here and in Brisbane than his figures suggest, swinging the ball and locating a good length.

As a footnote, there was another untidy moment when Ryan Harris was given out lbw following a review, despite some evidence that he had hit the ball. I've got a meeting with Haroon Lorgat, chief executive of the ICC, on Saturday night, and I'll tell him the Decision Review System is not working in my view. There are still controversies about dismissals, which is precisely what this system was supposed to stop.

DAY 32　4 December 2010, Second Test – second day

It is an early start to take part in a Stockman's breakfast at the Adelaide Festival Centre. Two hundred farmers or 'Bushies' – many sporting dense goatees and moustaches and wearing Stetson cowboy hats – have descended on Adelaide from the far reaches of South Australia. And they are on the beer early – 7 a.m, in fact. I have always loved outback Australia, and escape to the more remote parts of South Australia – to Parachilna and beyond – whenever I can. I engage in conversation with the fellow sitting next to me who shares my love of flying light aircraft. He tells me he has ninety landing strips on his land. Ninety! Annoyingly, I won't be doing any flying on the trip. The tour is just too crammed. Also present is Daryl Harper, the Australian Test umpire, and the early morning alcohol-fuelled question and answer session is both lively and entertaining.

Morning session: At lunch – England 90/1, Cook 35*, Trott 39*

England recover from the shock dismissal of Strauss to the third ball of the day to which he offers no stroke and is bowled by Bollinger for 1. Had Doherty run out Cook on 6 from a similar position in the field to Trott yesterday, the morning would have a very different feel to it. As it is, it is starting to look like Brisbane revisited – with Cook and Trott seemingly well set at lunch, although Trott was missed low in the gully by Hussey on 10.

Haroon Lorgat, the chief executive of the ICC, is my lunch guest on *Test Match Special.* He is much more forthright on the subject of the impending hearing against Butt, Asif and Amir than I expected. He tells me the ICC have a strong case, and that in his view there should be no mitigating circumstances for age or inexperience. We talk about the Decision Review System and my reservations, but I will get my real chance to address those when I meet Haroon privately this evening.

> *"One of the things I introduced as England captain was that, when you were out, you had to sit on the balcony with your team-mates. There was no hiding away. Look at Simon Katich yesterday; he sat on his own in the crowd all day. It sends out another little sign that all is not right in the Australian camp."* MICHAEL VAUGHAN, TMS

Afternoon session: At tea – England 198/2, Cook 90*, Pietersen 14*

It is a boiling hot afternoon with the mercury showing 37 degrees in the shade, and a reprieve for Cook, who was given out caught down the leg side, does little for Ponting's humour. Trott is dropped on 76 as he hooks Harris, but two runs later he flicks the same bowler to mid-wicket. He and Cook have added 502 for 1 in the last two innings. KP arrives to a chorus of boos, but no change there.

> *"Quite a few seagulls now strutting round the outfield. Maybe Ponting can give one of them a bowl."* TOM FORDYCE

Evening session: At the close – England 317/2, Cook 136*, Pietersen 85*, England lead by 72

This is a massive session for England as they take the match by the scruff of the neck. Neither batsman gives a chance as they put on 141 before the close, with Cook reaching his fifteenth Test century. Ponting takes the new ball, but it makes no impression at all and his bowlers – Bollinger particularly – are struggling. Doherty, the left-arm spinner, looks miles out of his depth and offers Ponting no control.

Haroon Lorgat is a very pleasant, bespectacled and quietly spoken South African with an impossible job. As ICC chief executive he has to preside over the self-interest of the rich members and the financial woes of the poor, and manoeuvre cricket through the post-Commonwealth political minefield that is still very much in evidence today. He is also a firm advocate of the Decision Review System, so I know I am wasting my time when we meet up for a drink after the day's play. Well, I have a couple of glasses. Haroon is teetotal. I illustrate my reservations about the system based on our experiences of it, but he gently breaks the news that it will be used during the World Cup and, almost certainly thereafter, throughout one-day cricket. It is a robust discussion, but the ICC has clearly invested too much in the system to abandon it now.

A full and contrasting day that began with the 'Bushies' and ends with the man who is responsible for running world cricket.

END OF DAY REPORT

In Adelaide on Saturday, England took a huge step towards securing what they came to Australia to do – retain the Ashes.

They are on course to build an enormous lead and the best Australia can hope for is a draw. If they don't manage that, it leaves them needing to win two of the last three Tests to regain the Ashes and that would be a very tall order indeed.

Once again Alastair Cook was England's main man and the Essex opener is in the form of his life. He has been England's rock and deserves all the praise that comes his way. He is racking up the records and the beauty is that he does not even know he is doing it. He is not interested in that sort of thing. He just wants to bat, and he is doing that pretty well. Everyone who plays international sport for their country goes through dips in their form and technique. Cook experienced that last summer when he was planting his right foot in front of his stumps and having to play round his legs to hit the ball, which is very difficult. He was getting out lbw a lot, and was often caught in the slips.

All he is doing now is moving his front foot down towards the pitch of the ball and coming forwards to the ball rather than across his wicket. He has started playing the cover drive, which is a shot he hardly ever plays. The reason he can play that shot is because his front foot is out of the way.

Australia had not bargained for Cook playing that shot. I think they had him down as a back-foot player so they have bowled quite full at him, which is the right thing to do. But because Cook's footwork is so perfect, he is just smacking them for four. Australia need to do some more homework on Alastair Cook and work out how they are going to bowl at him.

Cook was ably supported by Kevin Pietersen, who put together a very important innings for himself and the team. He had to wait a long time to get out there and was a little bit wild to begin with but he played really straight, which is something he hasn't been doing. He's now 15 runs away from breaking that unhappy sequence of 18 Tests without a hundred.

England's primary objective on day three on Sunday must be to see off that new ball and bat for the rest of the day. With eight wickets still in hand, they should be able to build a colossal lead, and take it from there. There is some bad weather around, which could come in on Monday and Tuesday and have an impact on the game, but England have put Australia out of this match, which is exactly what they set out to do. Australia will face the same situation as England did at the Gabba and I certainly wouldn't back them to do it.

Finally, a word on Australian spinner Xavier Doherty, who had a really poor day. He bowled 15 overs for 70 and I would be surprised if he keeps his place. He had no control, bowled far too short and was regularly punished by Cook and Jonathan Trott. If he is dropped, Australia will have changed their two lead bowlers and their spinner, which tells its own story.

Jeff Thomson has said this is the weakest Australia attack for 30 years and it is certainly the weakest for a generation. You have to go back to the 1980s to find them so short of quality in the bowling department. They need to take a long, hard look at themselves and work out where they are going to find some better players.

DAY 33 5 December 2010, Second Test – third day

Just five more days until Emma arrives and I have to acknowledge that my ambition to lose a stone has been a laughable failure. This despite denying myself one of Adelaide's unique culinary offerings: in the press area at the Oval, they serve two-bite meat pies that are simply beautiful. In the Australian way you inject the tomato source in to the top of the pastry and devour them in two bites. They are incredibly moreish and I have not had a single one of them, even though their enticing smell comes straight through to the commentary box, and all my colleagues are forever diving in.

An early morning jog results in an unexpected meeting on the banks of the Torrens with Gavin Darby, who is a serious runner and was also one of Vodafone's big players when the company sponsored the England cricket team. I invite him to my Boycott evening tomorrow, and he seems pleased.

Morning session: At lunch – England 449/3, Pietersen 158*, Collingwood 40*

Cook's stand with Pietersen comes to an end at 175 when Cook is caught behind off the inside edge for 148. He faced 269 balls, and this is his first dismissal in over seventeen and a half hours at the crease. Meanwhile, this is the best I have seen Pietersen bat. Gone are the over-ambitious flicks through the leg side and there are no moments of madness that have been responsible for his downfall in the past. This is a brilliant innings in which he plays methodically and beautifully straight. If he always batted like this, no one would ever get him out. There is a bizarre passage in which Siddle and Bollinger take it in turns to pound in with three fielders in the deep for Pietersen's hook shot. He thrashes Bollinger over mid-wicket for 6 off the front foot and then takes the rise out of Siddle by premeditating a pull shot for four. His 150 comes from 210 balls. Ponting has really lost the plot this morning as a staggering 132 runs come from 26 overs. This is a Test match!

> *"If a bowler's asked to bowl with a 7-2 field, he's entitled to throw the ball back to the captain and say 'You bowl it yourself.'"* Ian Chappell, TMS

Afternoon session: At the close – England 551/4, Pietersen 213*, Bell 41*

Pietersen duly reaches his double hundred from 282 balls – the tenth Englishman to score a double century against Australia. He loses Collingwood for 42, lbw to Watson after a stand of 101, but the day is cut short by rain, which is already forecast to return on the final day and could yet save Australia from what is now a hopeless position. Strauss will have to judge his declaration carefully tomorrow and leave his bowlers with enough time to dismiss Australia a second time.

The hotel bar is really buzzing this evening with delighted England supporters, for many of whom this is a trip of a lifetime. It is always a good reality check to share a minute or two with those who are not lucky enough to see every match England plays. But it does wind me up when people carry on about my job; of course it is a wonderful way to make a living, however there appears to be an assumption that anyone can do it – that it's just a case of turning up. I would not be so presumptuous, but there's no point arguing about it.

The rest of the evening is spent with David 'Bumble' Lloyd and Mike Atherton. Bumble is a great friend (even if he still hasn't forgiven me for taking his wicket more than thirty years ago when he was a senior cricket figure as Lancashire's opening bat and I, barely out of school, was bowling in my first ever first-class match) and one of the great characters on tour. I sometimes feel he is wasted on television where commentary really focuses on what's happening out in the middle. Bumble has always got an eye for something going on – a silly hat or someone asleep in the crowd and the wonderful laconic northern vocabulary to describe it with warmth and humour. He adds colour – a quality in broadcasting that really belongs on radio – which is why people love him.

Until recently, Bumble was a keen Twitterer, but dropped it because of a lot of bad language that was doing the rounds. I find this really sad; he is not in the least bit an abusive character and had really embraced what Twitter is all about – making contact with a community, something he is brilliant at fostering. I hope he reconnects with his many followers again soon.

By the end of the evening, Michael, Bumble and I have firmly concluded that Australian cricket is in for a rough ride over the coming months.

> "If you see me betting on a draw, I'll be wearing someone else's trousers because I won't be betting with my own money." Ian Chappell, TMS

END OF DAY REPORT

The third day at Adelaide was another one-sided affair, which once again exposed the paucity of bowling options at Australia captain Ricky Ponting's disposal. Poor old Xavier Doherty has been shown to be a crazy selection. He is 28-years-old and has hardly played any first-class cricket, and that is for a reason. He is simply not good enough. His shortcomings have been exposed in the full glare of everybody on a flat pitch. He has bowled far too short. He could not control it, Ponting could not set fields for him, so I do not think we will see him again.

Ryan Harris bowled well. He has a lot of bustle about him and bowled a good few overs at Kevin Pietersen that were very aggressive and very hostile. He knocked Pietersen off his feet once, and could have had him caught hooking. It is no coincidence that he is the one frontline bowler who has not gone for 100.

Doug Bollinger and Peter Siddle are honest and hard-working but the ball did not do anything for them. To see them trying to bowl short to Kevin Pietersen with three men on the leg side was a sad sight and Pietersen absolutely destroyed Siddle because he knew what was coming.

But I do not think Ponting did a huge amount wrong today. He tried things but he has not got the firepower to bowl bouncers and he has not got a skilful spinner. When your bowlers are haemorrhaging runs and the score is ticking over, you have to be inventive and I do not blame him for trying to bowl the ball wide of off stump. As it happened, Pietersen just let them bowl out there for a few overs and when they drifted in, he inevitably just hit it for four.

In these situations, it is always the bowlers that get it in the neck but in fact the fault for Australia's predicament has been the batsmen. Their first innings total was well below par and that is why Australia are in this horrible position. Nonetheless, the spotlight may fall on Australia bowling coach Troy Cooley. He certainly has not got the ringing endorsement from Australian onlookers that he had when he revolutionised the way England bowled in 2005.

It doesn't reflect well that he has not been able to straighten out Mitchell Johnson and it may be that he is judged on what happens with Johnson because clearly Australia would love to have him out there, bowling well.

Ian Chappell is not alone in struggling to name the Australia attack for the Third Test. I suggested to Shane Warne that Nathan Hauritz would have to come back but he said they should go for leg-spinner Steve Smith. That would be a huge call because he is not an accurate bowler at all. He bowled for Australia A against England in Hobart and got marmalised – Ian Bell just took him to the cleaners.

There is a dearth of Australian cricketers at the moment, but they must not judge those who are around at the moment against the recent generation of brilliant cricketers – they are not going to come round again any time soon.

The Aussie public are not very happy with what they are seeing and have said all sorts of things over the last couple of days but all that does is put more pressure on the players.

Meanwhile, Pietersen's innings was the best I have ever seen him play. It looks as if the kick in the pants he got through being dropped in the summer has paid off. He looked hungry for this, he was absolutely determined and he did not offer any chances to the fielders. He played so straight, and from his celebration at the end you could see what that meant. He worked so hard and showed wonderful control to reign in what has been his rather compulsive nature in the past.

England are in total control of the match and it would be a crying shame if Australia escape because of the weather.

I hope England declare overnight and get on with it because with a lead of more than 300, Australia would have to bat long into the final day to make the game safe. Graeme Swann has a big role to play because the ball is spinning a bit out of the rough. He bowled pretty well in the first innings and will be a key figure in this match.

DAY 34 6 December 2010, Second Test – fourth day

It is reported that there was a dust-up between Ian Chappell and Sir Ian Botham in the Adelaide Oval car park after play yesterday and that they were 'at each others' throats'. The *Daily Mail* says that they 'had to be pulled apart'. The pair have never spoken after an incident at the bar of the Melbourne Hilton in 1977, so to read of an incident between them is not necessarily surprising. However, they both strenuously deny the events as reported, which is definitely the first time Messrs Chappell and Botham have been united over anything for more than 30 years!

Speaking of the *Daily Mail*, I suffer my own embarrassment this morning. On opening my laptop, I discover that I have been somewhat misquoted. A while ago, in the course of plugging my book, *Thanks, Johnners*, I was interviewed by *The Times* for their health section. Frankly, when you are trying to promote a book you say yes to every imaginable interview and end up answering all sorts of interesting questions. I was asked by a reporter on *The Times*, "Is sex important to you?" I was also asked whether I had any interesting ailments and so mentioned that I had Dupuytren's contracture (a condition of the hand where the fingers bend towards the palm and cannot be fully straightened). A couple of days ago this was picked up by the *Daily Mail* who, in return for a generous plug for my book, asked to speak to me about the condition.

A very nice lady called one evening, and we talked about Dupuytren's contracture at some length. It is inconvenient, annoying, can be painful and requires several operations to correct. As a sufferer you are always looking for cures and answers, anything that might solve it and that's why, in the spirit of giving other people who might have it the benefit of my experiences, I was happy to chat away.

In the course of the interview I mentioned that *TMS* scorer the late Bill Frindall had had a finger amputated as a result of the condition and that a lot of cricketers have it, in particular David Gower and Graham Gooch. Job done – I was expecting a very nice piece.

This morning the article has appeared, and half way through it states that England batting coach Graham Gooch has had his finger amputated. Graham is, of course, on this tour – in fact I had dinner with him only a few days ago. I know that it can't have been easy for the *Daily Mail* reporter to hear me because I was actually eating my dinner in a noisy restaurant when she called, but this is all very embarrasing. I know I will spend the next two weeks avoiding Graham and hoping that no one in his family has actually read the blessed article.

Morning session: At lunch – England 620/5 dec, Australia 78/0

Strauss decides to bat on, which is a decision not universally popular in the media centre. Already leading by 306 at the start of the day, England will also have seen the weather forecast that indicates it will definitely rain on the last day, the rain due to start in the afternoon. I like the thought of England rubbing Australia's noses in it for a while and, with Broad out of the game, Strauss has to be mindful of tiring out his two remaining seamers, Anderson and Finn.

England add 69 in 9 overs for the loss of Pietersen for 227 – his highest score in Tests. Trying to hit Doherty out of the park, he gives a catch to Katich who is fielding at slip because he has an injured Achilles tendon. It is Doherty's only wicket in the innings and, I suspect, will be his only scalp in Test cricket at a cost of 158 runs. Bell and Prior rattle along adding 52 in 34 balls before Strauss declares with England having passed 600 for only the second time ever in Australia. The lead is 375. Australia are left with a task slightly less imposing than England's in the previous Test, but this time the Australians will be batting on a wearing pitch. The limping Katich and Watson see out the remainder of the morning.

> *"England wouldn't expect Australia to roll over and let them win the game easily. It's going to be difficult – but they've definitely got the tools to do it."*
> MICHAEL VAUGHAN, TMS

Afternoon session: At tea – Australia 160/3, Clarke 36*, Hussey 14*

Swann settles in at the Cathedral End and starts to make the ball talk. Katich is his first victim, edging to Prior for 43 and then comes the big wicket of Ponting. He sweeps for four, but a Swann 'slider' which goes on with the arm, finds the edge and Collingwood grabs an outstanding catch low to his left at slip. It is truly brilliant piece of cricket and Ponting departs for just 9. Watson is taken by Strauss at first slip off Finn for another fighting half-century, but Clarke and Hussey look determined. Australia are only three wickets down at tea, but it is still England's session.

> *"It's the kind of pitch where you can get a cluster of wickets. If Graeme Swann gets one wicket, he could go bang, bang, bang."* MICHAEL VAUGHAN, TMS

Evening session: At the close – 238/4, Hussey 44*, Australia are 137 behind

There is definitely rain around, and an hour is lost in the session, which helps Australia to make it almost to the close without losing any more wickets. Then high drama when England are convinced that Clarke, on 80, has given a catch to Cook at short-leg off the very last ball of the day, bowled by, of all people, Pietersen. The umpire says not out. England review the decision and there is clearly a big nick on to Clarke's pad before the ball loops over Cook's head and, as he turns and tumbles, into his hands. It is a massive wicket – and a hugely embarrassing moment for Clarke, who feels guilty enough at his obvious misjudgement in refusing to walk, to later issue an apology for his actions via Twitter, which in turn is scorned by many Aussie fans.

It will be an early start tomorrow to make up for lost time, but the weather, and Hussey, are both against England.

At the dinner table, Sir Geoffrey is in great form, holding court. I opt for the other end of the table. I've heard his many stories about the Yorkshire heydays before. In company he knows and trusts he is very entertaining. His wife, Rachael, who adores him, is clearly a kindly and hugely patient woman.

"Outstanding day's play. Aussies played well. They will be doing rain dances all over Adelaide tonight. Only chance they have." MICHAEL VAUGHAN, TMS

END OF DAY REPORT

A surprise wicket for Kevin Pietersen, off the last ball of day four, has made a massive difference to this absorbing Adelaide Test match. Australia are 238/4 in their second innings and still 137 runs behind after England's first innings declaration on 620/5.

Michael Clarke and Michael Hussey played so well in their partnership, and were starting to frustrate England, with nicks not going to hand. If Australia had been only three wickets down at stumps, they would have felt they had a real chance of saving the game, but that one wicket really does swing things.

England do not have to take the new ball immediately when it becomes available on the final morning, and indeed I would suggest that they avoid doing so, with Graeme Swann bowling pretty well. He should fancy his chances. Even though Hussey has had a start, there will be two left-handers on strike when he is joined by Marcus North, and Swann likes bowling to left-handers.

Pietersen, who does spin the ball and gets a lot of bounce, will also be an option, and on a wicket like this he could be important, especially given that there is an issue over Stuart Broad's fitness. No one wants to get out to KP, but Michael Clarke did, on 80, and his dismissal showed just how much spin there is out there.

England's plan for Tuesday should be to get amongst the Australians early with the old ball, while in the back of Andrew Strauss's mind will be the knowledge that he can take the new ball, and if Broad is not quite fit, then Anderson and Steven Finn will share it.

Broad's injury brings with it one or two complications, but Paul Collingwood, with his cutters, is also there as a potential partnership breaker. On this kind of wicket, however, Pietersen has probably earned the right to come on before him.

The one thing that will prey on England's mind overnight, and the one thing that could stop them from achieving a richly deserved win – even if the Australian fans don't want to admit it – is the weather. We have already had interruptions, and Tuesday's forecast from the local Met Office is light rain around in the morning, and more of a showery variety in the afternoon with the possibility of a thunderstorm.

England just have to get on with their job, and try not to think about the weather. There is a possibility of stoppages, but we do have an early start.

Australian fans will be pleased to have seen a significant innings from Clarke, who was determined to bat his way out of a poor run with some positive cricket. At times it became a little frenetic, but generally he was somewhere between the two. He came down the pitch and used his feet well to Swann in a good little tussle, but the best battle of the day was between Swann and Ricky Ponting.

The Australian captain is obviously a big wicket and he was out there on a king pair, with the pressure mounting. He managed to punch one away through the on-side for four but then got a ball that really turned and bounced. The very next delivery skidded on. It was one of those that was rolled out of the hand, not spun hard. Ponting had to play it, and it took the edge. Collingwood's catch at slip was brilliant – in fact all of England's catches were good, even Alastair Cook's at the end.

Strauss's take off Finn to remove Shane Watson was another good, clean catch – and it's so good for England that all these chances are sticking.

Australia did show a lot of fight on Monday. There were the two big stands, one between Watson and the injured Simon Katich, who refused to use a runner, and then the Clarke-Hussey stand.

They will not lay down for England, but England should still manage to win this match.

DAY 35 **7 December 2010, Second Test – fifth day**

Mischievously, when I wake up, I immediately post on Twitter that the weather in Adelaide is awful. After a few minutes to allow that news to be absorbed by everyone at home who are excitedly anticipating an England win, I follow it with a photo taken from my hotel window that shows blue skies and sunshine. Cue a mixture of relief and gnashing of teeth from the other side of the world. That's the joy of Twitter. You can play with people and have a lot of fun in doing so.

The talk at breakfast is all about the weather, and the various forecasts people have seen. Everyone is agreed: it will rain heavily this afternoon.

What a heartbreaker – Stuart Broad is out for the series, and the one-day internationals. It is terrible news, and a devastating blow to poor old Broad. All that training and preparation to no avail. A scan shows he tore something in the side of his abdomen while bowling round the wicket yesterday. In the short term it means that England are now a bowler down in this game, which they are so well poised to win. It is a good thing that the pitch is starting to take spin as Swann should be able to tie up one end and Broad's absence won't be felt so strongly.

Morning session: Australia 304 all out, England win by an innings and 71 runs

In twenty overs it is all wrapped up. Australia surrender meekly and haplessly, losing 6 for 66 to give England their first victory by an innings here for 24 years. Hussey makes a rare misjudgement and is caught at mid-on, aiming to pull Finn, for 52 and that opens the floodgates. Anderson nips out Haddin and Harris, who completes not merely a king pair (out first ball in both innings) but becomes surely the first batsman ever to do so having unsuccessfully reviewed both lbw decisions! Swann takes the last two wickets to finish with 5 for 91 and, clutching my producer Caroline – who has never experienced anything like this before – I head on to the outfield to broadcast the presentation ceremony and conduct the post-match interviews.

Ponting is magnanimous as always, and Strauss pays tribute to his team. But the most striking interview is with Pietersen, the man of the match, who tells me that this is the way he is aiming to bat from now on. No more rushes of blood. Hitting the ball straight down the ground. It is a fresh start. "This is music to every English fan's ears, Kevin," I say. He reaffirms his absolute determination that this is the future.

Shortly after lunch, when I am back in my room bashing out the various reports on my long list of commitments, a clap of thunder rocks the hotel to its foundations. Moments later, the rain hammers down. I am on the nineteenth floor and cannot see the pavement below, it is raining so hard. Had Australia held on for a couple more hours, the match would have been washed out.

The celebrations are many and varied. Collingwood chooses to dash from the England dressing room wearing only his underpants for some puddle diving on the saturated outfield, while Giles Clarke, the chairman of ECB, throws a dinner party to which I am invited for us all to savour the moment. No one who witnessed this demolition can surely imagine anything other than England retaining the Ashes.

END OF MATCH REPORT

England's first win over Australia by an innings and more for 24 years certainly ranks among the greatest victories I have seen overseas.

Andrew Strauss's team are a fantastically drilled, very fit outfit playing at the height of their abilities. Their fielding in Adelaide was exceptional and apart from Matt Prior's tough chance, when he dropped Mike Hussey off Graeme Swann's bowling early on the final day, they caught everything. Jonathan Trott's superb direct hit to dismiss Simon Katich in the first over of the match set the tone for a thoroughly clinical performance.

But for me, the one individual who stood out above the others was Kevin Pietersen.

I interviewed him after he received his man-of-the-match award and what impressed me was his new-found approach to batting. He now understands the value of his wicket and how important it is to score big hundreds, all the things we have wanted to hear since his arrival in the England side.

Graeme Swann's return to form also illustrated just what a class act he is. After his performance in Brisbane, where he said he 'bowled like a 12-year-old', he has once again shown why he has reinvigorated finger spinning. He gives every delivery a serious tweak, but has a superb arm ball, perfectly illustrated by the sliders that dismissed Ricky Ponting and Xavier Doherty – he is a brilliant spin bowler.

England's celebrations will be tempered by the news that Stuart Broad is out for the series with a stomach strain. Broad has made a huge contribution in this series with the ball, even though he hasn't taken a lot of wickets. So who will England choose as his successor? I think Tim Bresnan is ahead of his rivals at the moment. For the Perth Test England will want a third seamer to bowl into the wind, known as the 'Fremantle Doctor'.

Bresnan is more of a traditional swinger than Yorkshire team-mate Ajmal Shahzad or Chris Tremlett, which works in his favour, although the WACA is traditionally the fastest and bounciest pitch in Australia, which will suit the bowling styles of the other two seamers.

The selectors will have a chance to consider their options when England play Victoria in a three-day match in Melbourne, which begins on Friday.

Their dilemma is relatively minor compared to Australia, who are in complete disarray.

With Simon Katich ruled out with an Achilles injury, Australia are likely to turn to opener Phil Hughes, who was dumped after two Tests in last year's Ashes in England. The 22-year-old is a high-risk player at the top of the innings and England won't be scared of him because they have successfully devised plans to get him out.

As well as a new opener, Australia will need a new spinner and changes to their pace attack because Ricky Ponting will want fresh bowling options in Perth. I suspect they may bring back Nathan Hauritz in place of the ineffective Xavier Doherty and drop Doug Bollinger, who was poor in Adelaide, with Ben Hilfenhaus returning to the pace attack.

Australia's chairman of selectors Andrew Hilditch is under immense pressure. It seems they have no long-term plans, judging by their depleted reserves of talent, and the Australian media want answers.

This saga will run and run. There have even been calls for the return of Shane Warne and it is all very demoralising for the hosts. Warne is not going to be playing in this series, those who want him in the team need to face up to reality.

AUSTRALIA v ENGLAND
2nd Test

Result: England won by an innings and 71 runs

Played at Adelaide Oval, Adelaide on
3,4,5,6,7 December 2010

Toss: Australia
Referee: JJ Crowe

Umpires: M Erasmus & AL Hill (TV: BR Doctrove)
Man of Match: KP Pietersen

AUSTRALIA	Runs	Mins	Balls	4	6		Runs	Mins	Balls	4	6
SR Watson c Pietersen b Anderson	51	127	94	7	1	c Strauss b Finn	57	174	141	10	-
SM Katich run out (Trott)	0	2	0	-	-	c Prior b Swann	43	108	85	6	-
RT Ponting c Swann b Anderson	0	2	1	-	-	c Collingwood b Swann	9	21	19	2	-
MJ Clarke c Swann b Anderson	2	7	6	-	-	c Cook b Pietersen	80	170	139	11	-
MEK Hussey c Collingwood b Swann	93	299	183	8	-	c Anderson b Finn	52	154	107	5	1
MJ North c Prior b Finn	26	100	93	4	-	lbw b Swann	22	56	35	3	-
BJ Haddin c Finn b Broad	56	148	95	3	1	c Prior b Anderson	12	24	21	2	-
RJ Harris lbw b Swann	0	4	1	-	-	lbw b Anderson	0	1	1	-	-
XJ Doherty run out (Strauss/Cook/Prior)	6	25	19	1	-	b Swann	5	17	9	1	-
PM Siddle c Cook b Anderson	3	24	21	-	-	b Swann	6	28	22	1	-
DE Bollinger not out	0	7	3	-	-	not out	7	14	16	1	-
Extras (lb 6, w 1, nb 1)	**8**					**Extras (b 5, lb 1, w 5)**	**11**				
TOTAL (85.5 overs)	245					TOTAL (99.1 overs)	304				

ENGLAND	Runs	Mins	Balls	4	6
AJ Strauss b Bollinger	1	4	3	-	-
AN Cook c Haddin b Harris	148	428	269	18	-
IJL Trott c Clarke b Harris	78	213	144	11	-
KP Pietersen c Katich b Doherty	227	428	308	33	1
PD Collingwood lbw b Watson	42	92	70	5	-
IR Bell not out	68	151	97	8	1
MJ Prior not out	27	25	21	2	-
SCJ Broad	-	-	-	-	-
GP Swann	-	-	-	-	-
JM Anderson	-	-	-	-	-
ST Finn	-	-	-	-	-
Extras (b 8, lb 13, w 8)	**29**				
TOTAL (for 5 wkts dec) (152 overs)	620				

Eng	O	M	R	W		O	M	R	W	
Anderson	19	4	51	4		22	4	92	2	
Broad	18.5	6	39	1		11	3	32	0	
Finn	16	1	71	1 (1 nb, 1 w)	(4)	18	2	60	2 (1 w)	
Swann	29	2	70	2	(3)	41.1	12	91	5	
Collingwood	3	0	8	0		4	0	13	0	
Pietersen	-	-	-	-		3	0	10	1	

Aus	O	M	R	W		O	M	R	W
Harris	29	5	84	2 (1 w)		-	-	-	-
Bollinger	29	1	130	1 (2 w)		-	-	-	-
Siddle	30	3	121	0 (1 w)		-	-	-	-
Watson	19	7	44	1		-	-	-	-
Doherty	27	3	158	1		-	-	-	-
North	18	0	62	0		-	-	-	-

FALL OF WICKETS			
	Aus	Eng	Aus
1st	0 (2)	3 (1)	84 (2)
2nd	0 (3)	176 (3)	98 (3)
3rd	2 (4)	351 (2)	134 (1)
4th	96 (1)	452 (5)	238 (4)
5th	156 (6)	568 (4)	261 (5)
6th	207 (5)	-	286 (7)
7th	207 (8)	-	286 (8)
8th	226 (9)	-	286 (6)
9th	243 (10)	-	295 (9)
10th	245 (7)	-	304 (10)

ADELAIDE MILESTONES

Ⓜ **Ricky Ponting became the fourth** player to appear in 150 Tests. The first three were Allan Border, Steve Waugh and Sachin Tendulkar. Ponting replicated Waugh's first-ball duck in his 150th match.

Ⓜ **Simon Katich was run out** without facing a ball in Australia's first innings. He was the fifth Australian to suffer this fate in a Test:

Name	Against	Venue	Season
AF Kippax	South Africa	Adelaide	1931/32
WM Lawry	South Africa	Port Elizabeth	1966/67
RM Hogg	England	Birmingham	1981
WB Phillips	West Indies	Port-of-Spain	1983/84
SM Katich	England	Adelaide	2010/11

Ⓜ **Alastair Cook followed up** his 235* in 625 minutes in the second innings at Brisbane with 148 in 428 minutes. His 1,053 minutes between dismissals is an England record, passing the 1,021 by Nasser Hussain v South Africa in 1999/00. West Indies' Shivnarine Chanderpaul, who has remarkably batted on four separate occasions for over 1,000 minutes between dismissals, holds the world record of 1,513 v India in 2001/02.

Ⓜ **Cook's 383 runs between dismissals** is also an England record, passing the 365 by Wally Hammond in 1932/33 and 1933.

Ⓜ **Cook and Trott added 173** for the second wicket, an England record for this wicket at the Adelaide Oval, passing the 169 that John Edrich and Keith Fletcher added in 1970/71. Following on from their 329 unbroken stand at Brisbane, they had added 502 in partnerships before being dismissed and this was a record for England passing the 411 that Colin Cowdrey and Peter May added in one partnership v West Indies at Birmingham in 1957. It was the third best in the world:

Runs	Batsmen	Details
624	KC Sangakkara and DPMD Jayawardene	624 v SA, 2006
576	ST Jayasuriya and RS Mahanama	576 v Ind, 1997/98
502	AN Cook and IJL Trott	329* & 173 v Aus, 2010/11
495	SM Gavaskar and DB Vengsarkar	344* & 151 v WI, 1978/79
489	Inzamam-ul-Haq and Ijaz Ahmed	352* v SL, 1998/99 & 137 v Aus, 1999/00

Ⓜ **Kevin Pietersen's 227** is the highest score for England at Adelaide, passing the 206 that Paul Collingwood made on the previous Ashes tour in 2006/07. It was his first century in 18 Tests since making 102 v West Indies at Port-of Spain in 2008/09. In the intervening 17 Tests he scored 904 runs at an average of 36.16 with six fifties and a best of 99. His career average had dropped from 51.09 to 47.75 in that time.

Ⓜ **Ian Bell passed 4,000 Test** runs during his innings of 68* in England's first innings.

◫ **Ryan Harris completed a king pair** in Australia's second innings, joining Adam Gilchrist (v India at Kolkata in 2000/01) as the only Australians to have done this in Test cricket. Harris was out lbw in each innings and unsuccessfully had the decision reviewed each time.

◫ **This was Australia's first innings defeat** at the Adelaide Oval since England beat them there by an innings and 230 runs in 1891/92. It was England's first innings win over Australia since the Melbourne Test of 1986/87, which England won by an innings and 14 runs.

FIVE

SECOND TEST INTERLUDE

"On this tour so far England have out-bowled them, out-batted them and out-fielded them."

GEOFFREY BOYCOTT

DAY 36 **8 December 2010**

With the Adelaide Test now over, I can pass the baton to Mark Pougatch who leaves with the team and my colleagues for Melbourne and a first-class match against Victoria. From so much hustle and bustle, the hotel is strangely quiet as I settle in to wait for Emma's long-awaited arrival. Because of the amount of travelling my job involves, we are apart a great deal, and being away so much is tough on family life. I've lost count of the number of my daughters' birthdays I have missed over the years and I reckon this will be the eleventh time I've been away for Christmas in the last 20 years.

Communications and my employer's attitude to touring have been transformed since my early days as a broadcaster. Peter Baxter, the then *Test Match Special* producer, told me that I was entitled to one telephone call home per week. And every fulltime cricket journalist covered every day of every tour: it was just the done thing. It is impossible to do that now and maintain any semblance of a home life, and this is recognised sympathetically and respected by our employers. Meanwhile, texting, Skype and the Internet have revolutionised the way we stay in touch with our families. Webcams mean you can actually see the people you are talking to so far away, making it feel like they are with you in your hotel room for a while at least.

But there is also a positive side to this in that absence really does make the heart grow fonder, and I believe that our marriage is stronger for the anticipation and sheer joy of being reunited after, in this case, six weeks apart. It will be longer at the World Cup in the spring.

I have booked four days on Kangaroo Island, which is a short hop from Adelaide and is somewhere new for us to explore. These breaks are a great opportunity to clear the head, escape from the constantly ringing phone and also to provide a source of material for the commentary of the next Test. We stay in a delightful lodge overlooking one of Kangaroo Island's many pretty bays, and spend the days in a four-wheel drive exploring an island of wonderful natural and unspoiled beauty. The only shame is the amount of road kill, the sight of which really hits the unprepared visitor hard. Kangaroos, possums and even koalas litter the sides of the dirt tracks. Driving at dusk really is very hazardous indeed.

We certainly didn't miss anything at Melbourne where a slow, flat track produced a lifeless draw. On to Perth.

FOUR OTHER GREAT ENGLAND WINS

Oliver Brett| 7 December 2010

Tuesday's Ashes win in Adelaide will resonate powerfully as a landmark England victory. Delivered by the crunching margin of an innings and 71 runs, it was the first to be achieved Down Under with the series still up for grabs since Mike Gatting's victorious tour in 1986-87. The 2-1 series success from 24 years ago did not release the floodgates for a great run of form from England, in fact it was much the opposite. By the time new captain Nasser Hussain's side were beaten on home soil by New Zealand in 1999, they were ranked at the bottom of the pile in the Test rankings.

After that woeful summer, Duncan Fletcher was installed as a full-time coach and results have generally been much better since then, despite a post-2005 Ashes blip. The win in Adelaide, which moves England up to third in the latest edition of the ICC's Test Championship ladder, is potentially hugely important.

Since the dawn of the millennium there have been some splendid victories for England on foreign soil across the globe, and here follows a selection of some of the best.

Karachi, December 2000 - England 388 & 176-4 beat Pakistan 405 & 158 by six wickets

Summary: After two drab draws on flat, slow wickets, England pulled off a thrilling run chase as they battled the impending darkness to pull off their first Test triumph in 39 years in Pakistan, and end a five-series drought against those opponents.

How they did it: The match appeared to be heading towards another stalemate until Pakistan collapsed to Darren Gough, Ashley Giles and Craig White either side of lunch on the final day. England were left to chase 176, and crucially earned the sympathy of umpires Steve Bucknor and Mohammad Nazir while Pakistan captain Moin Khan employed some questionable delaying tactics. Finally, with everyone struggling to see the ball, an inside edge from Graham Thorpe (who scored 64 not out) just missed the stumps and England scampered the winning runs.

Kingston, March 2004 - England 339 & 20-0 beat West Indies 311 & 47 by 10 wickets

Summary: Mercurial pace bowler Steve Harmison enjoyed his finest hour in an England shirt, recording an extraordinary 7 for 12, as West Indies capitulated on the fourth morning. The result set up a 3-0 whitewash for Michael Vaughan's team.

How they did it: A match that had been keenly contested for three days exploded into life when West Indies resumed on the fourth morning at 8/0 in their second innings, trailing by just 20 runs. Using his natural height and pace to maximum effect, Harmison found a perfect length from the start, and the West Indies batsmen either nicked everything or missed the straight ones. With the frontline batsmen blown away in next to no time, Vaughan had eight slips and a short-leg to the last few batsmen. With nobody able to launch any sort of a fightback, the final West Indies total of 47 all out remains their lowest ever.

Johannesburg, January 2005 - England 411 & 332-9d beat South Africa 419 & 247 by 77 runs

Summary: This was the fourth of five Tests in an engrossing and competitive series won 2-1 by England. With only the last two sessions of the Test to bowl out South Africa, Matthew Hoggard with 7 for 61 led the way with an irresistible burst of swing and seam bowling.

How they did it: For four days, these two high-quality sides appeared to have batted each other to a standstill, but Marcus Trescothick resumed on 101 not out on the final day and a plan was laid. Trescothick played with brilliantly controlled aggression before falling for 180, adding significant runs with the lower order, whereupon Michael Vaughan declared, leaving South Africa to chase an improbable 325 to win. With much of the attack either injured or out of form, Hoggard, according to Matthew Engel in *Wisden*, "carried the team on his shoulders like Atlas". He nabbed the last wicket just in time and later dressed up in a cowboy hat and a cigar for photographers eager to mark his 'Magnificent Seven'.

Mumbai, March 2006 - England 400 & 191 beat India 279 & 100 by 213 runs

Summary: Despite England's gradual resurgence over the last 11 years, India have remained a fiendishly difficult opponent to overcome whether at home or away, but Andrew Flintoff's often-criticized captaincy worked a treat in this rare triumph.

How they did it: An Andrew Strauss century and James Anderson's 4 for 40 ensured a healthy first innings lead and when play resumed on the final day, India were 18/1 chasing 313 to win. Desperate to end the series with a 1-0 win, India never considered going for the runs, and were three wickets down at lunch. But with Johnny Cash's *Ring of Fire* played at full volume in the England dressing room at the interval, the tourists suddenly seized the match by the scruff of the neck, with the last seven wickets falling in just 15.2 overs. Flintoff opened the door with the critical wicket of Rahul Dravid, before unheralded 37-year-old spinner Shaun Udal blew it off its hinges with four of the last five wickets. Udal was never picked again.

WHERE DO AUSTRALIA GO NEXT?

Tom Fordyce | 9 December 2010

They have just lost a Test by an innings and 71 runs. For the first time in two decades, they have failed to win a single one of their last five Tests. Four opposition batsmen have an average in the series of more than 100. So do four of their own bowlers. They are also taking a fearful pummelling from public and pundits alike. So, with the Third Test only a week away and needing to win at least two of the remaining three Tests to regain the Ashes, how can Australia bounce back from here?

There are issues over selection, tactics, the team's attitude and the captaincy of Ricky Ponting, let alone a toothless bowling attack and struggling top order. By contrast, England will head to Western Australia off the back of their most impressive overseas victory in memory, full of runs and wickets and bursting with confidence. "It's going to be tough, no two ways about it," says former Ashes-winning skipper Mark Taylor. "There are plenty of questions and about a thousand answers to each question."

Team selection

"The first thing they need to do is find a replacement for the injured Simon Katich. I daresay that will be Phil Hughes," says Taylor. "He can play and he's back in some sort of form. But it's in the bowling that they're really struggling. To me, Doug Bollinger doesn't look quite fit. He struggled in Adelaide and I think Ben Hilfenhaus will have to come back in. Ryan Harris will be retained because he bowled OK. The people around the team have to sit down and say, right, what's our best team for Perth, let's pick it and go from there. I'd like to see some young players coming through."

Australia's chairman of selectors Andrew Hilditch is due to announce his squad on Friday. Spinner Xavier Doherty is the man most likely to be dropped, with the axe also hanging over Marcus North, Peter Siddle and Bollinger. There are even rumours that Mitchell Johnson, discarded after his wayward performance in the First Test at the Gabba, might be recalled.

Steve Waugh was a young all-rounder in the last Australian team to lose an Ashes series at home. He then starred in eight consecutive series wins, the last two as captain. "I don't know what the selectors are going to do because they have chopped and changed probably too much in the last 12 months. You just look at the bowling. They've got through so many bowlers: Clint McKay, Peter George, then we've got Hilfenhaus and Johnson. Where do you go if you've just discarded these guys? Nathan Hauritz , do you bring him back now? I was totally against Hughes being dropped at the time. I think it was a short-sighted decision and I think it's proven to be so if he gets picked right now. He's got that fire in the belly and you can see something in his eyes."

Former Australian skipper Ian Chappell averaged more than 40 in Tests against England and led his side in four Ashes series. "What happens if they bring Johnson back in and he goes for plenty in his first three overs? You're then stuck with a bloke who the captain doesn't want to turn to and who could be a liability. He needs to go off and get some wickets in Shield cricket before they even think about it."

Tactics

Should Australia opt for a policy of all-out attack? In the two games so far, they have taken only 17 wickets, 10 of which came on the very first day. "What I would like to see from Australia is tactics that are a bit more conservative," says Taylor, who scored 2,496 runs in five winning Ashes campaigns from 1989 to 1999. England have flourished because their tactics have been pretty simple: bowl line and length and set your field accordingly. At stages in Adelaide, Australia had three men on the hook shot or three men on the drive. It is very hard for bowlers to bowl to that sort of field. Be consistent in your plans and at times be boring. Australia don't have the cattle at the moment. What Ricky Ponting has to do is remain as positive as he can. And be a bit more relaxed. There's been a lot of talk from Ricky about being fit and how every day is the biggest day of your life. Well, it's a game of cricket and I think Australian teams play their best when they're relaxed."

Attitude

With the exception of the first day in Brisbane, the Australian players have looked a shadow of their aggressive, self-confident selves. "It's almost like the shoe is on the other foot, we've reversed roles," says Waugh. "I'd like to see us have a bit more spring in our step. I know it's hard when you are not taking wickets but someone has got to lift the team in that situation. They've got to find some sort of aggro for their attack," believes Taylor. "Johnson's been out of form – there's no doubt about that – but by not having him in the side they've lost that bit of aggro that's always been part of Australia's way of playing. They've either got to bring him back or find someone who can do that kind of job."

Chappell disagrees. "Aggro doesn't get you wickets. It's no good having a bloke who's just going to shout his mouth off. You need batsmen who can score runs and bowlers who can take wickets. You don't get self-belief from making great speeches, otherwise Winston Churchill would have been the best cricket captain England could ever have had. You get it from playing well and winning matches. Ponting can't just conjure it up from nowhere for his players."

Leadership

What of captain Ricky Ponting, who scored only nine runs across two innings in Adelaide and faces the dismal prospect of becoming only the second Australian captain in history to lose three Ashes series? "He is in a really tricky position," says former England skipper Michael Vaughan. "His bowling unit is not what it was and you can see a captain just trying to prove to everyone that he should be the captain. He is trying to come up with a tactical masterstroke too often. He is changing his field regularly and changing his bowlers regularly. He is not really sticking with a plan for a period of time to allow it to develop. He is under a huge amount of pressure but Ricky Ponting has to stay as captain for Australia to get back into this series and he has to go to Perth and score runs. So far in this series, he has scored an unbeaten 51 in the second innings in Brisbane, failed in the first innings (10) and failed twice in Adelaide. I really feel he has to concentrate solely on scoring as many runs as possible. The only way, I believe, Australia will get a big score is if Ricky Ponting contributes with the bat."

There have been comments in some Australian newspapers that Ponting might have to step down as captain, both to focus on his own batting and freshen the side up. "I think it would be the wrong move," says Vaughan. "I think he is an extremely good leader. Tactically, I think we can all question him but this bowling unit does take some captaining. I think he is actually playing OK. He is making one error and getting out but that happens in cricket. If he continues to move his feet like he has done, I am pretty sure he will get a score. But England know if they get him cheaply at Perth, the Australia team will definitely wobble once again because the leader is so important."

Chris Tremlett came in to replace Broad in Perth after a Test absence of more than three years and made an immediate impact, picking up three wickets in Australia's first innings and five in the second. With his steep bounce, he would look dangerous every time he bowled in the series.

Mitchell Johnson was brought back into the Australian side after Adelaide and restored his confidence with a counter-attacking 62 as England failed to reinforce their advantage, having had Australia 69 for 5 at one stage.

Johnson turns destroyer with the ball. A combination of the fast Perth wicket and a favourable breeze, courtesy of the 'Fremantle Doctor', made his inswinging yorkers virtually unplayable. He ended England's first innings with six wickets, including the scalps of Trott, Pietersen and Collingwood, all trapped in front of their stumps lbw.

In England's second innings, Ryan Harris is the chief destroyer with six wickets. He appeals successfully for an lbw decision against Alastair Cook.

Sadly for Ricky Ponting and Australia, the injury-prone paceman broke down early on the fourth day of the next Test and was out for the rest of the series, possibly from Test cricket altogether. He was Australia's most consistent and dangerous bowler throughout.

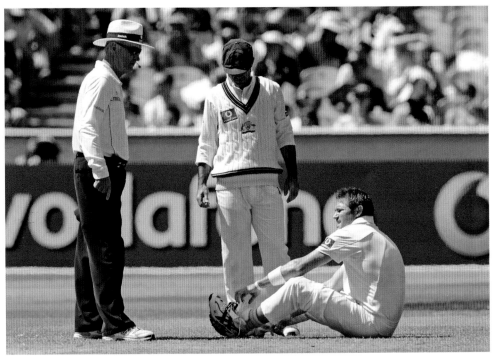

Mike Hussey looked as if he could bat all series as he followed up his runs in Brisbane and Adelaide with another excellent century in Perth. His 517 runs made him the leading run scorer on both sides at the end of the Third Test.

Steven Finn is the last man out, caught by Smith in the gully off Harris. That proved to be Finn's last contribution of the series. Even though he was England's leading wicket-taker to date, he made way for Tim Bresnan in Melbourne and Sydney.

Jonathan Trott declared he had been looking forward to playing at Melbourne for the past six months. His unbeaten 168 was a study in composure, technique and application, despite having to bat for the latter part of his innings in considerable pain.

The Australian captain played in Melbourne with a broken finger. Two more low scores, a prolonged altercation with umpire Aleem Dar over an unsuccessful review against Kevin Pietersen, for which he was fined 40 per cent of his match fee, and another innings defeat made this a Test to forget for him.

The Fourth Test in sport-mad Melbourne traditionally starts on Boxing Day. With the series level, some 84,000 spectators turned out to ensure that it would be an intimidating atmosphere. However, no one in their wildest dreams could have imagined England bowling out Australia for under a hundred in just 42 overs before tea on the first day. As the match progressed, the home support dwindled away until by the end, the England supporters pretty much had the huge arena all to themselves.

In a series where the review system played a key part, Matt Prior's reprieve after being caught behind off a no-ball from Mitchell Johnson, which umpire Aleem Dar requested after the event, was crucial as Prior went on to score 85.

Tim Bresnan underlines England's strength in depth in the fast-bowling department as he takes his fourth victim in Australia's second innings, a wicket that ensured England retained the Ashes.

Pitch

The pitch at the WACA is traditionally a fast, bouncy wicket, although the pitch that England played on in their warm-up game in Perth was slower and lower. Can an Australian attack that has shipped more than 1,100 runs in breaking England's last five partnerships take the 20 wickets it needs to win a game on a track like that?

"I don't see how Australia can come back into this series unless they produce a green wicket in Perth that has plenty of bounce and allows the likes of Siddle, Johnson, Harris and Hilfenhaus something to bowl on," says Vaughan. "If they think they are going to try to beat us on flat wickets with a bit of spin, that is just going to play into the hands of England and Graeme Swann. They have to get some life into the pitches. England lost a game last year at The Wanderers in Johannesburg when Morne Morkel and Dale Steyn twice bowled us out cheaply. That is the way I would play against England. But this England batting order is playing well and it wouldn't surprise me if they scored runs on anything at the moment."

Prognosis

"The immediate future for Australia as I see it is pretty bleak," laments Chappell. "Those of us who remember the mid-1980s will recognise it but I think a lot of other people are going to have to get used to the idea that Australia might be in a slump for a while yet."

"Our people aren't used to this," admits Taylor. "We're used to being impregnable. There's no doubt that you can't stay at the top forever, whatever you do. We probably fell off the perch two years ago. I just hope it's not a cycle that takes us 30 years to get right because there's been too much time, money and effort invested."

HOW TO WIN AT THE WACA

Tom Fordyce | 14 December 2010

Less than 48 hours to go until the Third Test gets under way, and the tension is ratcheting up. Should England win here in Perth, they will hold on to the Ashes urn for another two years. Should Australia come out on top, the series is wide open again going into the final two matches over Christmas and New Year. England, dominant for all but two days of the series so far, have a problem. Historically, they have never worked out how to play well at the WACA.

Of the 11 Ashes Tests staged here, they have come out on top just once, in 1978, when Australia's team had been decimated by the breakaway World Series. Australia have no such issues. They've won every one of the last five Ashes Tests at the ground, including the 206-run thrashing four years ago.

So what is the secret to winning at this idiosyncratic arena on the banks of the Swan River? What special skills do batsmen and bowlers need to succeed here?

"The thing about batting here is that, while it can be a batsman's paradise, the margin for error is a lot smaller than at other grounds," explains former Australian opener Justin Langer, a Perth native who scored 711 runs, including two centuries, in 10 Tests at the WACA. "If you nick it, it usually carries to the slips, so you have to be very careful when driving. The trick is in being selective. Make sure you're in a perfect position or you'll be caught behind. If you're going to drive, you need to strike the ball as under your eyes as possible. If the ball gets outside your eye-line, because of the bounce and big carry through behind, you can get yourself in trouble. Technically you need to be quite correct, because if you're loose the extra bounce will also find you out. You have to keep it all nice and tight.

"The rule of thumb is to play the ball as late as possible. Playing with soft hands is a big thing. If you're watching the ball onto your bat and playing late, you'll have those soft hands naturally because you're not as far through with the shot. People talk about hard hands, but you mainly play with hard hands when you're hitting the ball away from your body."

Langer has scored more runs at the WACA than any other batsman in Western Australian history. He also shares the record for the highest Test partnership at the ground, the 327 he put on with Ricky Ponting against Pakistan in 1999-2000.

So what shots bring the most reward for batsmen on this track?

"It's a great place to play the pull shot, even with the extra bounce, because that bounce is so true. It's the same with the cut shot. The cut is a very aggressive shot, and if you play it here you can afford to play it as hard as you like. On most grounds if you don't quite get it, it will fly off to third man, whereas here the bounce is so consistent that you can feel confident behind it. You will also get great value for your shots because the outfield is so quick, it's like an ice-rink. But you have to watch the ball right onto your bat."

The WACA is famous for the 'Fremantle Doctor', a wind that blows up from the west and buffets the ground from mid-afternoon onwards. While it's better known for the impact it has on bowling conditions, it also affects the way batsmen must approach their innings. "That wind can be a nightmare," admits Langer, now Australia's batting coach. "It's a very strong breeze, so as a batsman you're almost getting pushed backwards at the crease. That's how strong it is. As a batsman, you always want to be coming forward at the bowler. If the quicks have got that really strong wind up their backsides, it gives them such an advantage. The flipside of that is that at the other end you're getting pushed towards the bowler, and they have to fight their way into that breeze.

"Good batting is all about balance. As long as you get your balance right at the crease here, you don't need to change your stance or set-up because of the wind. But you do need to have in your mind that you've got a guy coming in at you fast with the breeze at his back, and it'll be a lot harder for you to be positive with the bat. For example, it'll be a lot harder to hit down the ground because you're hitting into that wind."

What must bowlers do to take wickets and keep the run-rate down?

"It depends how strong the wind is and how regular," says former Middlesex seamer Simon Hughes, in Australia as an analyst for *Test Match Special*. It can blow you off-balance as you come into your delivery stride, and that messes up your timing. And bowling is all about timing. If it's in your face it pushes you back as your arm comes over, which means you can bowl too full, and if it's at your back it can push you through your action and make you bowl too short.

"You have to make it work for you. If the wind is coming across you from leg to off, you might bowl more bouncers because if a batsman plays a pull shot, the ball can get held up and he may get caught. A cross-wind will also affect a swing bowler. If you're a right-armer with a good outswinger, you don't want to bowl into a wind coming from off to leg, because it can straighten out any swing. So you might have to set the ball off wider to compensate for the effect of the wind. Other swing bowlers will enjoy bowling into the wind, because it holds the ball up and so allows it to swing a little more. But bowling into it will tire you out. Not only are you fighting your way through it when you bowl, but it pushes you back to your mark much faster, so your recovery between deliveries is shorter."

England have yet to announce which of Chris Tremlett, Tim Bresnan or Ajmal Shahzad will replace the injured Stuart Broad for this Test. Should the physical builds and track records of the three bowling in windy conditions come into the selectors' minds?
"Someone like Bresnan would be able to push through a strong breeze because of his leg power," says Hughes. "For that reason he might get the nod. It wouldn't have suited Broad, because he's willowy even though there's still a lot of him. It might not suit Steven Finn either. The difficult thing is that the Doctor doesn't always call. Sometimes there's very little wind; sometimes it blows all day and sometimes it only comes mid-afternoon."

Is there a particular line or length that tends to reap dividends?
"Some bowlers get a bit carried away with the bounce here," believes Langer. "You don't very often see the ball go through to the wicketkeeper above head height, but you do here, so bowlers can sometimes bowl too short. But you actually have to pitch the ball up a little more because of that advantage with bounce. You're pushing the batsman back because of the pace and lift in the wicket, but you want to bring him forward because that's where those nicks will come into play."

The highest wicket-takers in Tests at the WACA are all pace bowlers; Brett Lee, Merv Hughes and Craig McDermott, with the top of the pile (52 scalps in 12 Tests) being Glenn McGrath, who liked to bowl exactly the sort of delivery Langer describes, just short of a length on off-stump or just outside, drawing the batsman forward to take the edge.

"At most grounds around the world now blokes can just get on the front foot and play with ease, because there isn't that bounce there any more," says Langer. "At the WACA it's a bit different. You can't be as confident going forward. For me, while I was looking to get forward and looking for the full ball, I knew I couldn't go with the same confidence as elsewhere. If the ball is only coming through waist-high you're not so worried.

"Good off-spin bowlers can do well here, particularly right-armers, because they can get their flight into the breeze. What's brilliant is that from the other end against an offie, you feel as if you can hit every ball for six, because you've got the wind at your back, and they're putting some flight on it. Leg-spinners don't tend to have as much success; the great Shane Warne never had much joy at the WACA. But the margin for error for all bowlers is very small, because of the true bounce and fast outfield."

What of the specific conditions for this match?

On Tuesday lunchtime the Test pitch here looked much greener than expected, with a little more grass than traditional WACA wickets. Groundsman Cameron Sutherland expects it to offer something for both bowlers and batsmen. "In the first 10 overs, the quicks have been getting a bit of movement here, and there's been some swing. It will still have a bit of colour come Thursday, but I don't think there'll be much seam movement off it, there'll be a little nibble, but it won't go excessively either way. We'll get cracks, no doubt, it just depends on the weather as to how big and when they will appear. Spinners can play a role, there'll be some bounce for them. Given the WACA's history we're hoping it can produce a result. We've only had the one draw here, and that was a pretty dead pitch."

15 December 2010

The WAGs have arrived! The issue of wives and girlfriends on tour is a contentious one, but the timing of this seems right to me. The players have got the tour on the road, and for the best part of two months have devoted their energies entirely to that. Now it is time for their families to join them. The dynamics of the team do change from now on. I notice, for instance, that Monty Panesar is by himself at breakfast. So too is Ajmal Shahzad. They will be seeing a lot of each other because most of the others have babies and children in tow and understandably spend all of their free time with them. Indeed, the sight of Pietersen carrying young Dylan in his arms is a common one in our hotel lobby. Chris Neale, the wife of the team operations manager, Phil Neale, reveals to me that she is no longer the 'mother hen' for the WAGs, and has handed over the responsibility to Chantal Bastock, Ian Bell's girlfriend, who is always a friendly and cheerful face on tour.

It has been confirmed that Stuart Broad will be joining us in the *TMS* commentary box during the Perth Test match, which is great news. His mother and step-father had always been planning to come to Perth in the hope of seeing him play, so it makes sense for him to remain here to meet up with them. I have been told Andy Flower doesn't want him to do it, so he won't be a full-time expert summariser because that would be too difficult a balancing act for him to pull off, with one foot still firmly in the dressing room privy to things that the coach wouldn't want him to talk about. Now Stuart is intelligent enough not to do that, but it will also be quite difficult for him to be openly critical of his team mates. If he came out and said, "Old so and so has bowled badly," it would be all over the back page of the tabloids before you could mutter the word 'disloyal'. But he will give his thoughts at the end of sessions and during drinks breaks, and I am looking forward to working with him.

The question of who will replace Broad on the field has been the major talking point around the England camp. It won't be announced until the morning of the game, so it gives everyone a chance to give their views.

The Australians announce that Johnson will return to the team in place of Bollinger, who looked absolutely knackered at the end of the last Test. Selector Greg Chappell makes the absurd statement that

Johnson had merely been rotated. That certainly was not the impression anyone formed, including Johnson himself, during his press conference at Adelaide. Rod Marsh weighs into the captaincy debate with a slightly left-field observation. "How can a bloke [vice-captain Michael Clarke] captain Australia with tattoos? It's just not on."

Meanwhile the selection of the entirely unknown spinner, Michael Beer, has caused widespread amazement and amusement. This is his first season of first-class cricket, and you would have thought that after the Doherty experience, they would want a reliable spinner who could hold up one end. Brad Hodge, the former Australian spinner, says the Australian selectors are "giving away baggy greens for free." It is reported that Nathan Hauritz, meanwhile, has flogged his Australian sweaters and assorted paraphernalia in a car-boot sale outside his flat in Sydney. "I don't play for them anymore," he is reported as saying. I can't help but feel that the story has been tickled up a bit.

During my pre-match interview with Ponting I have to take a deep breath and ask him about his future as captain. As usual he doesn't duck it. "It's entirely out of my hands," he says. "Those who appointed me can take it away at any time."

I arrive at a restaurant in South Perth for dinner with the Marks to be greeted by a variety of friendly and familiar faces. Courtney Walsh, Mike Gatting, Barry Richards, Mike Brearley, Steve Bucknor, Alec Stewart – in they all come. It is when I see MCC chief executive Keith Bradshaw that I realise this is the MCC World Cricket Committee. Steve Waugh approaches and I remind him he is due on *Test Match Special* tomorrow lunchtime. He is one of my favourite interviewees, and I think he enjoys the platform to express his views on the game.

> "Excited to be part of the TMS team at the WACA come Thursday! Appointed official tea maker. @aggerscricket @vaughancricket, milk no sugar?!" STUART BROAD

EVE OF MATCH THOUGHTS

England can retain the Ashes this week and the team hotel is buzzing with good cheer and genuine optimism. With their wives and children now firmly on board, the players are very relaxed, yet focused. It will be a major surprise to me if they fail in their mission over the next five days.

It is not Andrew Strauss's style to name his team until the morning of the match, so we were not expecting news of Stuart Broad's replacement during his press conference. It is not a straightforward decision; like-for-like points the finger firmly at 6ft 7in Chris Tremlett, but with only four bowlers to turn to, Strauss has to be convinced of his reliability under pressure as well as his ability to bowl a meaningful spell or two into the strong breeze, which is such a feature of cricket at the WACA. This is where Tim Bresnan will come into consideration, and would be my preference.

The pitch is green and hard enough for Ricky Ponting seriously to consider playing a four-man pace attack. This might also have something to do with the unbelievable decision by Australia's selectors to choose Michael Beer. Nothing against Beer, who bowled steadily against England in the warm-up match here six weeks ago, but it smacks of absolute panic and uncertainty – and has left Australia's cricket followers with gaping jaws.

Ponting was left searching for control at Adelaide – and failed to find it. To usher in another spinner of such inexperience is extraordinary under the circumstances. Steve Smith is only a part-time leg-spinner, who was dismantled by Ian Bell in the match against Australia A. He is not yet capable of playing the role of the solitary, lead slow bowler in a Test line-up but he is a decent batsman.

It may be, however, that the selectors should have eyed up the pitch and kept Marcus North in the squad before jettisoning him completely.

If the pitch has the pace and bounce that its colour and appearance suggests it might, it will test the discipline of England's batsmen and bowlers. The extra bounce and carry takes time to adjust to for all the batsmen who must have patience at the start of the innings to get used to what are, for English players, very alien conditions.

They have performed poorly here in recent series not merely because of shortcomings in the way they have batted, but because the fast bowlers could not hit the right length. When the ball flies dramatically through to the wicketkeeper, it is very tempting to get carried away and bowl too short.

Australian batsmen, being fine players off the back foot, are quite comfortable cutting and pulling and this is another reason I would opt for Bresnan, whose natural length is a little fuller and more reliable than that of Tremlett. Were England contemplating five bowlers, I would think differently.

With Australia in such disarray that they will field an entirely different attack for the third time in this series, and make up to five changes from the last match, they do appear ripe for the taking.

England have the confidence and the form behind them finally to bury their unhappy recent history and become the first team to win the Ashes here in a generation.

SIX

PERTH TEST

"There are definitely lessons to be learnt from this game. It would be wrong for us to wash our hands of it completely. But it's all about bouncing back now. We've done it well in the past."

ANDREW STRAUSS

DAY 44 **16 December 2010, Third Test – first day**

Morning session: At lunch – Australia 65/4, Hussey 28*, Smith 5*

There is grass on the pitch and with Tremlett confirmed as the replacement for Broad, who is watching anxiously from our box as Strauss wins the toss, England choose boldly to put Australia in to bat. New opener Phillip Hughes plays an awful shot to leg and is bowled by Tremlett for 2 in the tall fast bowler's opening over. Tremlett could not ask for a better start. Watson is reprieved by the Decision Review System following a dreadful decision by umpire Doctrove who had given him out caught behind, but Ponting on 12 then falls to the catch of the series so far – and there have been some good ones. Pushing at Anderson, Ponting edges high to third slip's right hand where Collingwood hangs on to a one-handed screamer. Another failure for Ponting, and he is quickly followed by Clarke who is caught behind for 4 chasing a wide ball from Tremlett. Watson is lbw to a Finn yorker for 13, and the Australians are already reeling at 36/4, but survive further England inroads, reaching lunch without losing another wicket

Steve Waugh duly appears on *TMS* at lunchtime to discuss primarily the new working party, which he is heading, to rid cricket of corruption. This includes the proposal to introduce lie detector tests. Naturally I enjoy the rare opportunity to sympathise with him over the decline of Australian cricket, which he takes well.

> *"Australia just look like a beaten team. You can go a long way to losing a Test in the first session of a match."* MICHAEL VAUGHAN, TMS

Afternoon session: At tea – Australia 179/6, Haddin 52*, Johnson 25*

Another poor decision by umpire Doctrove almost allows Hussey to escape a confident appeal for caught behind off Swann; Prior confidently calls for a review and Hussey is sent on his way to the pavilion after a fighting 61. Supporters of the Decision Review System regularly point to the success of the system in detecting right or wrong decisions, but the fact is that Doctrove has given two decisions in the first 39 overs that are not worthy of Test cricket. Root out the poor umpires, I say. The irony of this is that Aleem Dar, probably the best in the business, is relegated to third umpire, while Doctrove is out in the middle. Bonkers. Tremlett deals with Smith, who looks out of his depth, but Haddin and Johnson add 42 before tea to rescue the situation somewhat from 137 for 6.

> *"From half an hour after lunch this pitch has looked an absolute belter to bat on. England's catching has been outstanding again. The pitch is just starting to bake a little bit. The green tinge this morning was brighter than it is now."* MICHAEL VAUGHAN, TMS

Evening session: At the close – Australia 268, England 29/0, Strauss 12*, Cook 17*

Geoffrey Boycott thinks the Australians have got too many. Their last five wickets add 199 with half-centuries from Haddin and Johnson and a brave 35 not out from Siddle at number 10. England would probably have settled for this at the start of play, but I agree with Geoffrey – they were 69 for 5 and should have been bundled out for 150.

> *"Mitchell Johnson has it in him to get Australia back into the series, so it's important we get him down early."* MICHAEL VAUGHAN, TMS

It was a bold, confident decision by Andrew Strauss to put Australia in to bat at the WACA, which will have been partly motivated by the presence of grass on the wicket but also the lack of confidence in the Australian batsmen. With Australia having chosen four quick bowlers, Ricky Ponting would have had to put England into bat had he won the toss, but England do not have such an attack and did not have to do so.

The tourists can see how low in confidence the Australian top order is and this was backed up by the way they played today. Michael Clarke's shot was poor and Phillip Hughes' stroke was appalling for a man who is just back in the Test side and with a lot to prove, but this is what happens when you are playing badly as a side.

The problem for Australia is that the openers are simply not providing the platform they need and that is why Ponting and Clarke are being exposed to the new ball far too early and are being swept away.

This is not a 268 all out pitch by any means. With the score at 69/5 England may feel they should have rolled them out for 150. However, the fact that almost all of the lower order Australian batsmen got runs shows that once the shine is off the new ball it is a pretty decent pitch. England will look at that and think they should score 450, which is no doubt what they will aim to do on Friday.

Before the match Ponting was pointing to Chris Tremlett's inclusion and the possibility that James Anderson might be tired – he travelled to the UK for the birth of his child in the break between Tests – as potential weaknesses for England, but there were no signs of this.

Tremlett bowled extremely well. I favoured Bresnan to be picked because of the length he would bowl, but Tremlett bowled a full length. He got a nice early wicket, which geed him up and he went on to perform superbly.

England's fielding was again brilliant. There were two truly outstanding slip catches, firstly from Paul Collingwood to dismiss Ponting and then Graeme Swann to end Brad Haddin's innings. A catch like Collingwood's is totally deflating for Australia. It took Ponting an age to drag himself away from the wicket afterwards – he couldn't believe it. But these are the sort of catches you take when your team is on top, full of confidence and playing well.

England have worked hard at their fielding, but it does not always happen for you. It happens when everything else clicks. Australia will have been working just as hard at their fielding but because their confidence is so down and they are playing badly as a team, their fielding has deteriorated.

In 12 overs at the end of the day, we saw at least two fumbles in the field by the home side. They used to set the standard but now England are arguably the best fielding side in the world. Former Aussie pace bowler Terry Alderman said to me that he has never seen an England side field like this and he is right.

Friday is going to be a huge day as it could well be a case of England batting through, building a big lead and heading into the third day that could see Swann's spin come to the fore. Australia have got an awful lot of hard work to do tomorrow if they are to keep this series alive. The pressure is mounting on Ponting. He cannot keep failing to score runs and seeing his team lose.

His time in charge may well be coming to an end. Who knows what might happen if things continue this way into Sydney? If the situation determines that the Ashes are gone and he can't score a run, he might well feel that he has had enough by then.

DAY 45 17 December 2010, Third Test – second day

I have never seen morale so low in the Australian ranks. The *Herald Sun* amused me over breakfast: 'If the fat lady sings any louder for Ponting, she will shatter a window.' An online bookie based in Sydney announces that it will be paying out now on an England Ashes win, to the tune of £250,000. Chief Executive Matthew Tripp: "We'll be paying out anyway so the punters might as well have their cash for Christmas."

> *"Australia will know that if England get away today, the Ashes are gone."*
> GEOFFREY BOYCOTT, TMS

Morning session: At lunch – England 119/5, Bell 13* Prior 3*

Australia promised to be much more aggressive in this Test and after Strauss and Cook put on 78, Johnson produces a stunning spell of 4 for 7 in 27 balls to rip the heart out of England's batting line up. He swings the ball into the right-handers at formidable pace, and looks an entirely different proposition from the wayward scattergun we saw not merely at Brisbane but also in England on the last Ashes tour. Cook drives low to Hussey in the gully for 32, Trott looks completely distracted and is lbw for 4. Pietersen aims one of his casual leg-side flicks and is lbw third ball for a duck and Collingwood is trapped lbw following a searing bouncer for 5. In all, with Strauss caught behind off Harris for 52, England lose five wickets for just twenty runs. This spell has brought the Ashes back to life. Great tension.

Afternoon session: At the close – England 187 all out, Australia lead by 81

Bundled out, losing all ten wickets for just 109 runs, England are on the receiving end of a brilliant spell by the mercurial Johnson who finishes with 6 for 38. Ian Bell again stands out, and certainly looks to be batting too low at number six where he scores a defiant 53. He is eighth out after Prior is bowled off his body from round the wicket by the aggressive Siddle, who gives Prior a verbal send-off. Shouting over his shoulder as he departs, Prior appears to invite Siddle to continue hostilities in the car park. Suddenly, it has all become more heated, and England are losing their grip. They have been blown away, and no one appears more surprised than the players. In the commentary box, Stuart Broad has been an enlightening and enthusiastic summariser. I ask him how he is feeling about missing the rest of his first Ashes tour, having geared his entire cricketing life around these three months. "You have to look at the positives," Broad replies rather sadly. But from our detached position as observers, he also senses trouble ahead for his England team mates that no number of his 'positives' during commentary can disguise.

> "I've said all along that although 268 was OK, England should have bowled Australia out for 200, and that may come back to haunt them." Geoffrey Boycott, TMS

Evening Session: At the close – Australia 119/3, Watson 61*, Hussey 24*, Australia lead by 200

England need to get amongst the wickets to have any chance of fighting back: they deal with Hughes (12), Ponting (1) and Clarke (20). Ponting is given not out to an appeal for a catch down the leg side, defiantly shaking his head as England review the decision. Even when Hot Spot confirms England's confident appeal and the umpire's finger is raised, Ponting has to be dragged from the crease to a chorus of Barmy Army boos. To be dismissed that way twice in six innings is unlucky, and there have also been two superb slip catches by Collingwood, but the fact is Ponting has now scored only 83 runs in six outings with 51 of them coming in one innings. He will be cheered though by his team's position at the close. They are two sessions away from batting England out of the game.

> *"You can tell it's much harder to bowl people out than it was for England in the first innings. Batsmen who are good front-foot players like Watson are getting forward with ease, when they were quite tentative doing it on the first morning."* GEOFFREY BOYCOTT, TMS

END OF DAY REPORT

One of the Australian national newspapers tore into their national cricket side on Friday morning in response to how one-sided the Third Test had been so far.

Early on the second day, when an edge from Andrew Strauss flew between wicketkeeper and first slip with no-one getting a hand to it, it appeared a case of 'here we go again' and we all assumed England would be well on the way to racking up a sizeable lead by the evening.

But a very special spell from Mitchell Johnson has turned this match on its head and lifted the entire home team. Suddenly, the Australians are believing in themselves again.

When we were looking forward to this series, it struck me the one thing that was missing, from a classic Test series point of view, was a genuinely fast bowler who can rapidly blow a hole in a batting line-up.

The reason I thought this was that we had not seen Johnson bowl anything like his reputedly match-winning best in any Test match he has played, either against England or in England against Pakistan.

The Australian media have talked him up, but he was very ordinary at the Gabba and was dropped. Johnson looked like a different man on Friday. His was a devastating spell of bowling, up there with the best of anything we have seen in recent years.

He bowled with genuine pace, he was nasty, he roughed up Jonathan Trott and Paul Collingwood and he swung the ball at great speed on a pitch that clearly had bounce that visiting batsmen are not used to. We now know why he was the ICC's player of the year a few years ago.

There are one or two dismissals you may look at and pick holes in – Trott for example could have played straighter – but when you are undone by 90mph deliveries swinging into your pads that early in your innings, you have to say 'fair play'.

Ian Bell again played beautifully and with lots of confidence. He was out chasing a wide ball, trying to move the score on as he was batting with the tail. This is the problem with batting at six. I would not have thought England would change things immediately, but Bell does look wasted there.

There is still the faintest hope for England. Ryan Harris supported Johnson but there was nothing much from everyone else. If you look at the rest of the Australian attack it is workmanlike, and lacking a spinner.

Recent history suggests that batting late on in the game at the WACA has not been a problem. We're only at the end of the second day so the pitch is still a decent one. If England have to chase 350 then they will certainly have enough time to do it. Whether they are able to do this remains to be seen.

First they have to bowl Australia out tomorrow and they will have to do it just after lunch. They need to take those seven wickets before the Aussies score another 150 runs.

However, the England bowlers look tired, which is to be expected. They put everything into yesterday and didn't expect to be bowling again this afternoon. We've had two hot days and it is hard work. That is one of the issues with playing four bowlers and it is on occasions like this that the debate over whether five bowlers should be selected returns to the fore.

It was not all positive for Australia. Skipper Ricky Ponting failed again and his determination not to walk before a review showed he had gloved a catch to Matt Prior off Steven Finn shows how desperate he is at the moment. He averages only 16 and that is only because of an unbeaten half-century at the Gabba.

Michael Clarke produced another frenetic innings, with a loose shot that brought about his downfall. If Australia lose this series, people like

Clarke will be looked at very closely. But on Friday, he and others have been saved by Johnson's amazing burst.

Lovely dinner spent beside the river with the ABC commentary team. The Shiraz flows, and they all seem in a better mood than of late. Can't think why.

DAY 46 18 December 2010, Third Test – third day

"The one plus side to this Test match so far is that Mitchell Johnson will once again return to being an awful bowler as soon as he leaves the WACA." Anon, SMS

Morning session: At lunch – Australia 211/4, Hussey 60*, Smith 16*, Australia lead by 292

The first hour passes and Australia add 46 without loss. Hussey, on his home ground, is in the form of his life and England simply have not yet worked out how to get him out cheaply. He leaves the ball brilliantly. Watson inches towards his century but falls five short when Tremlett traps him lbw. That is the fourth time he has been dismissed in the nineties; he has only two Test hundreds to his name. It is England's only success, although Doctrove gives Smith out caught at slip only to be overruled – again. This is not a case of the players being reprieved by the system, but the umpire.

I don't see how England have a cat in hell's chance of winning the game and there's only one chance in a lot of saving it." Geoffrey Boycott, TMS

Afternoon session: At tea – Australia 297/8, Hussey 111*, Siddle 3*, Australia lead by 378

Hussey has ensured that the game is up. Barely half-way through the match in terms of overs bowled, England will do well to take this into the final day, although there are still people who think England can score these runs! Let's not forget they have only ever scored 300 plus batting last to win a Test three times in their entire Test-playing history. Hussey pulls his way to his third hundred of the series and receives a tremendous ovation. Smith falls to Tremlett for 36 but Johnson and Harris are brushed aside. There's still plenty in this pitch, but the application shown by Watson and Hussey has been the difference – and that brilliant spell by Johnson.

> *"Mr Cricket [Mike Hussey] is the star man of this Australian side. When he gets into that rhythm, he just takes every ball on its merits and is difficult to dislodge."* MICHAEL VAUGHAN, TMS

Evening session: At the close – England 81/5, Anderson 0*, England are 309 behind

A disastrous session confirms that the series will be levelled tomorrow. Hussey finally perishes for 116 when he pulls Tremlett to deep mid-wicket where Swann takes the catch and then, indicating that he believes there is still something to celebrate, Swann performs a brief Sprinkler for the benefit of the crowd behind him. If he really feels upbeat about the situation, he won't at the close, 26 overs later. Tremlett finishes with his first five-wicket haul in Tests, but doesn't over-indulge in one of those triumphant, ball brandishing exits from the field.

There's no question that England are not happy in a hostile environment and facing the short ball, as was suggested before the match by the former South Africa coach, Mickey Arthur. Cook is lbw to Harris for 13 and Strauss edges Johnson to second slip for 15. Pietersen hangs on for a jittery 22 balls but a poor firm-footed prod to first slip gives Hilfenhaus his first wicket since the third ball of the series. Trott edges Johnson straight to Ponting at second slip who, most unusually drops it, only for Haddin to cling on to the rebound. Ponting has damaged his finger [which is later confirmed as a fracture] and leaves the field. England are 81/4 when Collingwood edges the last ball of the day to third slip. England have lost 15 wickets for 190 runs in the match, and have been blown away by a combination of aggressive fast bowling and their own tentative batting.

There is a real change in atmosphere in the hotel this evening. The players have gone to ground and, as expected, there are various *sotto voce* muttering amongst the supporters about the 'coincidence' of the players' families arriving in Australia and England's poor performance. I don't think that's the reason at all, but the past four days have been a big wake-up call.

Earlier in the day I found myself in an awkward position from a broadcasting perspective when Geoffrey Boycott was at his most strident with Stuart Broad. The three of us were summing up the end of the Test and Broad clearly found his position extremely difficult. He is still very much a part of the England set-up, but is now having to be honest in the face of a chastening defeat. It was the scenario that Andy Flower had been concerned about.

Broad knew that England had been outplayed as much as the rest of us, but could not say so without feeling that he was letting down his team mates, so he adopted the much favoured fall-back position of 'taking the positives' out of the situation, regardless of how actually hopeless the situation might be. This was like a red rag to a bull to Geoffrey, who publicly shredded poor Broad, telling him in no uncertain terms that Stuart was talking utter nonsense. It all became rather too personal for my liking.

I felt I had to apologise to Stuart when I saw him on an adjoining table that night. Stuart took it perfectly well. He knows from his dad, former England opener Chris Broad, what Geoffrey can be like. Personally, I get on with Geoffrey extremely well, and this was forthright Boycott making his ground absolutely clear. To be fair to him, his main criticisms of England's performance were entirely valid and he was perfectly right to take issue with someone else in the box attempting to water them down. It is a good object lesson in how difficult it is to have someone from the current dressing room as an expert summariser on radio or television, because they can't do a completely honest job when the team plays badly.

"Defeat is acceptable, going down this weakly is not. The demons are starting to resurface." Anon, SMS

END OF DAY REPORT

After the euphoria when England saved the Test in Brisbane and their emphatic win in Adelaide, an inevitable Australia victory here in Perth means the Ashes series is set for a phenomenal finale.

The WACA is a one-off, unlike any ground around the world. It is a venue Australia have made their own – England have won only once in 11 matches, and that was against an Australian side weakened by the World Series defections in the late 1970s.

England have not become a poor team overnight, but a number of poorly judged shots in the second innings – Kevin Pietersen and Jonathan Trott in particular – have not helped their cause. However, a lot of praise must be heaped on Mitchell Johnson, who has once again bowled with pace and fire, and at times has been very nasty to face on what has been a lively pitch. Johnson's success in Perth may well force Australia to review their strategy and adopt a four-man pace attack for both Melbourne and Sydney.

The WACA pitch has benefited Johnson, who plays his Sheffield Shield cricket for Western Australia, and we could well see more grass left on the wickets at the MCG on Boxing Day and at the SCG for the New Year Test.

This particular tactic works two-fold in Australia's favour. One, the hosts believe England's batting line-up are uncomfortable against short-pitched fast bowling, exemplified by their collapse against South Africa in Johannesburg at the start of the year. And two, it would force England to review their tactic of playing three seamers alongside Graeme Swann for the remainder of the series.

The spinner had plenty of assistance in Adelaide, with rough outside off stump for both the left- and right-handers on a dry, cracking pitch. But here in Perth, Swann has had almost nothing to work with, which was reflected by second-innings figures of 0 for 51 from nine overs. Mike Hussey, in particular, played him beautifully, using his feet as he has done throughout this series to get to the pitch of the ball.

So if England find themselves up against another grassy, seam-friendly pitch, can they go into back-to-back Test matches with only three front-line fast bowlers?

Sydney is traditionally the Australian ground most receptive to spin but SCG groundsman Tom Parker has been preparing grassier wickets for New South Wales' Sheffield Shield matches, so it can be done. But would England drop Swann, the world's best spinner, from their line-up? It is unthinkable.

Watching the morning session, I was disappointed to see Andrew Strauss set a 7-2 off-side field when James Anderson was bowling to

Shane Watson. The ball was still swinging but with a field like that, you can't bowl straight because anything on middle stump will be worked away to the leg side. Watson is an lbw candidate, as his first-innings dismissal suggested, but because of the heavy off-side field, Anderson's line was on off stump and just outside, enabling the Australia opener to shoulder arms to a number of deliveries.

I understand England didn't want Australia to get off to a flyer, but I would have liked to have seen England on the attack, moving a man from the off side into the leg side and enabling Anderson to bowl a middle-and-off-stump line. Instead the tactics were a little too negative for my liking as England's seamers wasted a lot of precious energy on deliveries, which Australia's batsmen left without any trouble.

Once again Hussey batted beautifully with superb judgement on the ground where he has played the majority of his cricket. He became the first player in history to score 50 runs or more in six successive Ashes Test matches by choosing which deliveries to leave and which to dispatch to the boundary.

England's top order could learn from Hussey's astute judgement.

DAY 47　19 December 2010, Third Test – fourth day

"I've decided to call Ian Bell 'The Shepherd' as he's continually having to shepherd the tail." MICHAEL VAUGHAN, TMS

Morning session: England 123 all out, Australia win by 267 runs
England's spineless collapse on the fourth morning mirrors that of Australia in Adelaide. It needed only 50 minutes for the last five wickets to fall for 42 runs with Harris grabbing four of them for 25. Ponting does not take the field, but comes on to congratulate his men the moment the last wicket is taken. I take some consolation in the knowledge that the WACA is an awkward place to play if you are not used to it – even for Australians. Watson is the only eastern Australian to have contributed with the bat, while Hussey and Johnson (formerly from Queensland but who now plays his cricket for Western Australia) stand out with the bat – as, clearly, does Johnson with the ball.

As is usual at the end of the match I head down to the outfield to interview the captains. I am using the new 3G gizmo, which is a marvellous piece of kit, but with its in-built delay, means I cannot speak to anyone back in the commentary box. These on-the-field broadcasts are always a bit of a trial of nerves, there is not a great deal of organisation and they have something of a suck-it-and-see quality. After a few minutes I am on the air and interviewing Andrew Strauss, who is very good – quite forthright about England's defeat, but also firmly confident that they will come back again. Nevertheless, I can see how angry and disappointed he is.

I thank Andrew and turn around to talk to Ricky Ponting, but Sky's Michael Atherton has grabbed him. So now I am on my own and I know there will be at least five minutes before Ricky is free. The nightmare of every broadcaster has descended upon me – five minutes to fill (an absolute eternity when standing on your own with nothing but a microphone, no script and the sound of silence in your headphones). I look at my notes and do the old: "If you are just joining us, the score is," followed by: "This is what happened today …" In desperation I look at the scoreboard, which is in front of me, and chat about that, then it's a mention of the Barmy Army who I explain have gone a bit quiet.

Bloody hell, Atherton is still talking to Ponting.

I look round and actually there is Strauss still waiting for his slot with Sky, so, in desperation, I go over to him again and say, "I know you've just talked to me, but let's just have another couple of questions." To be fair to him he responds with, "Yeah, OK." Whether it's as a result of my barely subdued panic or a misplaced attempt at humour, I stupidly blurt out: "There's Ricky, it's his birthday today you know." Andrew looks at me firstly in studied amazement and then his face changes and with a 'if looks could kill expression' (thank goodness this is radio) and in a voice barely escaping from his gritted teeth, the words "Happy Birthday Ricky" emerge.

Dear old Andrew had done me a great favour and in return I make the duff observation of the tour. And people think this job is easy.

It will be very interesting to see how England pick themselves up from this, but the impact Australia's win will have on the series is going to be massive. They are already talking about the biggest crowd ever turning up at the MCG for a Boxing Day Test.

My co-commentators and I head back to the hotel bar to drown our sorrows and are joined, late in the evening, by a number of the England players who have been to see the band U2 in concert in Perth. I'm glad I wasn't there to hear Bono talk of his delight at Australia beating England: "We're all on the same side here tonight," he announced. "We're united in passion, we're united in high-mindedness and we share an overwhelming desire to stick it to the Brits!" The players didn't seem to mind too much, and it was probably a good distraction after such a disappointing week.

Alastair Cook and I have a lengthy conversation about fast bowling, during which he tells me that after watching Michael Holding on old television replays, he is surprised at how slowly he appears to have bowled. "I'll give you Joel Garner," he continues, "but I'm not convinced Holding was that fast."

It is certainly an interesting point of view. I suspect Alastair is basing his argument on two things: firstly, it is widely accepted that most professional sportsmen and women, including cricketers, are running faster and generally performing to higher standards these days because of superior training techniques and improved levels of fitness. Secondly, I am pretty sure Alastair has only watched Michael bowling off his short run, he can't have watched him in his pomp. In fact, I'm not having it! I have been playing and watching top-class cricket for over 30 years – and not through rose-tinted specs, either. Holding was one of the fastest there has ever been in that time, and I say to Alastair: "Go to YouTube and key in four words. Holding. Close. Old Trafford. Then tell me Holding wasn't fast." It is late in the evening, and it has all been good-natured banter. It is also another reminder of the healthy relationship that exists between England's cricketers and members of the media – even in the midst of defeat.

> "Australia are back. It's been brutal this morning – fast bowling and good catching. It's England who have questions to answer now." MICHAEL VAUGHAN, TMS

END OF DAY REPORT

England's performance on day four was rather predictable given the way they played throughout the match. It is disappointing when a team subsides quite as dramatically as that but I think they got themselves into the mindset where they knew they were going to lose. But that's no excuse for giving it away quite so lamely. Ryan Harris is a wholehearted sort of fellow but he ripped through them much too easily. It was a disappointing end to a very disappointing performance by England.

England are going to have to reassess their line-up – they need to think hard about the balance and make-up of the side. Do they really, honestly think that four bowlers is the best way to go, particularly if there is grass on the pitch and Graeme Swann is going to be ineffective? I believe the answer to that is no.

One of the reasons England lost this game is because Australia got away from 69/5 to 268 all out in the first innings. We didn't have that extra person to come in and apply the killer punch. They are expecting an enormous amount of bowling from three fast bowlers, two of whom are very inexperienced. If they do bring in an extra bowler, the obvious thing is that Paul Collingwood would have to make way for Tim Bresnan. Collingwood's batting is all over the shop. He has taken great catches, but he's not making any runs.

England have been so doggedly determined about four bowlers that I know they will be reluctant to change their policy. I'm not calling for wholesale changes because I still believe England are the better side. But an extra bowler would keep up the pressure on Australia's batting, which is extremely frail.

Indeed, it is Australia who still have all the problems in terms of form.

Ricky Ponting's finger injury will be a distraction and he won't be able to practise just when he needs to rediscover his touch. Should they continue with Steve Smith at six? Mitchell Johnson remains a mercurial player – can he get it right in two consecutive matches? And they still haven't got a spinner.

The real question is how much confidence has been given to Australia from their Perth victory and how much has been taken away from England? Do England still believe they are the better side or are Australia now the more confident side?

It is difficult to know what to expect in Melbourne for the Boxing Day Test because it is a drop-in pitch and they are notoriously unpredictable. They usually have a bit of damp about them and the one England played on last week was horribly flat – it might have been made in Karachi. The weather is unpredictable – and until we get there and look at the forecast, the machinations are hard to know.

It all bodes for an absolutely fantastic spectacle in Melbourne. There is probably going to be the biggest crowd ever to see a day of Test cricket on Boxing Day – up to 90,000 or so. It is going to be massive and Australia still have to win one of these next two games if they are going to win the Ashes.

England have taken a knock but they have to get themselves back on the horse and prove what a good side they still are.

AUSTRALIA v ENGLAND

3rd Test

Result: Australia won by 267 runs

Played at WACA Ground, Perth
on 16,17,18,19 December 2010

Toss: England
Referee: JJ Crowe

Umpires: BR Doctrove & M Erasmus (TV: Aleem Dar)
Man of Match: MG Johnson

AUSTRALIA	Runs	Mins	Balls	4	6		Runs	Mins	Balls	4	6
SR Watson lbw b Finn	13	72	40	1	-	lbw b Tremlett	95	221	174	11	-
PJ Hughes b Tremlett	2	10	6	-	-	c Collingwood b Finn	12	51	31	1	-
*RT Ponting c Collingwood b Anderson	12	11	10	3	-	c Prior b Finn	1	17	9	-	-
MJ Clarke c Prior b Tremlett	4	13	10	1	-	b Tremlett	20	21	18	4	-
MEK Hussey c Prior b Swann	61	139	104	9	1	c Swann b Tremlett	116	296	172	15	-
SPD Smith c Strauss b Tremlett	7	46	37	-	-	c Prior b Tremlett	36	83	62	2	-
†BJ Haddin c Swann b Anderson	53	119	80	6	1	b Tremlett	7	17	10	-	1
MG Johnson c Anderson b Finn	62	117	93	8	1	c Bell b Collingwood	1	5	4	-	-
RJ Harris b Anderson	3	8	5	-	-	c Bell b Finn	1	14	7	-	-
PM Siddle not out	35	69	59	3	-	c Collingwood b Anderson	8	33	26	1	-
BW Hilfenhaus c Cook b Swann	13	25	12	3	-	not out	0	8	5	-	-
Extras (lb 3)	**3**					**Extras (lb 6, w 4, nb 2)**	**12**				
TOTAL (76 overs)	268					TOTAL (86 overs)	309				

ENGLAND	Runs	Mins	Balls	4	6		Runs	Mins	Balls	4	6
*AJ Strauss c Haddin b Harris	52	125	102	8	-	c Ponting b Johnson	15	39	35	3	-
AN Cook c Hussey b Johnson	32	91	63	3	1	lbw b Harris	13	24	16	1	-
IJL Trott lbw b Johnson	4	7	8	1	-	c Haddin b Johnson	31	85	61	3	-
KP Pietersen lbw b Johnson	0	2	3	-	-	c Watson b Hilfenhaus	3	36	23	-	-
PD Collingwood lbw b Johnson	5	25	17	-	-	c Smith b Harris	11	38	27	1	-
IR Bell c Ponting b Harris	53	133	90	6	-	(7) lbw b Harris	16	32	23	3	-
†MJ Prior b Siddle	12	62	42	1	-	(8) c Hussey b Harris	10	19	9	-	1
GP Swann c Haddin b Harris	11	45	31	1	-	(9) b Johnson	9	8	5	1	-
CT Tremlett b Johnson	2	21	14	-	-	(10) not out	1	12	3	-	-
JM Anderson c Watson b Johnson	0	7	6	-	-	(6) b Harris	3	22	14	-	-
ST Finn not out	1	2	1	-	-	c Smith b Harris	2	6	7	-	-
Extras (b 8, lb 4, w 1, nb 2)	**15**					**Extras (lb 8, nb 1)**	**9**				
TOTAL (62.3 overs)	187					TOTAL (37 overs)	123				

Eng	O	M	R	W		O	M	R	W	
Anderson	20	3	61	3		26	7	65	1	(1 w)
Tremlett	23	3	63	3		24	4	87	5	(1 nb, 2 w)
Finn	15	1	86	2		21	4	97	3	(1 nb)
Collingwood	2	0	3	0	(5)	6	3	3	1	(1 w)
Swann	16	0	52	2	(4)	9	0	51	0	
Aus	O	M	R	W		O	M	R	W	
Hilfenhaus	21	6	53	0	(1 nb)	10	4	16	1	
Harris	15	4	59	3	(1 w)	11	1	47	6	
Siddle	9	2	25	1	(1 nb)	(4) 4	1	8	0	(1 nb)
Johnson	17.3	5	38	6	(3)	12	3	44	3	

FALL OF WICKETS				
	Aus	Eng	Aus	Eng
1st	2 (2)	78 (2)	31 (2)	23 (2)
2nd	17 (3)	82 (3)	34 (3)	37 (1)
3rd	28 (4)	82 (4)	64 (4)	55 (4)
4th	36 (1)	94 (1)	177 (1)	81 (3)
5th	69 (6)	98 (5)	252 (6)	81 (5)
6th	137 (5)	145 (7)	271 (7)	94 (6)
7th	189 (7)	181 (8)	276 (8)	111 (7)
8th	201 (9)	186 (6)	284 (9)	114 (8)
9th	233 (8)	186 (9)	308 (10)	120 (9)
10th	268 (11)	187 (10)	309 (5)	123 (11)

PERTH MILESTONES

Ⓜ **Australia made four changes to their team** from the eleven that played in Adelaide. This was the first time that Australia had made this many changes to a starting eleven within a series since the match against West Indies at Melbourne in 1984/85. Australia were 3-0 down in that series at the time.

Ⓜ **Four of Australia's main seam bowlers** in their squad for the series came into the match with long wicket-less streaks. Doug Bollinger (who did not play at Perth) had bowled 28.3 overs for 130 runs since dismissing Strauss with his third ball at Adelaide. Ben Hilfenhaus had bowled 50.3 overs for 142 runs since dismissing Strauss with his third ball at Brisbane. Peter Siddle had bowled 56.4 overs for 222 runs since dismissing Graeme Swann shortly after his hat-trick in the first innings at Brisbane. Mitchell Johnson had bowled 62 overs for 238 runs since dismissing Cheteshwar Pujara in the first innings of the Test against India at Bangalore. In total they had bowled 197.4 overs between them for 730 runs without taking a wicket.

Ⓜ **Johnson extended his wicket-less run** to 67 overs for 255 and then took 4 for 7 in his next 27 balls, dismissing Cook, Trott, Pietersen and Collingwood. He ended with 9/82 in the match and now has 30 wickets at an average of 18.13 in his four Tests to date at the WACA.

Ⓜ **In Australia's first innings** Johnson became the first number eight batsman to score a run in the series. The previous innings by number eight batsmen in the series were Johnson's 0 and Broad's first-ball duck at Perth and Harris's king pair at Adelaide.

Ⓜ **England scored 1,137 runs** for the loss of six wickets in the second innings at Brisbane and the first innings at Adelaide combined. Adding in the runs from the loss of the seventh wicket in the first innings at Brisbane to the loss of the first wicket at Perth, they scored a total of 1,278 while losing ten wickets. This is the most runs made by England while losing 10 wickets, beating the 1,223 they made against India in 1990. The world record is 1,494 by South Africa against New Zealand in New Zealand in 1998/99.

Ⓜ **Michael Hussey passed fifty** for the fifth time in five innings in the series when he scored 116 in Australia's second innings. Going back to the 121 he scored in the second innings at The Oval in 2009, he now has six consecutive scores over fifty against England. He thus became the first player to score fifties in six consecutive Ashes innings. Interestingly, the only previous time any Australian had scored five consecutive Ashes fifties was Hussey himself in 2006/07. The only Englishmen to score five consecutive fifties against Australia are Peter May (1954/55-1956), John Edrich (1968) and Graham Gooch (1990/91).

Ⓜ **James Anderson took his 200th** Test wicket when he dismissed Peter Siddle in Australia's second innings. He was the 13th Englishman to reach this milestone and the second youngest at the age of 28 years 142 days. The only Englishman to reach 200 wickets at a younger age was Ian Botham, 25 years, 280 days.

SEVEN

THIRD TEST INTERLUDE

"I've pushed him as hard as I can, and he's more aggressive, more ruthless, now, and he's taken that training and intensity with him over to Australia."

BARRINGTON PATTERSON, IAN BELL'S FITNESS COACH

REASONS TO BE CHEERFUL

Tom Fordyce| 19 December 2010

Beaten in an hour over four days. Thrashed by 267 runs. Failing to bat for 100 overs in their two innings combined. There are plenty of reasons to feel miserable after England's feeble capitulation in the Third Test. I could go on: having Australia at 69/5 on the first day and yet somehow managing to lose; a middle order that contributed just 54 runs between them in this match; Mitchell Johnson transformed from laughing-stock to living legend. I could, but I won't. What's the point in wallowing in the misery and horrors of it all? It's over, just let it go.

Instead, let us face the future with a spring in our step. Here, courtesy of English stars past and present, are myriad reasons to be cheerful. Before we know it we'll be wreathed in beatific smiles and skipping gaily towards the MCG on Boxing Day like members of some happy cricketing cult. Here are mine:

1. Winning the Ashes in a nail-biting finale, having heroically fought off the slings and arrows and battled through varied tragedies en route, will be far more satisfying than winning them at a canter having come up against only token resistance. By losing here at the WACA – which has always happened, and probably always will – England have only made the final victory all the sweeter. Think of an Ashes victory Down Under as the partner of your dreams. If she or he acquiesced upon your first

phone call, you'd only take them for granted. By emerging with them in your arms after a long, tempestuous courtship, you will cherish them for the rest of your days.

2. The last time England won the Ashes, they did so with victory at Melbourne. I know it's a more well-known fact than omen or forecast, but it's something nonetheless.

3. Ashes joy follows disaster with this England team as surely as the wise paparazzo follows Shane Warne. After the Nightmare of Cardiff, the Triumph of Lord's. After the Hammering at Headingley, the Ovation at The Oval. There's only one thing that can follow from the Whacking at the WACA: the Marvellousity of Melbourne. We'll polish up the name at a later point.

Michael Vaughan: former Ashes-winning England captain, *Test Match Special* expert summariser

1. At least five of the Australian players aren't in any kind of form. Phillip Hughes, Michael Clarke, Ricky Ponting, Peter Siddle, Steve Smith. And you would think all five of them will still be in the team for the Fourth Test in Melbourne.

2. Chris Tremlett bowled very well coming back into the team. He made the breakthroughs on the first morning and then took five wickets in the second innings.

3. Ian Bell has been batting beautifully. Personally I'd think about moving him up the order.

Alec Stewart: 133 Tests for England, BBC Radio 5 live pundit

1. We aren't playing another Test match at the WACA until the next series Down Under. England haven't dealt with this pitch well, but that doesn't matter as they won't need to worry about it until then.

2. We haven't lost the Ashes at the WACA on this tour. Normally we do. Four years ago it was all over by this stage, and eight years ago it was too. The Ashes are still alive.

3. There's no way Steve Smith should be batting at number six. At Test level he's a number eight at best. The fact that he didn't bowl a single over means they picked him as a batsman but he's not good enough to bat there. So England have one less top-class batsman to worry about.

Simon Hughes: former Middlesex fast bowler, *Test Match Special* analyst

1. Australia have never had such a bad opening pair. I think they are more vulnerable at the top of the order than since their current chairman of selectors Andrew Hilditch and Graeme Wood were opening in the 1985 Ashes series in England.

2. Michael Clarke is in the worst form I've ever seen. He often wears sunglasses on the back of his head, but he'd probably bat better if he wore them at the front. To be honest, he might even bat better if he took his stance with his back to the bowler, let alone his sunglasses.

3. Australia do not have a spinner. Their current pick is their worst bowler since Murray Bennett.

Stuart Broad, England fast bowler

1. Chris Tremlett did really well here. He took eight wickets in the match in his first game back, and that's an excellent return.

2. England's catching has been amazing over the course of the series. That brings wickets and lifts everyone's mood.

3. It might be 1–1, but that scoreline allows us to retain the Ashes. And anyway, the lads are playing good cricket, and they believe we can win over here.

HOW TO DISMISS MIKE HUSSEY

Tom Fordyce| 23 December 2010

Two centuries in this Ashes series so far. Three fifties. 517 runs from just three Tests – six times more than his skipper Ricky Ponting – and an average of over 100. How on earth can England stop the run machine that is Mike Hussey? Having been one bad innings away from losing his place in the Australian side, Hussey has gone on to dominate the series. He saved his team from deep trouble in Brisbane, nearly rescued them in Adelaide and then took them to the brink of victory in Perth. If England want to win the Ashes, Hussey is now the man they must stop.

Who or what might hold the key to dismissing the immovable 'Mr Cricket'?

A little digging through the scorecards reveals that Hussey has been out caught 54 times in Test cricket, bowled 16 times, trapped lbw 16 times and run out once. Compared to most batsmen, that's a slightly higher percentage of lbws than you might expect. Is there something there that England could attack? Bob Carter knows Hussey and his technique inside out. Having coached him when he was at Northamptonshire during his first stint in county cricket, he still speaks to him regularly and has been exchanging tips and advice throughout the series. Bob is now coach of Canterbury in New Zealand's South Island.

Can he identify any technical weakness that might be exploited?

"I honestly can't," he says, slightly dispiritingly. "Mike's got one of the best techniques I've ever had the pleasure to see or work with. At one time there might have been a little bit of self-doubt there, and that might be why it took him so long to reach the top. But there's no self-doubt there now. Mike's very aware of where his off stump is. The way he stands at the crease, his set-up and the way he gets ready to face the ball, he is very still, and plays every ball on its merits. His focus and concentration are also very good. It doesn't matter if he plays and misses or hits a four or a six, he'll play the next ball as if it's his first. Coupled with being very strong on either side of the wicket, and you have a complete player. At the moment, I can't see a chink in his armour. Getting a top batsman out is about creating the opportunity. It's quite generic

Graeme Swann leads the England team in the Sprinkler Dance as they celebrate going 2-1 up with one Test remaining.

Awaiting the nod before going to interview the victorious England captain Andrew Strauss after the Ashes are retained. Emma (centre) joins the *TMS* production crew on the outfield for this special moment. Vic Marks meanwhile holds the fort.

England wear pink caps for a team photo in recognition of Glenn McGrath (seated next to the captain) and his late wife Jane's cancer charity.

A caucus of would-be Richie Benauds auditioning for a commentary spot on Channel 9.

Having played five different spinners throughout the series, there were calls amongst some Aussie fans for a Shane Warne comeback. It was never going to happen.

American nanny Ashley @theashes Kerekes interviews Australian Prime Minister Julia Gillard before the start of play.

Michael Clarke took over the captaincy in Sydney but his poor form with the bat continued. Tim Bresnan dismisses him in the first innings for another single-figure score.

Ian Bell puts the Australian bowlers to the sword as he registers his first Ashes century. Together with Matt Prior, here celebrating his own hundred, they put on 107 for the seventh wicket, and in the process register the fourth England score over 500 in the series.

'He bowls to the left, he bowls to the right…' The Barmy Army relish Mitchell Johnson's discomfort as England rack up 644 while his first-ball dismissal in Australia's second innings (inset) prompted mass celebration from the visiting fans.

Steve Smith displayed some unorthodox technique during his spells at the crease. Despite making some useful runs in his three Tests, he was a long way from being considered an all-rounder in either discipline.

Philip Hughes was brought into the side in place of the injured Simon Katich after Adelaide but he never convinced at the top of the order. Here he is getting caught in the gully, playing away from his body.

Shane Watson also flattered to deceive throughout the series. He was regularly dismissed when well set and his running between the wickets caused uncertainty amongst his colleagues. This picture shows him stranded at the same end as his opening partner in Australia's second innings.

Paul Collingwood (out of shot) bowls Mike Hussey, not a bad last wicket to end one's Test career. Although runs were elusive, his fielding and catching were always of the highest order. Here he catches Ricky Ponting in the Third Test off the bowling of Anderson.

Chris Tremlett captures the last Australian wicket by bowling Ian Beer. It means England wrap up the series 3-1 and win in Australia for the first time since 1987.

For Ricky Ponting and Michael Clarke, senior players whose own contributions fell some way short of what was required, there were question marks raised about their futures.

For Matt Prior and the rest of the England players, it was a career-defining achievement. For captain Strauss and coach Andy Flower, the sign says it all.

at times, trying to hit the top of off stump or just outside, as you would say for Ricky Ponting. My plan would be to go across his off stump."

Could that line on off stump be the key? Is there anything Andrew Strauss should do with his field placings to help his bowling attack make the most of that opportunity?

I turn to former England captain Michael Vaughan. "Hussey's so strong on the back foot that you've got to bring him forward on or around off stump. If the ball comes back I think you can get him lbw; he can also be vulnerable to leaving the ball on or around off stump and being bowled. England will hope Swann can put Hussey under some pressure at the MCG. You can open up a batsman's off stump by getting him trying to drive through cover. For Hussey, I might leave a gap in the field at cover to try and draw a shot that might lead to an edge through to one of the slips."

So which bowler has dismissed Hussey more than any other player?

One name gradually emerges as the ultimate Hussinator, Adam Dale, once of Queensland, the Aussie one-day side and, briefly, its Test team too. Dale took Hussey's wicket eight times in Pura Cup and Sheffield Shield cricket. He's also been retired for seven years. Might he, I wonder, fancy coming out of retirement and switching sides in time for the Boxing Day Test at the MCG? "It would be fun, but I'm not South African so I'd probably struggle," he says with relish from his Melbourne home. "When I played against Huss he was a lot younger. Since then he's matured and grown into a far better player than he was at that point. He was probably only about eight-years-old when I bowled to him. If you put the player he is now back into that time frame, I wouldn't get him out and even if I did, he'd still have made a lot of runs by that point."

Yet what was he doing that got the young Hussey in such a pickle?

"My goal was to try to get him making a late decision," he explains. "Because he leaves the ball so well, and is probably the best in the business at playing to his own strengths, you want him to have to wait. If I could entice him and get him to hit to cover, I'd have a chance. Any time he hit to leg it would be run after run; anything too short and he'd punish you. But if you could get him to make a late decision to hit to cover, you'd have a chance. He's also so good that he knows where his off stump is. Being a swing bowler, the batsman's indecision becomes your big weapon: how far is it going to swing, when and which way?

"If you're bowling straight and can't move the ball, it becomes a much easier decision for him. But if the ball is swinging, it's much harder for him – does he let it go, does he let it hit his pads? Look to shape it across him, and then bring it back into him late. Mind you, that's the glory ball for every batsman, whether you're Michael Hussey or a Sunday cricketer. If you can achieve those sort of outcomes as a bowler and do it consistently, you throw the odds in your favour."

I thank Adam for his small betrayal and push on. In all three Tests so far, England have attacked Hussey with a short ball into the ribs. It got him out in the second innings in Adelaide, when he mis-pulled Steven Finn to Jimmy Anderson at mid-on, and also in the first innings in Brisbane, when he was pouched by Alastair Cook at deep square-leg.

Could the short-ball tactic be another option?

"I know they've got him twice out on the pull this series, but he's also scored very heavily with that shot," points out Carter. "Perhaps because of the form he's in, they're trying to look at something else." Vaughan is equally cautious. "I wouldn't rule out the bouncer, but make sure it's high. Don't bowl anything waist height or chest height, because he'll put you away. He got out on the pull in Brisbane because he only had the tail with him; the only mistake he's made in the series so far was on the final morning in Adelaide, but then Australia collectively were having a bad match."

Is there a particular type of bowler Hussey might struggle against?

Last summer In England he was trapped leg before by Stuart Broad on two occasions. Andrew Flintoff clean bowled him at Lord's, while Graham Onions achieved the Holy Grail by seeing him off for a golden duck at Edgbaston. The trouble is, none of those three players is available. Fred has retired, Onions is at home in Durham recovering from a stress fracture to the back and Broad is out of this series with a stomach injury. Steven Finn has dismissed Hussey twice in this campaign. But he was also put to the sword by Mr Cricket's blade, going at a run a ball at the WACA, and it may be that he will be rested for the Fourth Test at the MCG.

So what about Graeme Swann?

He got Hussey out twice in the 2009 Ashes (once caught at slip, once caught in the deep) and has bagged him twice this time around, caught at slip by Paul Collingwood (again), and pouched behind the timbers by Matt Prior. "It's quite difficult for a left-hander against a right-arm off-break bowler, when the ball is moving away from you, and Swann produced that wonderful ball to nick him out in Perth," says Carter. "The danger for England is that Mike has gone after him. That's been a great move from Mike. He's gone out there with a no-fear policy, and he's really flying. He's taken the upper hand and put the bowlers under pressure, rather than the other way round. Once a batsman gets on top like that you're in trouble."

Vaughan, intriguingly, has a slightly different take on this. "If I were captain I'd throw the ball to Swann as soon as he comes in. Hussey has only ever faced Swann once he's been in and set. He's faced seamers at the start throughout the series. So no matter what the situation is when he comes to the crease, get Swann on and see how he copes with it."

And if that doesn't work?

Vaughan again: "If Adam Dale got him out with inswingers, I wouldn't rule out using someone like Paul Collingwood, someone different to what he's faced already. For the rest of the attack, you've just got to keep your plans simple. When someone's in good form you have to accept that you'll have to bowl as consistently as possible. If you start chasing it, you're only going in his favour. One thing about Hussey is that he shouldn't really get on top of you. He won't intimidate you as a bowler by smashing you all over the place or putting you back over your head, so you should be able to block up an end by bowling dot balls. Build some pressure."

I have one last ace up my sleeve. Alec Swann, brother of Graeme, played with an impressionable young Hussey in his first season of county cricket. It was this unsung Swann who reportedly first came up with the Mr Cricket moniker, and clearly has an insight into his character.

Can he suggest any mind games that might work?

"Michael's a very personable chap. I never saw anyone who was able to ruffle him at all. He just went into his batting zone, and wouldn't bother saying anything to the opposition. My advice would be not to put him under any pressure at all. Every time he's in danger of being dropped, he comes out and scores a hundred, so make him feel as secure as possible. Tell him his position in the team is nice and safe, that he'll be playing for weeks to come. Then maybe he'll struggle."

So there we have it. Make him feel at home. Angle the ball across him, bend it back in if you can, don't drop short and don't bowl too straight.

DAY 52 **23 December 2010**

I think England only attend two proper sponsors' functions on this tour (excluding the one at the Gabba that caused all the unnecessary headlines). Today is an unavoidable commitment for the England camp. These can be pretty dreadful affairs – and this one is a particularly ghastly example of what happens when the marketing men are let out for the day from whatever circle of hell they traditionally occupy.

Taking place in a shopping mall, a horrible jokey raucous young disk jockey chap is interviewing some of the players and bowling a ball from five yards for Alastair Cook to slog into a crowd of bemused Christmas shoppers. What the sponsors get out of this is beyond me.

I take the opportunity to interview Ian Bell. I am particularly interested in how they are going to come back from the defeat at Perth, and in the fact that they haven't played or practised since. Ian explains that things are no different to the timings of, or the way in which they prepare for a Test match on home soil. "We are going to have our two-day practice – it starts tomorrow [Christmas Eve and Christmas Day], just like we always build up for every Test match, no different, nothing will have changed," he says.

Ian Bell has matured a lot, not just in the way he bats, but he has grown up as a person and I can't help thinking he is very convincing about the way the team will shrug off Perth. I do not believe he was just trotting it out because the England management had told him to say it. He genuinely doesn't feel there is a problem. It is most encouraging.

DAY 53 **24 December 2010**

England have the best part of five days off, spending time with their families in Melbourne before the Boxing Day Test. I am asked a lot about this by radio stations back home – is it right to have such a long lay-off after a heavy defeat? I'm more relaxed about this now than I used to be and still truly believe that Perth's defeat can be excused as a one-off.

It is impossible for the WACA conditions to be repeated in the last two matches, although I do believe that Australia would be best served by producing grassy pitches. Seam bowling is their strength, and they don't have a spinner, so why not? In fact it has given the newspapers plenty to chew on this week. One of many stories to make the back pages is the suggestion that the Melbourne groundsman – or curator as he is known in these parts – has ordered the pitch to be switched. There are tales of television camera positions having to be moved, which gives the story more credibility, but the curator clears up the debate by revealing that he decided to change pitches while the Perth Test was still being played, and that he certainly had not been ordered to do so by Cricket Australia.

The result is the same – there will be some grass and dampness on the first day. A good toss to lose, perhaps.

Sledging is still going strong, with Siddle now incapable of keeping quiet. We are given chapter and verse about the way he abused Prior and then has a go at Anderson for the nightwatchman's apparent refusal to take the strike at Perth, which resulted in Collingwood's dismissal to the final ball of the third day. Siddle is insinuating that Anderson did not fancy it. Frankly it is all getting a bit silly now, fuelled no doubt by the sudden rise in expectations within the Australian media.

Tonight Emma and I go to Carols by Candlelight at the Sidney Myer Music Bowl in Melbourne's King's Domain Gardens. It is something of an Australian Christmas tradition that has been going on since the 1930s, and the evening is great fun and very festive. From our vantage point we can see the MCG, which is all lit up and looks wonderful. A good omen for the coming week I can't help but hope.

Four years ago the weather in Melbourne at Christmas was appalling, 13 degrees and hailing. Emma has had a downer on Australian Christmases ever since. This year it has to be better.

DAY 54 25 December 2010

The players practise on Christmas Day, which happens to be Alastair Cook's birthday. When Simon Jones and Marcus Trescothick were on tour, there were three Christmas Day birthdays, something that must be a unique tour record.

At the MCG, after their break, the players are keen to show they are back in the business of preparing for a Test, and, rather sadly in my view, decline to wear the traditional Santa hats for the assembled photographers. Things must be serious. I interview Jonathan Trott, who is a straight-talking, no-frills individual. He tells me that he has been dreaming about playing in this match before an enormous crowd since the middle of last summer.

Rather depressingly, another old tradition has bitten the dust. For years players and press used to mix at a lunchtime cocktail party. England coach Duncan Fletcher saw that one off on his first tour here, and it's a great shame in my view. It didn't take long, and it brought everyone on the tour together in the spirit of Christmas. Many a hatchet was buried at those Christmas events. Not only do the players fail to wear Santa hats in the nets, they have also dispensed with the fancy dress, which was always an integral and much photographed part of their Christmas lunch. On this tour, with their families in tow, the players do entirely their own thing.

So Emma, Tom (my stepson) and I spend Christmas Day with some old friends of mine in Essendon, the club I played for thirty years ago. We pop in to Windy Hill, the cricket ground, on the way to lunch, which brings back lots of happy memories. That winter in Melbourne had been a wonderful experience and a good insight into the way Australians play their cricket.

The sun shines, the kids splash in the swimming pool and play cricket in the back yard, while we tuck into oysters and a huge roast followed by pavlova – the traditional Aussie Christmas pudding. It is a different sort of Christmas Day, and huge fun. But it's hard to push tomorrow entirely to the back of one's mind.

EVE OF MATCH THOUGHTS

The England camp is making the right noises, and most observers here still believe they will retain the Ashes, but there's no doubt that Australia have gained massively in confidence following their emphatic win in Perth. The media bandwagon has swung behind the team, and that result has done wonders for the public interest in the traditional Boxing Day Test, which is poised to break all records for attendance at a Test match.

The question of sledging has been high on the agenda all week – and there's no doubt that there were plenty of 'verbals' between some of the players at the WACA. But I do hope that there isn't a disintegration of what appears to have been a strong, healthy and competitive spirit into something boorish and unattractive.

Despite what some Australians have been saying including depressingly Paul Marsh, the secretary of the Australian Cricketers' Association, sledging or abusing the batsman is not an essential ingredient to playing good, tough Test cricket. I hope the umpires are strong enough in what will be a bullring of an atmosphere at the MCG to stamp it out quickly, if necessary.

That said, we did see a much more aggressive Australia at Perth and certainly we formed the opinion that a number of England's batsmen did not take much of a shine to the fast, short-pitched delivery. But can the Australian fast bowlers repeat that performance on one of Melbourne's drop-in pitches, and is Mitchell Johnson capable of stringing two consistently dangerous performances together?

The pitch has been the topic of great debate and although it has a green look to it, it seems most unlikely that any pitch in Victoria, with its large rainfall and temperate climate, could in any way replicate the strip on the other side of Australia. However, it would certainly assist Johnson, Ryan Harris, Peter Siddle and Ben Hilfenhaus if there is some movement off the seam.

England's selection dilemma hasn't been helped by the news that James Anderson has, at best, a stiff side and, at worst, a strained side muscle. If it is the latter, to play only four bowlers would be absolute madness. They have to be sure Anderson can get through five days irrespective of how many bowlers they play, but to leave Chris Tremlett, Graeme Swann and either Steven Finn or Tim Bresnan to carry the attack in the event of Anderson breaking down would leave England in a hopeless position.

Yes, this is a big game and yes, Anderson will want to play, but England simply can't afford to take the chance unless they pick five bowlers.

I still maintain that would be their best policy anyway. Ian Bell deserves to move up the order – it would be better for England if he does – and Bresnan's presence would lessen the workload on Finn who does have the happy knack of taking wickets.

With such a vast crowd expected, especially on the first three days, the team that can hold its nerve the best and remain calm under pressure should prevail. If I were Andy Flower, I would be reinforcing the point that to become distracted by silly sledging is the most likely road to ruin.

Focus, discipline and concentration helped England to save Brisbane and win at Adelaide. It is also what is required here.

EIGHT

MELBOURNE TEST

"I think we've done a very good job as a selection panel."

ANDREW HILDITCH, CHAIRMAN OF SELECTORS

DAY 55 **26 December 2010, Fourth Test – first day**

At breakfast at the hotel this morning, I find myself sitting with famous cricket lover and old friend Sir Michael Parkinson. Emma had said earlier, "I'm not going to bother with breakfast today, so you go down by yourself." Emma has always loved Parky, so while Michael and I were chatting away I got my phone out and texted Emma: 'I think you might like to come down after all, because I am having breakfast with Parky.' I had barely pressed the send button when a gust of wind blew through the restaurant and she was there! We all arrange to have dinner that night.

After breakfast I stroll through the park from the hotel to the vast MCG with Geoffrey Boycott, who does not seem to be brimming with festive spirit today. The enormous crowd is already gathering, with long queues forming at the gates as we make our way into the huge stand at the City End. This is clearly going to be an enormous day and even seasoned commentators are clearly excited as we all shake hands and exchange Christmas greetings.

"I'm amazed Australia haven't picked a spinner. From what I've seen of the pitch, it will definitely spin on days four and five." MICHAEL VAUGHAN, TMS

Morning session: At lunch – Australia 58/4, Clarke 12*, Smith 0*

England have replaced Finn with Bresnan. Strauss wins a critical toss and puts Australia into bat. After three inauspicious overs, in which England drop Watson twice and Tremlett is hit to the boundary a couple of times, Boycott announces on air that England are off the boil and that this match will be drawn. "But we've only been playing 12 minutes, Geoffrey," I say, surprised by his snap verdict that is outspoken (and mildly ridiculous) even by Geoffrey's standards. "That's why you're the commentator and I'm the expert," he replies with just the hint of a smile.

Finally a catch sticks when Watson is taken by Pietersen in the gully off Tremlett for 5 – the first time in 12 innings that Watson has been dismissed below 20. It is 15/1 when Ponting walks to the wicket. Hughes drives Bresnan to Pietersen for 16 and next over Ponting edges Tremlett to Swann at second slip, who catches the ball with two hands diving to his left. It's yet another failure for Ponting, who is batting with the handicap of a fractured finger. Australia decline to 58/4 when Hussey is caught behind off Anderson for 8. It is a massive wicket and entirely repays Strauss for his gamble in putting Australia in to bat for the second time in successive Tests.

> *"I can't see any way how England can win this Test from what I've seen so far. A draw would do. If you were an opener, you'd be queuing up to bat on this compared to Perth."* GEOFFREY BOYCOTT, TMS

Afternoon session: At tea – Australia 98 all out

A heavy shower of rain delays the resumption, and Australia then have to bat under floodlights. Conditions are not easy, but do not explain Australia's collapse to their lowest score against England on this ground, and their lowest anywhere against England since 1936/37. Every wicket in the innings falls to a catch behind from gully to wicketkeeper as the ball does just enough to find the edge. It is a rout with the wickets shared between Anderson, Tremlett and Bresnan as Australia lose 6 for 40 after lunch in 17 overs. I go off in search of Geoffrey.

> *"Jimmy Anderson, bowling on a pitch like this that swings, is one of the best in the world."* GEOFFREY BOYCOTT, TMS

> *"The ball was nipping around this morning, but there's no excuse for an Australian team to be bowled out for 98."* JUSTIN LANGER, TMS

Evening session: At the close – England 157/0, Strauss 64*, Cook 80*, England lead by 59 runs

As if the day isn't good enough already, England's openers stamp their authority on the match. It really is a case of rubbing your eyes and wondering if the whole thing isn't some sort of a dream. Has the outcome of a Test ever looked so clear so early? The attendance figure is announced – 84,345. A superb turn out, but actually not quite the record breaker everyone anticipated. And many of the Australian crowd decide on the evidence of what they've seen so far that the Boxing Day sales offer better entertainment, heading for the exits early, leaving the MCG at the mercy of the huge invasion of England supporters.

Emma's Christmas is made by having our planned dinner with Michael and Mary Parkinson. Mary is a particularly keen listener to *Test Match Special* while Michael was a very decent cricketer in his own right, playing as a young man alongside Boycott and Dicky Bird. It's a lovely evening of stories and reminiscences – and a shared delight at England's performance helped considerably by Parky's very fine choice of Pinot Noir.

> *"This is the most one-sided first day of a Test that I've ever seen – even including games with Bangladesh or Zimbabwe."* JIM MAXWELL, TMS

END OF DAY REPORT

England were simply superb as Australia crumbled in Melbourne.

To bowl Australia out for 98 and then come out and bat like that was remarkable. In theory it is possible to mess it up from here, but England are in an incredibly strong position. They will look to bat long, build a big lead and then their spinner Graeme Swann can come into play when Australia bat again.

The Australians will surely put up more of a fight second time around – they can hardly fail to – but England look set to retain the Ashes.

It was a day that England captain Andrew Strauss could have not dreamed of while his opposite number Ricky Ponting would never have imagined such a nightmare. For the tourists everything went right, starting with winning a toss that, while important, cannot be used as an excuse for Australia's collapse.

There was only a little help from the conditions, but the England bowlers all got the maximum they could from the pitch. Chris Tremlett bowled with real intensity and aggression to follow on from his performance in Perth. He has a glare and a presence now and he is such an enormous man he must be horrible to face.

Tim Bresnan also enjoyed a good day and he is someone I would have brought in for the last Test. In the past the Yorkshire star has been used as a new-ball bowler, which is the wrong role for him. He is a back-up bowler to come on first or second change. Given that role, Bresnan delivered and even bowled the quickest ball England produced all day.

But special credit must go to James Anderson, who just goes from strength to strength. There was a little bit in the wicket for the Lancashire paceman but it certainly was nothing like the helpful wickets he got against Pakistan in the summer. There was no movement through the air and in the past that might have taken away Anderson's threat but he is a different bowler now with many more strings to his bow.

He bowled accurately and with pace and he has the stamina to keep on performing, showing he is fully recovered from the slight strain he was carrying. He was simply outstanding and really is a formidable opponent.

The bowlers did their work and England will now look to build on Strauss and Alastair Cook's opening partnership, knowing that they are on the brink of retaining the Ashes. What the performance also did was to put the pre-match talk of Australia's improved fast bowling and how England would fold in the face of sledging into perspective.

In Perth, Australia chiefly relied on Mitchell Johnson and Michael Hussey while Shane Watson again impressed. What we saw in Melbourne is that if those players do not perform, Australia are liable to fold.

Throughout the series they have been rescued by Hussey, who has come in with the team in trouble and scored runs. Today England accounted for him quickly and, without their knight on a white charger, their innings simply home crumbled.

Of course, there should be some slight caution following Perth where, after day one, I said England were close to retaining the Ashes only for them to lose heavily. But if Australia are to somehow win in Melbourne, they will have to become the first Test side in more than 100 years to do so after scoring less than 130 when batting first.

England dominated but it should not be suggested that they got undue help. There was some grass on the track and these drop-in wickets can be a little damp, but the pitch certainly did not give England's bowlers much. Strauss's men bowled and batted with discipline while Australia had a nightmare that started with their selection.

It was understandable to go without a spinner at the WACA, but it made no sense to have an attack with five seamers in Melbourne. There was a little help for the bowlers, but the ball was not whooping around for either team.

Yes, the tourists had the better of the conditions as when they batted the sun came out, but the key difference was that they bowled line and length. They induced 12 nicks in total, Watson being dropped twice, and that was just through bowling in the right areas.

When Australia bowled they could not find the same discipline. Johnson reverted to being the wayward bowler of earlier in the series and under pressure they started conceding boundaries.

All this came despite the momentum supposedly having shifted to Australia after they won in Perth to level the series. The papers had gone crazy with all the sledging nonsense, their quicks were meant to have found form yet long before the end, the Australian fans were leaving in their droves. By the close, the MCG was less than half full as England brutally exposed the weaknesses in their team.

The hosts were rescued in Perth because Johnson blew England away, but with the Western Australian back to being a scattergun bowler there was little to trouble England's openers.

It all led to a day that people back in England will scarcely have believed possible. It was one of those magical days of Test cricket and happily it all went England's way.

I have always thought from the start of the series that England had the better team. Perth was a blip; I also thought they had it in them to retain the Ashes. It now looks like they will.

DAY 56 **27 December 2010, Fourth Test – second day**

"MCG about one-tenth full. Aussie public don't seem entirely convinced that their boys can turn this one around. From coliseum to county ground." TOM FORDYCE

Morning session: At lunch – England 226/2, Trott 31*, Pietersen 30*

Australia's only remote route back into the match is by taking early wickets, and within forty minutes of play both openers have been dismissed by Siddle; Cook caught by Watson at first slip for 82 and Strauss by Hussey high at gully for 69. Trott and Pietersen play busily to add a further 56 runs before lunch. England now lead by 128.

"Never mind all this talk of Shane Warne making a comeback, Australia don't need a leg-spinner, they need some batsmen, so maybe they should bring back Matthew Hayden and Justin Langer." MICHAEL VAUGHAN, TMS

Afternoon session: At tea – England 304/5, Trott 65*, Prior 12*

Once again, Ponting allows the pressure to get to him as he completely loses his cool with umpire Dar over a reviewed decision for a caught behind against Pietersen. At the time, only Haddin appeals while the bowler, Ryan Harris, appears to be surprised by his wicketkeeper's conviction. Ponting, fielding at mid-off, does not appeal either but is persuaded by Haddin to review Dar's not out verdict. With the replays now shown on the big screen, the players in the middle can see what the third umpire is reviewing but, in the case of the MCG, from a long way away. There does appear to be a Hot Spot mark on Pietersen's bat. But it is clear to everyone watching in the commentary boxes that this mark is nowhere near to the point on Pietersen's bat where the ball passed, so it is irrelevant to the review. When the third umpire confirms the not out decision, Ponting loses his rag. Gesturing to the umpire, he is clearly convinced that Hot Spot has condemned Pietersen. Siddle inexplicably joins in while Pietersen, impishly, winks at Ponting as the Australian captain storms past.

This enrages Ponting even more, and he has another go, this time at Tony Hill, the square-leg umpire who had nothing to do with any of the decision-making process. It is an unedifying, if revealing spectacle and Ian Chappell, on *Test Match Special*, immediately calls for Ponting's suspension. It remains the talking point of the day. Pietersen is unfairly booed when, moments later, he scores his 50 and then immediately afterwards plays rather distractedly across a straight ball from Siddle and is lbw.

Ashes cricket must be hard and tough, but it must also be played in a fair manner and within the right spirit. Passages of play such as we have just witnessed have no place in the game. Trott appears unmoved and scores only 34 in the session. Collingwood (8) and Bell (1) are both dismissed pulling Johnson, but Ponting's humour is sorely tested again when Prior – rightly given out caught behind on 5 – is recalled by Dar, who has asked for the possibility of Johnson having delivered a no-ball to be checked. And sure enough he had. England's lead advances to 206 at tea.

> *"I've got no idea what Ricky Ponting was doing arguing like that. If the ICC don't punish him, the Board should. The Australian captain shouldn't be allowed to behave like that."* IAN CHAPPELL, TMS

Evening session: At the close – England 444/5, Trott 141*, Prior 75*, England lead by 346 runs

It still seems unbelievable that any team should be in such a commanding position with so much time still remaining in the match. Maybe a Test featuring Zimbabwe or Bangladesh – but Australia? This is a profitable session with Trott batting more fluently now to reach his third Ashes century. It is reminiscent of Adelaide with Ponting's quick bowlers all running in gamely but with no edge while Smith, the leg-spinner, poses no threat whatsoever.

Today in the commentary box we became aware for the first time of the 'Mitchell Johnson Song'. This is a new addition to the Barmy Army repertoire, and reflects in a typically no-nonsense manner, the erratic nature of Johnson's bowling. When chanted in unison by several thousand England fans, complete with the appropriate arm signals, it is quite an ear and eye-catcher: *"He bowls to the left. He bowls to the right. That Mitchell Johnson – his bowling is shite!"* Poor old Johnson was taunted mercilessly throughout the afternoon. The

Barmy Army has been in good voice all tour, but today the singing was ruthless and highly effective. The Australians had nowhere to hide in the field, and how they must have hated every minute of it.

But let's not forget – the last time England won the Ashes in Australia, the Barmy Army didn't exist. They have waited as long as any of us to win here, and they know it will happen very soon.

I want to return to the wretched Decision Review System for a moment. My main objection to it is that it takes away the most fundamental aspect of cricket: the umpire's decision is final. He is the respected authority in the game, and to my mind the DRS undermines him.

We should remember that by allowing, at the highest level of the game, the notion that it is acceptable for players to question an umpire's decision, it gives permission for it to happen on club fields, school grounds, in fact it will happen everywhere now – mostly where there is no DRS technology in place. As a player I always accepted that the umpire's decision was final, you had to take the rough with the smooth. I believe that it is a very strong character-building component of cricket and to undermine such an important principle of the game is just wrong in my view. I really think the authorities are going to regret it. I am not anti-technology, but it has got to work and be more or less one hundred percent accurate.

At the moment it is creating more controversy rather than less, and clearly Hot Spot has been found badly wanting on this tour. Far from the purported great saviour many people claimed it to be, it clearly doesn't work effectively at all. And now the players know it.

"We wish we were waking up and today was Boxing Day." Justin Langer, TMS

END OF DAY REPORT

Ricky Ponting's outburst today betrayed his current state of mind as he allowed everything to boil over and get the better of him. Columnists and correspondents over here in Australia are starting to talk very seriously about his future as captain; his team are getting a pasting and he is in terrible form with the bat.

But his reaction to the umpire's decision was utterly inexcusable. You simply cannot behave like that. There was no possible reason for him having a go at the on-field umpires and he fully deserved to be fined 40 percent of his match fee.

I've always felt that with the review system you have to show it on the big screen so people watching live can see it. It does not seem right to me that people paying the entrance money are denied seeing what people at home get for free on their televisions.

But I'm having second thoughts about that because Ponting clearly made up his mind based on what he saw on the big screen. The ICC has been reluctant to put replays on the big screens for that very reason. You can imagine the uproar in Mumbai if Sachin Tendulkar was given out in similar circumstances.

The incident did not add to Ponting's humour on a day when everything seemed to go England's way. Jonathan Trott escaped being run out by one frame and Matt Prior was caught behind off a no-ball – all of those things combined to leave a rather bitter taste in Australian mouths. But it is the way things are going for England, and you do make your own luck. They were all entirely correct decisions.

It was another great day for England, with the only blot on the landscape being Paul Collingwood. You can forgive Ian Bell playing one rash shot because he has played beautifully all series but Collingwood's form is clearly a big concern. I suspect they will probably keep him in the team in Sydney but it will be a big game for him. He will be playing for his immediate future.

Meanwhile, Trott showed wonderful discipline, focus and determination. He is not the prettiest batsman to watch but he is mightily efficient. Someone had to go out today and make a big hundred and he took it upon himself to do just that.

England knew exactly what they had to do today – they have been so well organised throughout the series apart from the Perth Test match which was clearly an aberration.

A superb partnership between Trott and Matt Prior has firmly shut the door on Australia. They have no chance of getting back into the match and you would expect them to suffer a very heavy defeat. The only disappointment from a neutral point of view is that the Melbourne Test has not been much of a contest and that has had an impact on the attendance. Australians don't take poor performances very well. At the start of the first day, there was a massive crowd but half of them had walked out by midway through the afternoon. And today numbers were down even more.

It seems a bit odd saying this but for summer it is very cold here. Temperatures have been down at around 13 degrees with a biting wind. It is not much fun sitting in a big ground like this with virtually no sunshine, freezing to death. The conditions are not ideal for watching cricket, which is a shame for such a big match.

I think we could be in for a similar situation to the Gabba where there are more England supporters in the ground than Australians by the end of this match.

DAY 57　28 December 2010, Fourth Test – third day

Ricky Ponting has issued an explanation for his row with umpire Dar. He says he accepts his punishment, but it falls a long way short of a proper apology.

"I understand I overstepped the mark. I realise it didn't look good but the umpires vouched for me. I didn't show any malice or aggression, it's just the discussions went on longer than they should have done. I accepted the 40 percent fine straight away. I guess that one flaw in the system is that replays are shown on the big screen, we could see an obvious Hot Spot mark and I wanted to clarify how the third umpire got to making the decision he made. But I got caught in the heat of the moment and it went on too long."

The match referee, Ranjan Madugalle, calls Ponting's behaviour 'unacceptable'.

> "Even if England lose their last five wickets for 30, the real meat and potatoes today will be when Australia bat." VIC MARKS, TMS

Morning session: At lunch – England 513 all out. England lead by 415 runs

Once Prior misses out on what would have been a much-deserved century, the lower order is swept away before lunch, leaving Trott undefeated on a magnificent 168 from 345 balls. He is an extraordinary man. Even when the last wicket goes down, and the innings is all over, he still rakes at the crease with his boot?! Prior holes out to mid-on for 85 and Siddle runs through the rest to finish with 6 for 75 while Harris has to be helped from the field with an ankle injury which will clearly rule him out of the Sydney Test. Australia have 66 overs left to bat on the third day.

Afternoon session: At tea – Australia 95/1, Watson 50* Ponting 19*

Australia's openers make a good fist of their reply, albeit in hopeless circumstances, by scoring 53 runs from 12 overs before disaster strikes and Watson, who is a dreadful judge of a run, runs out his partner Hughes when he pushes Swann to Trott's left at cover. As we saw at Adelaide, Trott has worked hard on his fielding, and another arrow-like throw to Prior is enough to see off Hughes, who leaves the vast stadium head bowed, clearly wondering if he will play Test cricket again. Watson continues apparently undeterred while Ponting, having entered the fray to sustained and raucous booing from the Barmy Army, scratches around for 70 balls to tea for his 19. England merely have to be patient.

> *"I would think it would be very difficult to bowl Australia out here. If I was an Australian supporter and they didn't make 450 on this pitch, I'd be very disappointed."* GEOFFREY BOYCOTT, TMS

Evening session: At the close – Australia 169/6, Haddin 11*, Johnson 6*, Australia are 246 runs behind

Now it is Tim Bresnan's turn to demonstrate just how spot on England's selections have been in this series by producing the spell of bowling that will comfortably seal Australia's fate within four days.

Watson reaches another half-century but perishes almost immediately when he offers no shot to Bresnan and is lbw. Ponting edges into his wicket for 20 – another unlucky dismissal he would say, but a classic way for an out-of-sorts batsman to lose his wicket. Two runs later, Hussey drives Bresnan straight to Bell at short extra-cover for a duck. Clarke might have been stumped on 2 – a rare blemish by Prior behind the wicket – but on 13 he is taken by Strauss fielding at gully for the spinner who creates tremendous pressure by conceding only 23 runs in his 22-over spell from the Southern End. The icing on the cake comes when Smith, who gives us glimpses of quality in a fighting 38, drags a short ball from Anderson on to his stumps. All that remains is for the Barmy Army to celebrate a momentous day by welcoming Johnson to the crease with a deafening rendition of his song. He survives, but Australia know it is only a matter of time.

> *"England may have lost form at the WACA, but they've come back with a true professional performance. They look so much a better team than Australia, who look beaten and battered."* MICHAEL VAUGHAN, TMS

END OF DAY REPORT

With the Ashes now certain to remain in England's hands, the spotlight is falling on the future of Australia captain Ricky Ponting. He is having a ghastly time with the bat, the pressure is clearly getting to him and his team is performing woefully. But the issue of who should succeed Ponting, and when, is anything but a straightforward one.

The main problem is that there does not seem to be another captain around for them at the moment. There is no one there hammering on the selectors' door saying: "Look we have a crisis here. Make me captain and I'll sort it out."

Vice-captain Michael Clarke is going through a horror story of almost the same magnitude as Ponting. Clarke does not look like the right person, with the bat at least, to take over the reins. He has no confidence and is averaging only 21 in this series.

There is talk about Cameron White coming in as skipper but it would be very un-Australian to pick a player who does not automatically get into the team. Brad Haddin is another option but I am not convinced he has the right character.

Another issue is what do you do with Ponting if he is not captain any more? It is not the Australian way to have a former captain remaining in the side, yet he is their best player, so what do they do about that? Before Ponting jumps or is pushed, there are lots of things to resolve.

The only thing they do have in their favour is that after this Test series they do not have another until August 2011. So if Ponting were to go after Sydney, they could delay naming a successor to him as captain and thereby give Clarke time to get back into some sort of form.

That Australia find themselves in this predicament is largely down to another superb bowling performance from England on day three in Melbourne, with Chris Tremlett and Tim Bresnan particularly outstanding.

For the first time in this series, reverse swing really came to the fore and Bresnan, who has only played two games since September, was superb. To take the wickets of Shane Watson, Ponting and Mike Hussey was probably the highlight of his sporting career. It was a spell of brilliant, high-class, reverse swing bowling.

Tremlett did not take a wicket but he certainly deserved one, having bowled with pace and a lovely, consistent off-stump line. He really has come on in leaps and bounds. There is so much more about him as a person and a player. He is much more assertive and more confident and that's there for all to see.

Shane Watson has suggested England were lucky to bowl on a greentop early on the first day, and lucky to bowl on a dry, abrasive pitch second time round, but that is nonsense. The gulf between the bowling attacks is colossal.

Peter Siddle ran in wholeheartedly for Australia and was rewarded with figures of 6 for 75 but they do not have anything like the control in their attack that England have.

England's bowlers were helped out by some very intelligent field placings from Andrew Strauss. The captain does not over-attack but he comes up with clever fielding plans, like bringing in the short extra-cover that caught Hussey. You do not have to have rows of slips lined up to have an attacking field; Ian Bell was there at short-extra to take a wicket. Hussey was not unlucky – it was a perfectly laid plan and it was executed to perfection.

England will be delighted to win this match but the message will be clear – the job is only half-done. They will celebrate retaining the Ashes but they will be absolutely determined to to win the series in Sydney.

DAY 58 29 December 2010, Fourth Test – fourth day
Morning session: England win by an innings and 157 runs

England retain the Ashes in Australia for the first time in 24 years. It is an unforgettable day. The last three wickets – Harris could not bat due to injury – hang around rather longer than the England supporters might have wanted, but with trumpeter Billy Cooper playing Slade's *Merry Christmas Everybody* from the massed ranks of red and white in the Great Southern Stand, the bowlers chip away.

Finally, on the stroke of noon in Melbourne, Hilfenhaus is caught behind by Prior, fittingly off Bresnan who has enjoyed such a fine match. It is another thumping win, too – an innings and 157 runs to lead the series 2-1.

Emma is with me in the commentary box, and I am determined that she is a part of the celebrations too. I have spent years of our married life away on tours to far-flung parts of the world, which has required huge patience and consideration on her part. I really want her to enjoy today so I grab a spare pass which allows her access to the ground and, with Victor and producer Caroline, we set off to broadcast the ceremony live and, of course, to interview the victorious players.

Again, I am clutching my 3G contraption that, albeit with a small but manageable delay, enables me to broadcast in perfect quality while moving around the outfield. It's a superb piece of kit (notwithstanding the nightmare of the Perth Ponting birthday debacle), and this is the first time we have been able to use it with such great effect.

Out in the cauldron-like middle, the atmosphere is extraordinary. There is a brilliant blue sky overhead, and it is easy to forget just how vast the MCG is from ground level. Having been used to the sealed glass windows of the commentary box, you don't appreciate quite how noisy it is too. Immediately as we step on to the grass I ask Christopher Martin-Jenkins to hand down to me – and away we go. Victor, as always, is perfect in this situation, happily talking away to the listeners while I am searching the ground for people to interview. He knows I am not really listening to a word he is saying, but he keeps going all the same.

The key man in a situation like this is James Avery, the ECB media man who will provide me with players to talk to, but also allows me more or less a free rein to pick off whosoever I can. Similarly, I have by now got on well with James's counterpart at Cricket Australia, Lachy Patterson, and following a series of silent mime-like gestures (all negotiations have to be done without the conversation going out over the radio, of course) and lots of nodding heads, Ricky Ponting strides over to me.

As always he is firm, business-like and honest. We talk about his failure to perform with the bat (113 runs at an average of 16) and he searches for the word to describe his series. Then, looking me straight in the eye, he says, "Horrible." I know it's silly, but I suddenly feel terribly sorry for him. He appears so sad and vulnerable, and I always hate it when any sportsman reflecting on what should be a truly memorable time in his life – win or lose – does so with evident unhappiness.

Emma is busy clicking away with her camera, clearly loving the atmosphere, and Strauss appears grinning from ear to ear. He talks about his pride in his team, naturally, but he also stresses that the job has not yet been done and that the main focus of the tour is to win the series.

My absurd promise to perform the Sprinkler has been reawakened by this win, and as a final question, I ask him for a few tips. "I'm definitely the wrong man to ask!" he confesses, before I thank him and he scampers off to the far end of the ground to join his team mates on their lap of honour.

A huge roar goes up from the Barmy Army as Strauss arrives and, led by Swann, the whole team then performs the Sprinkler Dance right in front of them. The noise really makes the ground shake and all we can do is stand there and describe the rather absurd scene in front of us until Swann and Cook are ushered towards us for a brief chat.

What is so striking is just how nice the members of this team are. That is not offered in a hand-wringing sort of a way, but I have dealt with some teams over the years who have been neither approachable nor friendly. To a man, these players have been open, friendly, mature and decent from the very start of the tour, which makes their success all the more deserved and enjoyable, in my view.

By mid-afternoon our work is complete and it is time to think about how we will celebrate this wonderful achievement. Giles Clarke, the chairman of the ECB and always a very generous host, has already sent me a text inviting Emma, Tom and myself to what promises to be a splendid dinner at the same swanky restaurant on the river we had been with the Parkinsons a few evenings before. However, I am already in a very difficult position in that, months ago, I promised to speak at a fund-raising dinner for the Australian Cricket Society.

The fourth evening of the Melbourne Test had seemed to be a safe bet then, but now it is a disaster. Of course there is no escape, and having jealously dispatched Emma and Tom to the Rockpool, I head off for my dinner with two hundred Australians. To think I have waited twenty years to celebrate what I have been witness to today, and this is how it turns out! To be fair, they are delighted that I have kept my promise despite everything that has happened, but I make it a strict condition that I am done, dusted and on my way to the other dinner party by a quarter past nine. The deal is struck and by a quarter to ten, I am with the Clarke party and the celebrations, from my point of view, can really begin.

It is a fabulous evening and a fitting way for the day to end. Giles and I have had our differences over ECB policy at times – terrestrial television, the Stanford affair, and the amount of international cricket now being played are three such areas – but credit where credit is due. Four years ago he sat and watched the appalling performance by England in Australia and vowed it would not happen again. Under his chairmanship, England won the Ashes in England in 2009, and have now retained them too.

> "What's quite surprising is that Swann, Anderson and Siddle are the only bowlers who have played in all four Tests." VIC MARKS, TMS

> "Congrats to the England cricket team on retaining the Ashes. It has taken 24 years for England to do it in Australia. Well done." SHANE WARNE TWEET

END OF MATCH REPORT

After Australia were dismissed for 98 in the first innings and England put on 159 for their opening wicket, this Test match was only ever going to end one way – with an England win. It was simply a case of waiting for them to seal victory – and the special moment arrived on Wednesday morning, sparking wonderful scenes as England retained the Ashes for the first time in 24 years.

Their last series triumph Down Under came in 1986/87. My first tour to Australia was in 1991, so I have covered five unsuccessful series. That painful run has finally come to an end. There have been occasional happy moments along the way but generally it is a collection of bad memories and frustration.

Of course, we come here to report impartially but if you are English you want to see England win. So for me, after 20 years of reporting on Australian victories, this was a tremendous thrill. To be out there savouring the moment, being part of the noise and the colour, speaking to the players so soon after the match... it is the reason we all do this job.

Casting my mind back over the English defeats I have witnessed in Australia, the tour here four years ago must go down as the worst of the lot, which makes this result all the more special. Many of us saw the 5-0 reverse coming in 2006/7. We felt the hard work had not been done and there was no excuse for that. We knew how Australia would respond to their 2005 loss, we knew what sort of bulldozer would hit England in Brisbane.

For some reason, England did not see it coming, they had no idea, no preparation at all. It was a totally unprofessional tour. The wives and girlfriends were out there from the start. There was no proper focus. It was a stinker. Many of the other tours left me with a similar feeling. I would crawl into the commentary box of Australia's ABC radio to apologise and make excuses for what was going on in the middle. It was embarrassing and my Australian colleagues would have a good laugh.

But this time the boot is on the other foot and, to be fair, the Aussies have taken it really well. Hopefully they realise it is actually good for them to have lost the Ashes.

They will hate to admit it but they have got so many issues within Australian cricket that need addressing and it is a defeat like this that brings those matters to a head. It means administrators and selectors have to take action rather than only think about taking action. A good old defeat does not do anybody any harm and the Australia fans will be out in force when England return in 2013/14, desperate to see their side win the Ashes on home soil. This result breathes new life into one of sport's greatest rivalries.

Meanwhile, the travelling supporters will be celebrating for some time to come. To put it into context, the last time England won a series in Australia, the Barmy Army had not even been formed! During the intervening time since their formation on the Ashes tour of 1994/5, they have paid all that money, spent all that time, chanted all those songs and drunk all those beers without seeing England win. Twenty-four years since the last success is a very long time indeed.

I am not sure the players fully appreciate the magnitude of their achievement. During the tour, they have been so focused on the here and now that they have not had the chance to look ahead. They would have walked out on Wednesday thinking: 'Let's finish them off'. Suddenly, bang! It has happened and now they will be asking themselves: 'What do we do? How does it feel?' The attitude and spirit within the squad has been spot on.

Team director Andy Flower again showed himself to be an outstanding coach and a superb man manager. But the key to their success has been preparation. It was hopeless in 2006 but this time round they have used it really well, there was no messing about. It generated team spirit and brought players into form. He and captain Andrew Strauss complement each other very well. Strauss is very much respected and liked by his team mates. He has had a very good series as far as the captaincy is concerned. He has made lots of good decisions and enjoyed a spot of luck here and there.

The backroom staff have had a massive impact. They are incredibly dedicated people, very clever, innovative and always looking to improve. They want England to be number one. People raised their eyebrows when Richard Halsall was appointed as fielding coach but just look at the results. England's fielding has been so much better than Australia's – and that has not been the case for 20 years. We used to laugh at Phil Tufnell letting the ball through his legs down in the deep!

It is now Australia who have to go away, look at what England do and try to emulate them in order to improve and catch up with us. That is new territory. For the last 20 years, we have had such talk about needing an academy because Australia have got one, or needing to reduce the number of first-class teams because Australia have not got so many. Well, now we are doing things right and certainly the investment in our coaching staff has paid dividends.

But the series is not over yet. On we go to Sydney for the fifth and final Test. Will England win the Ashes? At the start, I predicted England would win the series 3-1 and I am pretty confident that will still be the case.

AUSTRALIA v ENGLAND

4th Test

Result: England won by an innings and 157 runs

Played at Melbourne Cricket Ground, Melbourne
on 26,27,28,29 December 2010

Toss: England
Referee: RS Madugalle

Umpires: Aleem Dar & AL Hill (TV: M Erasmus)

Man of Match: IJL Trott

AUSTRALIA	Runs	Mins	Balls	4	6		Runs	Mins	Balls	4	6
SR Watson c Pietersen b Tremlett	5	14	12	-	-	lbw b Bresnan	54	136	102	6	-
PJ Hughes c Pietersen b Bresnan	16	59	32	2	-	run out (Trott/Prior)	23	49	30	2	-
*RT Ponting c Swann b Tremlett	10	52	38	2	-	b Bresnan	20	101	73	2	-
MJ Clarke c Prior b Anderson	20	89	54	2	-	c Strauss b Swann	13	81	66	-	-
MEK Hussey c Prior b Anderson	8	44	41	1	-	c Bell b Bresnan	0	9	7	-	-
SPD Smith c Prior b Anderson	6	18	15	-	-	b Anderson	38	91	67	6	-
†BJ Haddin c Strauss b Bresnan	5	23	16	1	-	not out	55	135	93	4	1
MG Johnson c Prior b Anderson	0	8	4	-	-	b Tremlett	6	23	22	-	-
RJ Harris not out	10	39	23	2	-	absent hurt	-	-	-	-	-
PM Siddle c Prior b Tremlett	11	25	15	1	-	(9) c Pietersen b Swann	40	70	50	4	1
BW Hilfenhaus c Prior b Tremlett	0	10	8	-	-	(10) c Prior b Bresnan	0	5	4	-	-
Extras (lb 2, nb 5)	**7**					**Extras (b 1, lb 6, w 2)**	**9**				
TOTAL (42.5 overs)	98					TOTAL (85.4 overs)	258				

ENGLAND	Runs	Mins	Balls	4	6
*AJ Strauss c Hussey b Siddle	69	232	167	5	-
AN Cook c Watson b Siddle	82	212	152	11	-
IJL Trott not out	168	499	345	13	-
KP Pietersen lbw b Siddle	51	127	89	7	-
PD Collingwood c Siddle b Johnson	8	27	15	1	-
IR Bell c Siddle b Johnson	1	19	13	-	-
†MJ Prior c Ponting b Siddle	85	201	119	11	-
TT Bresnan c Haddin b Siddle	4	22	17	-	-
GP Swann c Haddin b Hilfenhaus	22	51	28	3	-
CT Tremlett b Hilfenhaus	4	8	7	-	-
JM Anderson b Siddle	1	5	6	-	-
Extras (b 10, lb 2, w 3, nb 3)	**18**				
TOTAL (159.1 overs)	513				

Eng	O	M	R	W		O	M	R	W	
Anderson	16	4	44	4		20	1	71	1	(1 w)
Tremlett	11.5	5	26	4	(1 nb)	17	3	71	1	
Bresnan	13	6	25	2		(4) 21.4	8	50	4	(1 w)
Swann	2	1	1	0		(3) 27	11	59	2	

Aus	O	M	R	W		O	M	R	W	
Hilfenhaus	37	13	83	2	(1 w)	-	-	-	-	
Harris	28.4	9	91	0		-	-	-	-	
Johnson	29	2	134	2	(2 nb, 2 w)	-	-	-	-	
Siddle	33.1	10	75	6	(1 nb)	-	-	-	-	
Watson	10	1	34	0		-	-	-	-	
Smith	18	3	71	0		-	-	-	-	
Clarke	3.2	0	13	0		-	-	-	-	

FALL OF WICKETS			
	Aus	Eng	Aus
1st	15 (1)	159 (2)	53 (2)
2nd	37 (2)	170 (1)	99 (1)
3rd	37 (3)	262 (4)	102 (3)
4th	58 (5)	281 (5)	104 (5)
5th	66 (6)	286 (6)	134 (4)
6th	77 (4)	459 (7)	158 (6)
7th	77 (7)	465 (8)	172 (8)
8th	77 (8)	508 (9)	258 (9)
9th	92 (10)	512 (10)	258 (10)
10th	98 (11)	513 (11)	-

MELBOURNE MILESTONES

Ⓜ **Australia's first innings total of 98** all out came in 42.5 overs at a run-rate of 2.28 per over. Having prided themselves on increasing the tempo in Test scoring rates over the past decade, this was their lowest run-rate in an innings lasting 40 or more overs since they made 280 in 125.3 overs v Pakistan at Karachi in 1998/99 at a rate of 2.23 per over.

Ⓜ During his first innings of 69, **Andrew Strauss** passed 6,000 Test runs, becoming the 11th Englishman to reach this milestone. With the help of the proliferation of Tests in recent times, he is the fastest to reach 6,000 runs in terms of time from debut. He was playing Test cricket for 6 years, 220 days at the time. The previous quickest was South Africa's Graeme Smith who took 6 years, 287 days to reach the mark.

Ⓜ **England took a first innings lead** without losing a wicket. This was the 21st time that this had occurred in Test cricket and the fourth time by England:

Against	Venue	Season	Opp total	1st wkt	Batsmen
Australia	Adelaide	1911/12	133	147	JB Hobbs and W Rhodes
Australia	Melbourne	1911/12	191	323	JB Hobbs and W Rhodes *
Bangladesh	Lord's	2005	108	148	ME Trescothick and AJ Strauss
Australia	Melbourne	2010/11	98	159	AJ Strauss and AN Cook

* Hobbs and Rhodes did it in consecutive Tests.

Ⓜ **England finished the first day** on 157/0 in reply to Australia's 98 all out. This is only the second time in Test cricket that a team batting second had a first-innings lead and all ten wickets in hand at the end of the first day's play. The other occasion, which had a remarkably similar scoreline at the end of the first day, was New Zealand with 160/0 in reply to Pakistan 104 at Hamilton in 2000/01.

Ⓜ **Strauss and Cook compiled their tenth century opening partnership**. They were the second English pair after Hobbs and Sutcliffe and the seventh pair overall. The only other all left-handed pair with ten century opening partnerships is Matthew Hayden and Justin Langer. The most century opening partnerships after the Melbourne Test were:

Batsmen	Inns	Unb	Runs	Best	Avg	100	50
DL Haynes/CG Greenidge (WI)	148	11	6482	298	47.31	16	26
H Sutcliffe/JB Hobbs (Eng)	38	1	3249	283	87.81	15	10
ML Hayden/JL Langer (Aus)	113	4	5655	255	51.88	14	24
MJ Slater/MA Taylor (Aus)	78	2	3886	260	51.13	10	16
AJ Strauss/AN Cook (Eng)	86	2	3678	229	43.78	10	14
V Sehwag/G Gambhir (Ind)	61	3	3505	233	60.43	10	19
SM Gavaskar/CPS Chauhan (Ind)	59	3	3010	213	53.75	10	10

Ⓜ **Jonathan Trott became the sixth England batsman** to score three centuries in his first five Ashes Tests. The others are Wally Hammond and Herbert Sutcliffe (4 each), Bob Woolmer, Chris Broad and Michael Vaughan (3 each). Trott had a career record of 1,600 runs at an average of 64.00 after the Test. Only two England batsmen had better career averages after 17 Tests: Herbert Sutcliffe (80.90) and Wally Hammond (67.56).

Ⓜ **Matt Prior passed 2,000 Test runs** during his first innings of 85. He is the fifth Englishman to score 2,000 Test runs when playing as a wicketkeeper. As at the end of the Melbourne Test the Englishmen with most runs as a wicketkeeper were:

Name	Years	M	Inns	NO	Runs	HS	Avg	100	50
AJ Stewart	1990-2003	82	145	15	4540	173	34.92	6	23
APE Knott	1967-1981	95	149	15	4389	135	32.75	5	30
TG Evans	1946-1959	91	133	14	2439	104	20.49	2	8
LEG Ames	1929-1939	44	67	12	2387	149	43.40	8	7
MJ Prior	2007-2010	39	60	11	2030	131	*41.42	3	16

Ⓜ **Prior's partnership of 173 with Trott** for the sixth wicket was an England record at the ground. The previous best was 140 by Patsy Hendren and Maurice Leyland in 1928/29.

Ⓜ **England's first innings lead of 415** was their fifth highest in Tests and their second highest against Australia:

Lead	Venue	Season	Team	Totals 1	Against	Totals 2	Result
702	The Oval	1938	England	903-7*	Australia	201 & 123	England won by an innings and 579 runs
563	Kingston	1929/30	England	849 & 272-9*	West Indies	286 & 408-5	Drawn
424	Leeds	2007	England	570-7*	West Indies	146 & 141	England won by an innings and 283 runs
420	Lord's	2005	England	528-3*	Bangladesh	108 & 159	England won by an innings and 261 runs
415	Melbourne	2010/11	England	513	Australia	98 & 258	England won by an innings and 157 runs

Ⓜ In addition to taking two catches, **Peter Siddle** put in a sterling effort to take 6 for 75 in England's first innings. These were the eighth best bowling figures in Test cricket in a total of 500 or more:

Bowling	Name	Team	Against	Venue	Season	Total
8-143	MHN Walker	Australia	England	Melbourne	1974/75	529
7-109	MJ Hoggard	England	Australia	Adelaide	2006/07	513
7-153	GD McKenzie	Australia	England	Manchester	1964	611
7-159	DG Phadkar	India	West Indies	Madras	1948/49	582
7-187	B Yardley	Australia	Pakistan	Melbourne	1981/82	500/8*
7-188	Danish Kaneria	Pakistan	Australia	Sydney	2004/05	568
7-189	WJ O'Reilly	Australia	England	Manchester	1934	627/9*
7-220	Kapil Dev	India	Pakistan	Faisalabad	1982/83	652
6-75	PM Siddle	Australia	England	Melbourne	2010/11	513

NINE

FOURTH TEST INTERLUDE

"We have got to try to restore some pride in Sydney ... unfortunately the way we have played we might have turned a few people off."

SHANE WATSON

DAY 59 **30 December 2010**

Melbourne airport is pandemonium with thousands of English supporters all trying to cram on to flights to get out of Melbourne and up to Sydney in time for New Year. The airport is absolutely choked with supporters still in the mood to party and in great spirits. It feels like the time to put a false beard on. Mind you it does set the scene for an England triumph – this whole travelling circus flogging its celebratory way up to Sydney.

DAY 60 **31 December 2010**

New Year's Eve is always a very special event in Sydney and every four years we are lucky enough to be in town for one of the greatest fireworks displays on the planet. By far the best way to enjoy the spectacle is from a boat on the Harbour and the BBC contingent is invited aboard one such vessel, chartered by one of the many companies that are hosting cricket supporters.

It is a long evening – we have to be on the water at 7 p.m, and the small, appetising display at 9 p.m is to be followed at midnight by the main event. Then it is a scramble to get back to shore again and walk through the vast crowds that have packed the parks and shoreline to our hotel. If you love cricket, the traditional Sydney New Year celebration is hard to beat.

Ricky Ponting has already let it be known that he is unfit to play in the Sydney Test, in fact we hear that his fractured finger will require an operation in order for him to be fit for the World Cup, which starts next month. Michael Clarke is confirmed as acting captain, but we have been told that Ponting will remain in and around the dressing room throughout the game.

As a former player, this strikes me as very odd indeed. It gives new-captain Clarke very little breathing space or chance to exert his authority. But more becomes clear during Clarke's preview day press conference, which is bizarre to put it mildly.

The Cricket Australia PR machine is obviously aware of the talk about Ponting's long-term prospects as captain, and has made it clear to Clarke that he must say nothing that might be interpreted by the assembled media pack as him making a pitch now for Ponting's position. This reaches ridiculous proportions when Clarke, age 29, announces that all talk of him succeeding Ponting, age 36, is rubbish because he, Clarke, might very well retire before Ponting! It is all rather silly.

As has become the custom, I am allowed an interview with the captain in the absence of ABC, and I usher Clarke next door into a small unattractive storeroom with concrete walls and various items of unused furniture scattered about. "This is a very special room, Michael," I tell him as I turn on my recorder. He seems surprised and asks for an explanation. "It was here eight years ago that I interviewed Steve Waugh the day before the Test against England," I continue. "And we all know what happened next day, don't we?" Clarke clearly hasn't a clue. "He scored a brilliant hundred from the last ball of the day and saved his position as Test captain," I explain. It takes a moment for the penny to drop. "Oh right," Clarke replies. Then after a pause: "So which chair did he sit in?" I'm pretty sure I point out the right one and, like a shot, Clarke (averaging only 21 in the series) plants himself firmly into the chair, confirming that, like many cricketers, he is highly superstitious.

Interview over, it is time for two very unusual team photographs with both Australia and England lining up wearing pink caps. The Sydney Test has become completely associated with raising money for breast cancer research and support, and specifically for the McGrath Foundation, which was set up in memory of the late Jane McGrath, wife of great Australian fast bowler Glenn, who died from the disease in 2008, aged just 42.

Everything is pink, even the stumps and the match sponsor's logos (normally a bright red). The spectators are encouraged to wear pink during the match, but on the third day in particular as this will be the Jane McGrath Day. I have a quick chat with Glenn, who is clearly very driven and focussed on the aims of the Foundation. Unsurprisingly, he is most perturbed by the current slump in Australian cricket. However, he is not concerned enough to be tempted into coaching their bowlers. He has recently remarried and seems to be contentedly settling into home life again.

Also worthy of note is the fact that Ashley Kerekes (aka @theashes) has made it to Australia with her boyfriend on an all expenses paid trip. She is already tweeting away, plugging every manner of business that has sponsored her entirely unexpected holiday in Australia. It is hilarious, frankly – and I'd much rather @EllaW638, who is still up each and every night tweeting scores over by over, was recognised instead. This really says a great deal about today's commercially driven world. Anyway, Ashley and I will finally meet during the Test.

DAY 61 1 January 2011

A very pleasant day spent with the family on Bondi Beach – along with five thousand Australians. Sometimes this job has its perks.

It is only a couple of days before Emma and Tom go home and, with the advent of the New Year, I feel it is time to re-assess my on-tour fitness regime. The truth is I stuck to it pretty well until Emma arrived, and even while she has been here, I have done a bit. Looking back, I did run most days in Perth, Adelaide and Hobart. But once the Tests started in earnest, my efforts have dropped off somewhat, unlike the England management who really take their running seriously. Andy Flower often runs back from the ground to the England team hotel. In Hobart I once, a little shame-faced, came back in a taxi at the end of the day's play to spot Andy flogging across the Tasman bridge – an incredibly bleak, wind swept 1.4km traffic-filled monster. Other members of the England management set-up (the bowling coach, the physio and the doctor) ran up Mount Wellington and back. So my little twenty-minute jog around Hobart Quay is all rather pathetic.

However, I remember that when the England players were having breakfast in the hotel in Hobart, I walked past them very obviously while on the way out for a run with all my gear on. Goochy smiled and gave me a big thumbs up as well as an encouraging "Go on mate, good on yer."

I shall start my fitness program again when I arrive on the Subcontinent for the World Cup.

AUSTRALIAN CRICKETERS I HAVE FEARED

Tom Fordyce| 1 January 2011

I've never believed in aliens. I stopped being scared of monsters at the age of six, well nine. But there is a bogeyman who has struck fear into me for most of my adult life, and he wears a baggy green cap. An unrelenting destroyer of Ashes dreams, impervious to anything thrown at him, the Aussie cricketer was everything his English counterpart appeared not to be: hard-nosed, aggressive, and indomitable under pressure. The names changed and the series went by, but the menace remained constant. That is until now.

It first struck me on the final day in Brisbane, and then in the aftermath of that glorious, ghost-slaying win in Adelaide. Perth put it out of my mind, but it was there again from the first morning in Melbourne and hasn't gone away since: I am no longer scared of Australian cricketers. It isn't just that England have been left holding the Ashes in three of the past four series. Nor is it that, for the first time in almost a quarter of a century, they will leave these shores with heads held high rather than tails between legs. It's that, of the 17 players Australia are likely to have used by the end of the Fifth Test, not a single one makes me want to hide under the bed sheets.

Mike Hussey has been wonderful, of course, but he's more to be admired and liked than feared. The rest of them? Once upon a time, the sight of Ricky Ponting marching to the crease was enough to trigger dread thoughts of runs plundered and matches stolen away, but not any more. Shane Watson makes runs but seldom big ones. Ben Hilfenhaus looks like a student teacher, Phillip Hughes his errant pupil. Mitchell Johnson? *He's* more scared of what will come out of his hand than any batsman is.

It feels dangerous to talk in this fashion. Such is the power of Australia's decades-long dominance that even musing internally on such topics makes you afraid of some supernatural revenge, the mockers as surely placed on English hopes as if it were back at Trent Bridge in 1989 or Adelaide in 2006 all over again. It isn't, and you shouldn't be. Michael Clarke could yet hit a match-winning, captain's innings. Johnson may randomly shift into gear and blow the tourists' top order away again, resulting in England losing the match and ending the series tied. It could happen again but the old aura is strangely absent. Maybe in four years time the Barmy Army will be booing Steve Smith and Usman Khawaja to the crease, terrified of the hell they are about to unleash.

In the meantime, by way of laying some ghouls to rest and reminding myself how delightful it feels to be finally free of the shackles of the last 24 years, I've put together a list of those who scared before. It's OK, they've all retired.

Merv Hughes

How the young Fordyce laughed when a bloke who liked like a Victorian ironmonger first waddled into Ashes cricket and found himself promptly smashed all around the Gabba by a paunchy, mulleted Ian Botham. Hughes came into that 1986 Ashes tour having gone 1 for 123 on his Test debut and went out of it in no better shape, taking just 10 wickets for 444 runs across the series and going for 22 in that single Botham over alone.

With Bruce Reid at the other end, he formed a cricketing incarnation of Jack Sprat and his wife, a cartoon character with a figure to match and as much chance of becoming an international strike bowler as I had of marrying Kelly leBrock. When he insured the handlebar 'tache for a reported £200,000, his absurdity appeared to have no limits. How gullible could I have been? In the three Ashes series that followed, Merv the Swerve took 65 wickets, including 31 in the 4-1 thrashing of 1993 alone, and made mincemeat of knock-kneed English batsmen with a barrage of sledging almost more brutal than his bouncer.

Glenn McGrath

This bloke doesn't look all that threatening, I remember thinking. He's not that fast, his approach to the wicket is a bit pigeon-toed, and his track record as a kid wasn't all that good. Talk about false impressions. By the end, after 157 English wickets at a cost of just 20 apiece, even the sight of McGrath loosening up was sufficient to induce a crushing depression. His action looked nothing like the destroyers of the preceding years like Waqar Younis, Curtly Ambrose, or Malcolm Marshall but the result was the same. He dismissed Mike Atherton 19 times in 17 matches – that's a lifetime of dismissals! But to single out just one victim is to underplay the damage he did to legions of English stooges. The noise of ball hitting stump during that spell of 5 for 2 at Lord's in 2005 remains my aural definition of doom.

Steve Waugh

A large chunk of the school holidays of 1989 were spent staying with my Irish granny in her small bungalow on the Essex coast. Absentminded at the best of times, her extreme forgetfulness in those declining years meant that I could spend as much time as I liked watching that summer's Ashes on TV. There was nothing else to do, after all. Social workers should have stepped in. My memories of the period are now reduced to two things: Terry Alderman, trapping Graham Gooch lbw with such regularity that it might as well have been an endless replay of the same delivery, and Steve Waugh batting. And batting. And batting.

He hit 177 not out in the First Test, 152 in the next. At one point his average was over 250. Alderman popped into the Test Match Special box in Perth a few weeks ago. He was fat, and had a bad beard. It made me feel a little bit better. Waugh is not fat. Neither does he look a roadie for Fairport Convention. That summer was only the start for him. I could talk about the 16 consecutive Test victories, or the images of him hoisting the little urn aloft, or the way he belted Richard Dawson for four off the last ball of the second day at the SCG in 2003 to bring up his century when he was supposed to be finished. I could, but I'd rather not. It's better to move on.

Ian Healy

Australian wicketkeepers in the 1980s were as memorable as Big Fun, and lasted about as long. Instantly forgettable names like Wayne Phillips, Mike Veletta, Greg Dyer, and Steve Rixon. Then came Ian Healy. It wasn't so much his glovework that left deep mental scars as his batting. Just when you thought England had Australia on the ropes, with the top order gone, Healy would stroll out to turn the innings around with biff after bash. He only averaged 30 in Ashes Tests. I've had to double-check that, because it doesn't seem enough. That was his power. He could make even cold hard facts look like lies.

Adam Gilchrist

Thank the Lord for that, Healy's retired. This Gilchrist bloke looks alright, but he'll never be as good as Healy. No, he was much, much better. Did his 152 off 143 balls at Edgbaston in 2001 hurt more than his 57-ball century in Perth in 2006? You might as well ask whether I'd rather be punched by Muhammad Ali's right hand or his left. If his dismal trot of 2005 hadn't happened, I wouldn't be able to say his name out loud without my voice quavering. For that – and many other things – thank you, Freddie Flintoff.

Shane Warne

When he was spinning it he was terrifying to watch. When he wasn't, it was almost worse. How could we be getting out to a ball that wasn't even doing anything? It didn't matter. The combined forces of Merlin and Potter couldn't have cast a more effective spell over the English batsmen. To see Robin Smith, scourge of the West Indies, proud precursor to KP, reduced to thrusting his pad blindly down the line of an entirely different delivery was to see a hero unmasked. To see Gatting and Strauss left motionless as the ball turned sideways was to believe in witchcraft. Warne's future away from cricket wasn't bright. His future was orange. But with a past like that, who cares?

IN THE COMPANY OF A LEGEND

Tom Fordyce| 2 January 2011

It's been a giddy few weeks out here during this Ashes series. Innings victories, record-breaking partnerships, calamitous collapses and the urn retained by England for the first time in almost 25 years. The thrills and spills have been wonderful, but at times it's been hard to keep the heroics in perspective, which is why, today, I find myself in a small room at the Australia Club in the centre of Sydney, sitting opposite an avuncular 88-year-old Ashes legend by the name of Arthur Morris.

If you don't know who Arthur is, you're going to enjoy meeting him. In five series against England, three of them victorious, he scored 2,080 runs at an average of 50.74 with eight centuries. Only three Australians have a better average against England. The principal among them, Don Bradman, was Arthur's best mate.

He was playing grade cricket against adults at the age of 12, and on his first-class debut aged 18 he scored centuries in both innings, the first man in history to do so. All of which makes it somewhat surprising to hear that in his first two Tests, when he scored just 2 and 5, he was "scared as hell".

"It was quite something," he says. "When I walked out, I thought, 'what the hell am I doing here? I think I've got an inferiority complex. It probably comes from growing up in the country where you think everyone in the city must be so superior in every way to us country fellas. I would smoke a cigarette before going out to bat. It was the thing to do in those days, we got it from looking at the movies: the drama of it, standing on the balcony, drawing on a cigarette and saying, 'Ah, what shall I do today?'"

Never has self-doubt been less appropriate. Arthur announced himself in Ashes cricket with 503 runs in the first series after the Second World War, averaging 71 and scoring centuries at Melbourne and Adelaide, but it was during Australia's 1948 tour to England that he secured his place in the pantheon. These were the Invincibles, arguably the greatest side in cricketing history, unbeaten in 31 first-class tour fixtures, feted by royalty, watched by record-breaking crowds, 4-0 victors in the Ashes series and heroes to a nation for ever more. The tour lasted 144 days. They played on 112 of them. At five weeks, the boat journey to England alone lasted longer than most modern tours.

"Now that really is living," chuckles Arthur. "Somebody asked me one day, how did you keep fit on the ship? I said to him, 'Well, we'd get up at 9 o'clock and have breakfast, and then I'd wander up on deck and read for a while, and then the bar would open at 12 o'clock so we'd have a few drinks, and then we'd have a snooze for a few hours in the afternoon, and when you woke up you'd put your black tie on for the first cocktail party of the evening...' We'd have about three weeks after our arrival before we really started playing, so you'd play a bit of squash, practise as much as you could. It was a long tour, so you didn't want to be in shape to run 100 yards at the start of it."

Morris, a short, left-handed opener, was top scorer in the series, pulling and lofting his way to 696 runs at an average of 87 in Tests, and was the only player on either side to score three centuries. "A menacing bouncer colliding with Morris's bat was like a rocky fist against an iron jaw," wrote Australian journalist Ray Robinson.

"We had huge crowds everywhere, mainly because Don Bradman was the big star," says Arthur, still in tip-top shape as he approaches his tenth decade. "We were just the supporting actors. And so we should be, because he was a great player and a great man. It was a marvellous series – it was hard going, because playing six days a week wasn't easy. We had a very good team, and England had some great players too – Hutton, Compton, Edrich, Evans, Bedser. We were able to be a little bit better, and we did very well. The more you play the better you become."

Arthur's modesty tells a fraction of the tale. The team's finest hour came during the Fourth Test at Headingley. Set 404 to win from just 345 minutes on the final day, they were expected to capitulate by lunch. "Don wrote in his book, 'I fear we will be beaten tomorrow', and I thought that was an understatement," remembers Morris. "My feeling was, 'I'm bloody sure we're going to get beaten tomorrow!' It was a dry wicket, and the ball was starting to turn a bit."

When Bradman joined his young team mate at the crease, with English golden boy Denis Compton bowling his tweakers, 347 were needed in 257 minutes. "Don wasn't picking his wrong 'un. Jack Crapp dropped him at slip off a very difficult chance, but I was determined to get at Denis. After lunch I really got after him, and drove him off the back foot, lofted. I gave him a bit of a thump, a bit more than Don at that stage. But I had to get him out of the way, so we did. We really battled on the first morning, and we thought after lunch, there might be a chance we can draw this. We got on top, and suddenly there was this thought: we could win this. And that's how it happened. It's just one of those things. We were both on top of our games, we had a bit of luck early on, and their captain had to keep his field up because he was going for a win. So if you got one through the field it was four."

Bradman suffered a fibrositis attack during the innings and Morris had to shield him from the strike. Despite that the pair added 167 during the afternoon session. By tea Morris was on 150, his side 288/1. When he was eventually dismissed for 182, the partnership of 301 in 217 minutes had taken Australia to within 46 runs of victory. "It was a battle all the way through," recalls Morris. "It's never been done before or since, to get 400 on the last day to win a Test match." He beams at the memory. "I think it was the best I ever batted, and it gave me a great thrill, because when everybody believes at the start of play that you must be beaten, you do too. The English movie people were there, so I thought, let's see how this looks. But I've never seen one second of it. I think they got it and destroyed it!"

It took me a little time to track Arthur down, four weeks, in fact. There were old phone numbers, dead ends, out-of-date addresses and shrugged shoulders. Even Cricket Australia had no idea where he was. Then a week ago, during a trip to the National Sports Museum at the MCG, made possible by the early finish to the Fourth Test, I spotted a glass case containing his bat, whites and pads from the 1948 tour. A plea to the manager led to a word with the archivist and a number for a retirement complex two hours outside Sydney. Seldom has a little wait and effort seemed so worthwhile.

The last Test of that 1948 tour was also Bradman's final Test match. As every cricket follower knows, he needed to score just four runs to end his career with a Test average of over 100. Morris had the best view in the house. "Years later, I was at a luncheon, talking to a chap who didn't know much about cricket. He started talking about how Bradman got a duck in his last match. So I said, 'Yes, I was there.' And he says, 'Really? What were you doing over there?' And I said, 'I was up the other end.'

"He went, '"Oh. Did you make any runs?' I said, 'Yup – 196 '. And I thought I'd emphasise it, so I added, 'run out'. The fact of Don getting the duck was the big thing. Even if I'd got 450 I don't think people would have realised I was playing. When Don had arrived at the crease, the English players had all gathered round and sung 'For he's a jolly good fellow', and it was all very nice.

I don't think anybody knew what that duck meant. I'm not sure Don knew. He got two very good balls. The wicket was doing a bit, obviously, nice and juicy for Eric Hollies, and he bowled a leg-spinner and then a wrong 'un right on the right spot, and he bowled Don. There was silence, complete silence. I think if it happened today, the greatest player of all time out like that, poor old Eric wouldn't have got more than 20m before they'd all have tackled him and jumped on his back, and the place would have gone mad. But there was just silence, although I think I did hear one voice say, 'Jolly well bowled, Eric.'"

Bradman was a constant in Morris's life: childhood hero, team captain, and lifelong friend. "I'll never forget the first time I met him. My family lived in Dungog, a little town of 2,500 people. He was travelling through, and there was a little afternoon tea laid on for him," he says. "I'm eight years old, walking round in no shoes or socks, a kid in the country. My father, a schoolteacher, was mad-keen on cricket. He said to me, 'Arthur, meet Mr Don Bradman'. And my first words were, 'I'm pleased to meet you, Mr Bradman'. There I was, a child; never in a million years would I dream that I would play under him as captain."

As a baggy green stalwart, Morris enjoyed opening with Sid Barnes. But he loved batting with Bradman. In partnership the pair averaged 108, two boys from the backwoods putting the world's best bowlers to the sword. "We must have liked each other, because neither of us ran the other bloke out!" he smiles. "There was none of this going up and down the pitch talking to one another; we just left each other alone. Occasionally you might say something, like 'Help'!"

He laughs again, and looks out of the window across to the Opera House and naval dockyards at Woolloomooloo. "Don was everybody's idol," he continues. "To play with him was a wonderful experience; he was a great captain, a good friend, a person you could rely on. I had great admiration for him. He was a very private person, a very shy person too. He would come down to the pub with us for a couple of drinks after the day's play, but there wasn't really much he could do. He used to get 100 letters a day, at least, and he would answer the lot of them. He had this great belief that he wanted to represent Australia on the cricket field, and he wanted to be somebody who would be remembered and admired. Maybe it comes from our old days, but we wanted to prove that we're equal to everybody else, that we're good, decent people, and that's the way he was."

Morris could find cricket a difficult sport. "We'd go out to the middle as openers, Sid and I, and we'd discuss what we were going to do, but it was a nerve-wracking thing. Particularly when you get out for a duck, and you have to walk all the way back again, and you're waiting for them to clap but nobody does, and you can see them all thinking, 'What an idiot this bloke is...' You can feel all those little stabs coming at you from everywhere." But he also enjoyed himself immensely. The stories from those tours are legion: the adoration of a public starved of fun and frivolity by the preceding wars, trips to shows and nightclubs, the team bus stopping so often at pubs that its average speed was reported to be 16kph.

"Occasionally, as I was single, I might take a girl out for dinner or something... They never came off my tab, of course, they probably came off the captain or the vice-captain's tab, but anyway…"

It was on a trip to London's Victoria Palace theatre during the Ashes tour of 1953 that Morris first noticed a young English showgirl named Valerie Hudson, a dancer with the Crazy Gang vaudeville show. After a hurried courtship, the pair married. Valerie, just a few years after moving to Australia with her new husband, was diagnosed with breast cancer. She tried to keep the illness secret to prevent it distracting Morris from his cricketing career but failed. Her decline and death hastened his retirement at the age of just 33.

Half a century later, Morris is one of the three oldest Ashes combatants left alive, beaten to an unwanted honour by Sam Loxton and Reg Simpson. He has few regrets. "I would have liked to have captained Australia regularly, but it wasn't to be," he shrugs cheerily. "I was vice-captain to Lindsay Hassett for five seasons, and we were a good team. I never lost a game as vice-captain."

He can even laugh at the way he was sacked as skipper of New South Wales, informed by local pressmen rather than the committee, supposedly given the boot for the crime of being 'too genial'. "I know there were a couple of selectors who didn't like me," he says, chuckling again. "One of them certainly thought there was something of a stink about me. He said, 'Morris wears these suede shoes, and he even wears his jacket with a cut up the back or something'. He probably thought I spoke with an English accent, and that would have been an absolute disaster."

Morris was named in both Australia's Team of the Century and the country's Cricket Hall of Fame. As he sees me to the door, we discuss the series in progress and the prognosis for this week's Fifth Test at the nearby SCG. "The English side is one of the best sides I've seen," he says. "I think they're well run, the captain I admire very much: his attitude, his control of the game and the team. They've bowled well, they've fielded well and they've batted well. That's not to knock our fellas, they're a good side, but they've run into a really top one."

Frank Tyson called Morris "one of cricket's patricians... endowed with a genteel equanimity, without seeming aloof or less than cordial and friendly". John Arlott, doyen of *Test Match Special*, said he was "one of the best-liked cricketers of all time: charming, philosophical and relaxed". As I wave farewell at the door, I find myself smiling in silent agreement.

EVE OF MATCH THOUGHTS

The destiny of the Ashes has been secured until England and Australia meet again in 2013, but there is still a huge amount riding on this final Test. Michael Clarke, Australia's stand-in captain, is drawing strength and optimism on this being the start of a new year as he aims to draw the series. Andrew Strauss is talking more in terms of making history as the first England team to win a series here for 24 years as he stresses the point that merely to draw would now be a great disappointment.

Certainly, Clarke has the tougher hand of the two. Not only must he come from behind, but he does so with two debutants in key positions: Usman Khawaja at number three, and Michael Beer, the solitary spinner, who has played only seven first-class games in his life, and not one of them at the Sydney Cricket Ground.

However, as can often be the case with new managers taking over at struggling football clubs, simply the introduction of a fresh face can be enough to galvanise a beaten team. England need to show that they can string consistent performances together. Their recovery following their drubbing at Perth was very impressive, but equally as worrying was the manner in which they subsided in that game.

This is a terribly long tour with T20s, and a ridiculous seven one-day internationals to come before embarking on the World Cup. Much is made of momentum, and certainly tours can assume a life of their own. Who knows, another good performance here could be the spark to igniting a truly historic winter?

One of the most important and decisive differences between the two teams has been the platform provided by the opening batsmen. Apart from the first innings of the series, when Jonathan Trott walked out to the middle at 0/1, Strauss and Alastair Cook have generally laid a solid foundation, passing 100 together twice. In contrast, Australia do not have a single century opening stand to their name, and have been 5/1, 0/1, 2/1 and 15/1. This has exposed Ricky Ponting much earlier than he would like, and his poor form has also brought Clarke to the crease all too soon.

Their lack of runs is one of the main reasons for Australia's failure in this series – and let's not forget that Clarke carries that poor form with him into his first Test as captain. However, this is a big opportunity for him. Far from universally popular, he has the chance to show Australian supporters that there is a bright future.

There is a widely held view that for a team to head off into a brave new direction, new leadership is essential and if Clarke and Australia perform well enough to salvage some pride and reputation here, Ponting could well find himself eased out of his job in Test cricket.

TEN

SYDNEY TEST

"I don't think there's a crisis in Australian cricket at all."

Michael Clarke

DAY 63 **3 January 2011, Fifth Test – first day**

Holiday over and it is time for Emma and Tom to return home today. Normally this would be a really sad moment, but I am due to head back myself at the end of this game, so I'm sure I can survive another week by myself. We say our goodbyes, and then Geoffrey Boycott and I drive to the Sydney Cricket Ground (SCG). It is a short drive, but long enough to catch up with his latest adventures on the golf course.

> *"If England win the series, you have to go out into the middle and do it [the Sprinkler Dance]. That's what you've said."* Michael Vaughan, TMS

Morning session: At lunch – Australia 55/1, Watson 19*

There is some moisture in the pitch and cloud cover overhead, but Clarke decides to bat first. I wonder had this not been his first Test as captain if he might have been brave enough to put the opposition in? England certainly do not complain, but fail to take a wicket until the last over of the morning when Tremlett finds some bounce and Hughes edges to Collingwood at third slip for 31.

> *"The SCG's a good place to play spin on the first two days because of the bounce, the ball just sits up. Swann's got to work hard on his accuracy. But if Australia get a big score then the pitch will deteriorate and that will give Beer and Smith a chance."* Michael Vaughan, TMS

Afternoon session: At the close – Australia 134/4, Hussey 12*

Rain and bad light curtail the day but not before England have made serious inroads into Australia's middle order. Shane Watson gets another start, but edges Bresnan to first slip for 45. Steve Waugh's lucky chair fails to change Clarke's fortunes (maybe it was the wrong chair after all) and he is caught at gully for 4. After a promising start, and in front of his desperately anxious mother, Usman Khawaja makes 37 in his first Test innings – but then shows his inexperience by sweeping Swann to square-leg as light rain and bad light threaten. The umpires confer immediately and that is the last ball of the day.

After three weeks of having my family with me, the hotel room seems very quiet when I get back this evening. That said, a solitary evening with room service (the first in ages) is not so unwelcome either. I watch a fascinating documentary about Sir Don Bradman. My word, he played some shots. And his cover drive was second to none.

"Australia will want their tail to wag and I think 280-300, if they get it, will be a good score." Michael Vaughan, TMS

END OF DAY REPORT

Australia's stand-in captain Michael Clarke's decision to bat first was a brave one. But a more experienced captain would probably have chosen to bowl first. The overcast, murky conditions, the threat of rain throughout most of the day – it felt like a bowl-first day. And with Australia 134/4 at the close, Clarke might rue his decision.

My gut instinct was confirmed as the ball duly moved around off the wicket from the first over. However, the toss is a very different situation when you have your neck on the line for one match, with Australia needing to win to draw the series, just in case it backfires and ends your prospects of taking over from Ricky Ponting full-time. So it's easy to understand why Clarke went for the safer option, but Tim Bresnan confirmed after the day's play that England would have put Australia in to bat if they had won the toss.

England did not bowl as well as they have done in the previous four Tests and they were a little too short at times. But they also could have had three wickets before lunch. What was clearly noticeable was the Australian top-order's belligerence and determination in not playing any unnecessary shots. They were able to leave a lot of deliveries in the first session, too many in my opinion, but there was a palpable sense of cutting out any risky strokeplay and concentrating on a long stint at the crease. However, that said, in declining to play their shots, it meant the scoreboard moved very slowly.

This perfectly highlights the lack of confidence in the Australian top order. When the scoreboard is not ticking over and you lose two quick wickets, as they did before the rain set in, you're still in no-man's-land. Clarke's tepid series continued with a rash shot outside off stump but debutant Usman Khawaja showed plenty of promise during his 95-ball innings. One aspect of his technique he has to work on is his footwork, as he looks vulnerable on the off stump. He gets forward nicely but doesn't go back and squares himself up with both feet pointing down the track when the ball holds its line, which will cause trouble in the future.

His dismissal was probably down to inexperience more than anything else. England applied plenty of close-field pressure with Graeme Swann applying the screw and the young left-hander went for a big hit, but instead top-edged his sweep to Jonathan Trott at square-leg just before rain curtailed the day's play. Khawaja is a qualified pilot and has shown a good temperament for Test cricket. As a pilot you have to make decisions under pressure and he clearly has the right temperament to succeed.

Traditionally, Sydney has been the most helpful pitch in Australia for spinners. But Australia last played two spinners at the ground nine years ago when Shane Warne and Stuart MacGill were in their prime. And only India have used two spinners since then because the SCG surface is becoming more seam-friendly. New South Wales' Sheffield Shield games at the ground have been played on green-tops and the drier, dustier pitches are becoming an increasingly rare sight. But it's hardly surprising when Australia's spin resources are at an all-time low.

DAY 64   4 January 2011, Fifth Test – second day
Morning session: At lunch – Australia 230/8, Johnson 30*, Hilfenhaus 14*

Another morning dominated by England's bowlers – this really has been one of the patterns of this series. Only 9 are added before Haddin, who has been a constant source of aggravation for England both at the crease and from behind the wicket, edges Anderson to Prior for 6. With the new ball looming, Strauss tosses the ball to Collingwood in the hope that he can conjure up a bonus wicket, and the old campaigner succeeds in having Hussey play an innocuous delivery off the inside edge and inside thigh on to his wicket for 33. This makes Australia 171/6 and the timing is perfect as one end is now opened up, but although Smith launches a huge drive at Anderson and is taken at third slip for 18, Johnson digs in and with Hilfenhaus finds a determined partner. They add 41 before the interval after an extended session of 36 overs.

> "What gets me is the lack of technique in Steven Smith and Phillip Hughes. So much poor footwork. Usually Australian players have got pretty good techniques." GEOFFREY BOYCOTT, TMS

Afternoon session: At tea – Australia 280, England 73/0

I think Strauss makes a mistake after lunch and bowls Bresnan rather than Tremlett from the Paddington End, where there has been some sharp bounce. 19 runs are taken from Bresnan's two overs before he is relieved, but the 50-partnership has been raised. The stand reaches 76 before Johnson is bowled, slogging at Bresnan for 53 and Hilfenhaus is last out for 34 to give Anderson his fourth wicket. 189 for 8 has become 280 all out. As at Perth, Johnson has been allowed to add too many with the tail, and we all know what happened after that.

But England's openers again get off to a confident start – another pattern we have become used to – and by tea England are 207 behind after just 16 overs of their innings.

> "I'll give Australia a little clue: don't bowl short on this wicket. So far it's cost them about 30 runs. They should be just trying to hit the top of off stump as many times as possible." MICHAEL VAUGHAN, TMS

Evening session: At the close – England 167/3, Cook 61*, Anderson 1*, England are 113 runs behind

Australia fight back with three key wickets in the session to leave the match in the balance. Cook has a piece of luck on 46 when he is apparently caught at mid-on, which would have given Beer his first Test wicket, only for umpire Bowden to question whether Beer had, in fact, bowled a no-ball. One replay is enough to reveal that Beer has committed a spinner's cardinal sin and overstepped. He is devastated at being denied his first victim, but only has himself to blame. Cook, meanwhile, has become the youngest batsman, after Sachin Tendulkar, to reach 5,000 Test runs and beat the aggregate of 633 runs scored in an Ashes series set by Michael Vaughan in 2002/03.

With the score on 98, Strauss is bowled by a good delivery from Hilfenhaus to end a lively knock of 60 from only 58 balls. Trott is out to his sixth ball, edging Johnson on to his wicket and just before the close, Pietersen – who had scampered to 36 from only 20 balls – top edges a hook off Johnson and is taken by Beer at long-leg. It seems such a waste yet again. As nightwatchman, Anderson has not failed to survive until the following morning, and he does so again.

I dine at Woolloomooloo and spend much of the evening comparing photos of our dogs withthe host's wife. I am badly missing mine. Home soon.

> "If he doesn't swing it in, Johnson's a lovely bowler to face as you know he's going to give you something on a plate to hit." GEOFFREY BOYCOTT, TMS

END OF DAY REPORT

What a fascinating Test match – a good, old-fashioned, see-saw game in Sydney, the first time we have really seen anything like this in the series. Australia will possibly feel they had the better of the second day, especially following the enterprising 76-run ninth-wicket stand between Mitchell Johnson and Ben Hilfenhaus as well as the late wicket of Kevin Pietersen, but England had their opportunities and didn't take them.

At 189/8, England really should have had Australia all out for 220 or less. In no way should the hosts have been allowed to score 280, a total which could be so crucial in what is likely to be a low-scoring game. Australia were there for the taking. England know what Johnson can do with the bat, he's a dangerous hitter when he's on a roll.

But I don't understand the theory of pushing men back on the boundary when you are in such a dominant position. I don't like the tactic because as a bowler, it really is confusing and you start to question your own abilities, despite what the scorecard is telling you.

There was a point just after lunch when I thought England had lost a grip on the situation with Johnson and Hilfenhaus at the crease. A thick outside edge off Hilfenhaus's bat flew past gully's hand off James Anderson's bowling. However, the fielder didn't look right. England usually have two players who field in the gully, Kevin Pietersen or Anderson. Anderson was bowling, but it wasn't Pietersen standing there, it was Tim Bresnan. What was he doing there?

England like to stick rigidly to their plans, but at 189/8 with an unpredictable pitch, why do you make batting easier for the number eight? Why treat Johnson any differently from the top-order batsmen who have struggled? It's not so much about giving away the singles to get the number ten on strike but more the change of mentality from everyone in the field.

It's difficult to tell what a good score on this surface is – although Andrew Strauss made it look positively flat with a superb run-a-ball innings. It was only a fantastic delivery from Hilfenhaus that ended his innings. A total of 350 is possible, but England will need Alastair Cook to drop anchor, something he is more than capable of doing after surpassing a number of impressive records on the third day.

As ever, Pietersen's dismissal will divide opinions. After stressing his insistence he had become a more responsible batsman following his superb double century in Adelaide, he once again fell to a high-risk stroke at a crucial stage of the game. But that's KP. I have spoken about this particular subject on numerous occasions – and I doubt this will be the last time. It's not too dissimilar to watching David Gower in his pomp, when he edged a needless push outside off stump to the slips. It's more the frustration of being denied the pleasure of watching one of the best batsmen on the planet in full flow.

`DAY 65` 5 January 2011, Fifth Test – third day

It is often the case that by the end of a long tour I start to lose my voice, and it is now barely hanging on by a thread. It is simply due to talking too much and, what with doubling up on ABC, it is hardly surprising. The problem is that should England win this game, the commentary of the final ball will be played all over the world because it will be England's first series win here in such a long time. And my producer, Adam Mountford, has already told me that he wants me to be on air when it happens. It is time for the old favourite, honey [a natural antiseptic], lemon and hot water. A kind waitress in a street-side café in the Rocks provides me with the essentials, which I then take to the SCG. It is amazing what a difference this particular concoction makes to a croaky voice, and it's a preparation that has served me well all over the world.

Morning session: At lunch – England 277/5, Cook 130*, Bell 20*

The SCG is a vista in pink as Australia continue to fight hard. England lose Anderson for 7 and then Cook appears to give Beer his first Test wicket when, on 99, he turns the ball to Hughes at short-leg. The fielder immediately celebrates with the delighted bowler, but Cook is going nowhere and it is noticeable that Haddin does not look so sure either.

Replays, shown on the big screen of course, confirm that the ball bounced in front of Hughes, who is now roundly booed by the Barmy Army. In the television box, Sir Ian Botham says Hughes is cheating. This is a big call, but Cook survives and nonchalantly turns a ball to leg to complete his third hundred of the series. Finally, Beer gets a wicket when Collingwood launches a desperate slog and holes out at mid-on for an ugly 13, an innings and dismissal that says everything about his overall poor form and low confidence. In the press box there are already rumours circulating that Collingwood is to hold a press conference on the day after the game, presumably to announce that he is retiring from Test cricket. It wouldn't be a total surprise. England are still 54 behind with five wickets left when Collingwood is dismissed, but Cook and Bell inch England to within three runs of Australia's total at the interval.

> "If Alastair Cook can pass Wally Hammond's record of 905 runs in an Ashes series, I think England might win. Come on Alastair, come on." GEOFFREY BOYCOTT, TMS

Afternoon session: At tea – England 378/5, Cook 188*, Bell 62*, England lead by 98 runs

With the exception of Perth, Australia have failed to take the must-win sessions in the series, and this is another example. Presented with the opportunity to restrict England's lead to manageable proportions, they fail to take a wicket all afternoon – not helped, in our view in the box, by their persistence in bowling over the wicket to Cook. He is much more comfortable with this angle of attack, and with Bell adds 101 runs in the session. It is another reminder of Cook's transformation as a batsman from the one who was stuck in his crease and unable to score a run last summer, to this confident player off front and back foot. Batting is all about footwork, and there can be no better tutorial for a young batsman than the 'before' and 'after' videos of Cook. He might need them himself, sometime, if it all goes awry again.

Meanwhile I finally get to meet Ashley Kerekes, who is a confident and entertaining 22-year-old. She talks on *Test Match Special* with great enthusiasm and a measure of bewilderment about her sponsored journey from Westfield, Massachusetts to Sydney, Australia. She has spent the day sitting with Steve Waugh, who also gave her a personal tour of the Museum, and she has even interviewed the Australian Prime Minister, Julia Gillard. Whatever you think of her great good fortune in being flown half-way around the world to one of the greatest sporting arenas there is, it is an amazing story – both incredible and ridiculous in equal measure. I also consider it to be one-in-the-eye for the handful of people who had earlier, and in something of an unrestrained manner, accused me of 'cyber bullying' Ashley when I first mentioned her on Twitter in Brisbane. She is having a ball.

Evening session: At the close – England 488/7, Prior 54*, Bresnan 0*, England lead by 208 runs

Cook finally departs for 189, bringing his total time at the crease in this series to 36 hours and 11 minutes and his aggregate to 766 runs at an average of 127. What a triumph it has been for this delightful young man – who seemed nailed on for another double hundred until he drove Watson to Hussey in the gully.

Following their stand of 154, there is further controversy surrounding the dreaded Decision Review System when, on 67, Ian Bell is given out off Watson to a catch off an inside edge. The Australians and, indeed, umpire Dar are all confident Bell made contact with the ball, but Bell wanders down the wicket and holds a lengthy discussion with Prior mid-pitch before calling for a review. Yet again Hot Spot shows nothing, although there was a sound – clearly heard by the Australians. On the evidence of Hot Spot, Dar overturns his decision and Bell is reinstated. Minutes later, on our television monitors, up pops the familiar graphic showing Snicko had detected the sound of an edge: Dar's original decision had been correct. It seems that batsmen are now gambling on Hot Spot – hoping it will not betray them. I am convinced batsmen have come to the conclusion that it is worth the risk of a review when Hot Spot alone is the decider of their fate. A perfectly good decision has been overturned. I hate this system so much. The technology is simply not good enough yet and the administrators are currently chasing an impossible dream.

Not a single Australian applauds Bell when he reaches his first century in 18 Tests against them. I have noticed quite a lot of that in this series – it is a bad sign, indicative that the spirit of the cricket, as many of us understand it, is being eroded. But on this occasion the Australians have a right to be disgruntled. Bell is out just before the close for 115, highly satisfied, I'm sure, but I wonder if, deep down, his conscience is entirely clear.

I attend a supporters' evening with David Lloyd and Andy Stovold, the old Gloucestershire batsman, who I haven't seen for years. With fast bowler David 'Syd' Lawrence acting as master of ceremonies, it is a fun evening. These sessions always remind me of the importance of county cricket to English cricket lovers. I think we panellists find it difficult to answer the audience's many questions about the county game. Frankly, none of us simply see enough of it these days because England play so much. Nevertheless, morale is sky high amongst the loyal band who are enjoying the trip of a lifetime. More honey and lemon please.

"If England don't win this series 3-1 it will be a travesty. They have been so dominant in every facet of the game." MICHAEL VAUGHAN, TMS

END OF DAY REPORT

I can't see any other outcome other than England winning the Fifth Test and the series following another dominant day with the bat in Sydney. It's not a question of if but when – it could even happen on day four depending on how long England decide to bat on Thursday.

While Ian Bell stroked superlative off drives for his 12th career Test century, his innings was tainted by yet more controversy caused by the Decision Review System when, on 67, he nicked a catch to wicketkeeper Brad Haddin off Shane Watson. As many will know, I am not a fan of it and its implementation at all.

The trouble is that people now have entrenched views about the system – some people think it's brilliant and the answer to eliminating poor umpire decisions while the critics, like me, say it is creating more doubt and controversy, the very elements it is supposed to eradicate. My view is that the International Cricket Council has a panel of specialist full-time umpires who are the best in the world, and in whom they should have one hundred per cent faith and conviction regarding every decision they make. Unfortunately Aleem Dar, a brilliant umpire, was persuaded to overturn a correct decision because the technology proved inconclusive.

For those of you who ask why Snicko, the technology which detects the noise made by outside edges, was not used by third umpire Tony Hill, it's because it is not instantaneous. It requires up to seven minutes to process, too long for the ebb and flow of a Test match. However, its results show that Hot Spot is not the panacea for detecting outside edges.

It's the second time in this series that Hot Spot has proved inconclusive. Remember Michael Clarke on day three of the First Test? You could argue Bell's reprieve balances out Clarke's fortune at the Gabba, but it goes deeper than that. I think the players sense there is an inherent flaw in Hot Spot – we've seen it's not one hundred per cent accurate – and will do what they can to exploit that.

The ICC's implementation of the system is made the more baffling because it is not being used in the enthralling series between South Africa and India right now. Apparently, the Indian players are not keen on the system. If you are going to implement such an important development, then it should be used consistently and uniformly.

What didn't help Bell's cause was his reaction after he was given out by umpire Dar. He wandered down the pitch, had a chat with Matt Prior before signalling the 'T' some ten seconds or so later. If he knew he hadn't hit the ball, he would have instantly made the signal – like Alastair Cook did during his 148 in Adelaide when he was given out following a deflection off his shoulder. If you watch a lot of cricket, you get to know the reaction of players when they are out – and I think everyone knew Bell was out. But you can't really blame Bell in all of this – he did what any other batsman would do in that situation.

The error compounded a miserable day in the field for Australia stand-in captain Michael Clarke. He really showed his inexperience by constantly chopping and changing his bowlers around and using the wrong end, the Randwick End, for his quicker bowlers. It also showed Ricky Ponting's critics that changing the captain is not the sole answer to Australia's problems.

I thought Michael Beer bowled well in what was only his eighth first-class match. I like his attitude. However, the selection of Steven Smith continues to baffle. After he was moved down the batting order from six to seven because he was out of his depth, he didn't bowl his leg-breaks until the 102nd over. The only reason I can think why he was held back for so long was because Clarke wanted to keep control and not give away easy runs, which really doesn't say much about the captain's faith in the young leg-spinner.

As for Alastair Cook, what more can you say? He has never played as well in his life. It has been a phenomenal display of concentration and application of skill. That really is his game, although Australia have not bowled particularly well to him. And to think his place was in serious doubt in last summer's series against Pakistan after going eight innings without a score above 29. There had even been talk of moving Jonathan Trott to open alongside Andrew Strauss with Eoin Morgan slotting into the middle-order at the start of the tour following Cook's two failures against Western Australia. But ever since then, after a century against South Australia, Cook has never looked back and has shown what a wonderful player he is.

"So farewell then, Sgt Colly. I'll miss your catches, your rearguards and your ginger forearms." TOM FORDYCE

DAY 66 **6 January 2011, Fifth Test – fourth day**
Morning session: At lunch – England 636/9, Swann 33*, Tremlett 7*, England lead by 356 runs

Paul Collingwood chooses this morning to announce that he is, indeed, retiring from Test cricket. It is the right decision made at precisely the right time, which allows the focus tomorrow to be on England winning the series. He averages 40, which is not the benchmark it used to be with flatter pitches and fast, re-laid outfields, but he has been a terrific fighter who has used every ounce of his talent in England's cause.

Has a better fielder every played for England? I doubt it. He will, of course, continue to play for England in one-day cricket, but this sensible move allows him to call time on his Test career at the moment of his choosing, rather than, inevitably I suspect, being dropped next summer.

Prior presses on to his fourth Test hundred, batting in the bristling, aggressive manner that makes his absence from the one-day squad so frustrating – not least to him. He has had a really good tour behind the stumps, too. But the fact is that he has had plenty of opportunities in one-day cricket and has batted in just about every position in the order without taking his chance to make any of them his own. Typically his century comes from only 109 balls, and it really is the perfect innings for the occasion.

Australia look terribly ragged and undisciplined now, and after Prior is caught behind hooking a high bouncer for 118, the stage is set for Swann to rub salt into the gaping wounds. He flails the bat and at lunch England have their highest score ever in Australia.

> "Is this the innings where Khawaja can give the Aussie fans a little hope that they can build a side around him?" MICHAEL VAUGHAN, TMS

Afternoon session: At tea – England 644, Australia 77/2, Khawaja 4*, Clarke 19*

Hilfenhaus finally ends Australia's misery by dismissing Tremlett for 12 shortly after the break, to leave Australia 364 runs behind, and with 59 overs of the fourth day remaining. It has been a chastener – every Australian bowler has conceded more than 100 runs and it does show that a change of captain doesn't necessarily mean a change of fortune.

It is now merely a question of when England will win the game. Their task is made simpler by a crazy misunderstanding between Hughes and Watson – their second in consecutive games – which results, comically, in Watson being run out by the length of the pitch for 38. Hughes doesn't last much longer, caught behind off Bresnan for 13 and England's chanting supporters fancy the thought of it all ending today.

> *"I never thought I'd see the day when three or four Bangladesh players would get into this Australian team. Until they realise that, they're in denial." Michael Vaughan, TMS*

Evening session: At the close – Australia 213/7, Smith 24*, Siddle 17*, Australia are 151 runs behind

This is the final lesson for Australia from England's outstanding pace attack, and Anderson in particular. The subject is reverse swing, and the ball is hooping about all over the place. Unfortunately, almost always a reverse swinging ball raises questions about how the bowler is making the ball swing – is it by fair means or foul?

Umpire Bowden shows considerable understanding of the situation in what is still a febrile atmosphere. Applying a good deal of low-key common sense, he carries out periodic inspections of the ball, and no action is required. It is good professional umpiring; any suspicions the Australians might have had are quashed immediately.

The youthful Khawaja is dealt with brilliantly by several inswingers, and then the one that swings the other way, which he dutifully edges to Prior. Clarke also falls victim to Anderson for 41 and when Hussey cuts Bresnan hard to Pietersen at gully for 12, Australia are 161/5 and England start to think about claiming the extra half-hour to win the game this evening. Haddin makes 30 and with the shadows lengthening, in comes Johnson to a roof-raising rendition of the Mitchell Johnson Song. Bellowed in perfect unison, complete with thousands of swaying arms to the left and then to the right, it is an astonishingly hostile entry for an Australian to make on one of his home grounds. Take a look for yourself on YouTube. The poor man looks absolutely shattered and is promptly bowled first ball.

Smith and Siddle ensure that we must all come back tomorrow, which turns out to be a good thing for those of us who would otherwise have been out on the outfield for the presentations – minutes after the close of play, the heavens open. We would all have been absolutely soaked.

I am becoming seriously worried about my voice now. Please, I cannot miss out tomorrow on commentating on an England victory for the first time as correspondent, can I? I am supposed to speak to more supporters this evening, but cry off because I simply cannot take the chance. No wine tonight either – just plenty of honey and lemon. The matter of my foolish promise to do the Sprinkler Dance rears its head – again – on Twitter. Clearly there is going to be no escape; it is amazing how many people are adamant that I should make a fool of myself. I confirm that, come the end of the match, I will indeed perform the Sprinkler, but that I would like to do it with Swann. Can the power of Twitter sort it? With that, chuckling to myself, I lower the lid of my laptop. I hate to think how many messages Swanny will have in the morning!

> *"If I had ten innings batting on this pitch, I'd expect to get nine good scores."*
> GEOFFREY BOYCOTT, TMS

END OF DAY REPORT

Apart from the poor performance in Perth, England have been streets ahead of Australia and that was the case again today when the home side were given an object lesson in reverse swing bowling. Chris Tremlett, James Anderson and Tim Bresnan were all absolutely outstanding at getting the old ball to move both ways in the air. It is one thing to make the ball swing in reverse, it is another to do it with the skill, accuracy and variety that they did here.

They put intense pressure on Australia's two inexperienced batsmen Phillip Hughes and Usman Khawaja. They were all over them and it was another disciplined, ruthless and faultless performance by England in the field. James Anderson has become brilliant at hiding the ball during his run-up in the manner of great swing bowlers like Waqar Younis.

If you have a ball that is reversing, it is generally pretty obvious which is the rough side and which is the shiny side and any experienced batsman will look at that and know where the ball is going to swing, so part of the art is all about deception. Anderson runs up with the ball in his left hand, transfers it to his right, and manages to hide it right up to the moment of delivery. The whole thing is incredibly clever, all 'smoke and mirrors'.

Inevitably with reverse swing you get mutterings in dark corners about ball-tampering, but umpire Billie Bowden inspected the ball and was perfectly happy with the condition of it. England's seamers once again took the glory but off-spinner Graeme Swann has also played a crucial role in their success throughout this series.

At the beginning of the series we all expected the Australian tactic to be to get after Swann and try to knock him out of his rhythm, but most of the time the Australians have not been in a position to attack anybody. Swann has been able to come on and just bottle up an end, which is important when you are only playing four bowlers. This has allowed captain Andrew Strauss to rotate his quick bowlers.

Matt Prior also deserves credit today for his century, which saw England to a total of 644. He hits the ball hard and is incredibly strong square of the wicket on either side. He scores his runs quickly and that is exactly what England wanted. They wanted to make sure they weren't bowled out cheaply to give the Aussies a glimmer of hope but also wanted to rattle on and get as many runs as they could.

Prior has also been fantastic behind the stumps, making only one mistake all series, a missed stumping. Some 18 months ago he was in the West Indies and he was all over the place, but now he is up there as one of the best and it is all down to hard work. It will frustrate Prior that he is not in the one-day side but he has had lots of chances and has not taken them. He might argue that it was the old Prior who had lots of chances and not the new one, but first Craig Kieswetter came in and took his place and then Steve Davies.

Finally, a word on Paul Collingwood, who has announced his retirement from Test cricket. He has been a great servant to England. He was never the most talented batsman but he worked really hard at his game and got the best out of himself. His fielding has been brilliant and he has taken two blinding, match-winning catches this series.

His departure is the right thing to do because he has not shown any form at all here with the bat, but it is so nice for a sportsman to choose his own time and bow out on a high, rather than wait for the rug to get pulled away from under his feet by the selectors. Collingwood and England can celebrate having achieved something very special over here. It's going to be a huge party tomorrow.

DAY 67 7 January 2011, Fifth Test – fifth day

"The Barmy Army have had a huge effect here, particularly the effect they've had on Mitchell Johnson. They're going to have a great day."
Michael Vaughan, TMS

Morning session: Australia 281 all out, England win by an innings and 83 runs, England win the series 3-1

The quiet night in has done the trick. The voice is holding up and I am determined to do a good broadcasting job and to really enjoy everything about what is, after all, going to be a momentous day from an England perspective. I have spent five Australian tours apologising on ABC Radio for the sometimes quite abject performances by successive England teams – so today's outcome is going to be something to savour. I am not going to crow on ABC, but neither am I going to understate England's achievement. My first on-air slot is scheduled after the first 20 minutes of play, and I have been told that there is an ABC listeners' competition to select a composite team that matches the one selected by the commentators for us to chew over. Time for some fun with Kerry O'Keeffe, who I have loved working with all series.

First, I ask on air what the prize for the lucky winner is, and I am told it is a cricket bat autographed by the current Australian team. The same team, incidentally, pictured wearing their pink caps on the back page of today's *Sydney Morning Herald* under the headline 'Our Worst X1 Ever'. Ouch!

"Oh," I reply. "Well don't worry. A sheet of sandpaper will only set you back 50 cents. You'll have them off in no time."

Now it is time for the composite team: "Strauss or Hughes?" I ask. "Strauss," agrees Kerry. "Cook or Watson?" "Cook," agrees Kerry. And on we go with Trott and KP. "Number five is tricky," I concede. "Collingwood or Hussey? Catches win matches. Hussey hasn't scored a run for two matches and Colly also got Hussey out yesterday." Reluctantly Kerry agrees to come back to number five for further consideration, and we continue with Bell, Prior, Swann, Anderson, Tremlett and Bresnan with Finn twelfth man. "We need to get *one* Australian in," I taunt. "What about Blackwell?" There is a pause. "You know, Alex Blackwell. She scored 42 for the Australian women's side against England in Perth yesterday. She can be the Aussie." And with that I shake hands with Kerry and make my farewells to the ABC listeners as I leave the box. I only hope they took it in the spirit in which it was intended.

There is rain around, and with an estimated twenty thousand England supporters crammed into the Trumper Stand at the far end waiting for the big moment, Siddle and Smith make everyone hang around for a while. They put on another 44 before Swann removes Siddle for 43. Hilfenhaus edges Anderson to Prior and with one wicket left, Simon Mann graciously yields the microphone to allow me to end twenty barren years. (He can do it next time!)

Mercifully, the voice holds out just long enough for the dramatic moment. There is some pressure on because, as the commentator, you only have one chance to get it right – you simply cannot make a mistake like calling a wrong name. It needs to be a smooth twenty seconds or so, containing all the relevant information without any hesitation: it is going to be replayed goodness knows how many times in the future. I find myself leaning forward, focussing absolutely on the ball as it leaves the bowler's hand. In fact, the final dismissal is an unusual one – Beer plays Tremlett into his wicket, a method of dismissal that always takes a split second longer to register in the commentary box. I'm happy with the soundbite at the time, but make a mental note to have a listen later to make sure it is OK.

Then it is on to the outfield for the final time to report on the celebrations. It is bedlam down there as usual with stewards, photographers, players, officials and goodness knows who else rushing about but, again, I've got good old Victor Marks with me for support. We are standing just yards from the podium as Michael Vaughan hands Strauss the crystal urn. BANG! We are almost blown backwards by the explosion of brightly coloured paper, ticker-tape and tinsel that are launched dramatically skywards – it really is a blizzard. It makes opening our mouths and broadcasting extremely difficult. As it clears and the players stop jumping about on the stage and begin their lap of honour. James Avery gestures that we are free to join them and interview freely.

I start with Bell, who batted so well here and then move among the team as they walk slowly around the edge of the SCG soaking up the applause. The noise is absolutely deafening and it is one of those moments when my hair seems to be standing on end. I'm anticipating a Sprinkler performance when the team arrives in front of the Barmy Army, but they keep going. I talk to Prior and congratulate him on his innings and, moving on, to Swann who reveals that the team performance of the Sprinkler was a one-off at Melbourne, and won't be repeated here. "But Graeme…?" "And you can tell your Twitter lot to stop spamming me," he says. "I'm not doing it. But you make sure you keep your word."

The crowds on the field are thinning now. I find Anderson near the famous green-roofed pavilion. "Don't worry about the Sprinkler, Aggers," he says, "you're in decent nick for your age!" It begins to dawn on me that there really is no way of getting out of it. Finally I catch up with Strauss, who reveals that he has just broken the stem of the replica wooden urn in the course of the celebrations. Nevertheless, I doubt I've ever interviewed a happier man. All the hard work, the sleepless nights, the doubts after Perth, his own awful failure in the first over at Brisbane; now all firmly pushed into the background and he is able simply to enjoy the moment.

When we are finished, there is nowhere else to go. It really is now or never and I hand Victor my headphones, microphone and box of tricks, and Steve my iPhone, on which to record the full drama of my Sprinkler. The backdrop is the Members Pavilion, which is rather appropriate and with Victor commentating on *Test Match Special*, I duly keep my word – which is more than Shane Warne ever did with his bet about wickets. Later, when we are off air, I post the footage on Twitter and am dumbfounded by the number of hits. By early evening, it is well in excess of 100,000 helped, I suspect by Stephen Fry's post: *"Oh my lordy lord. Aggers does the Sprinkler. I've died and gone to heaven."* Amusingly, Strauss is captured on the film in the background having a conversation with ECB chief executive David Collier who draws the captain's attention to my hopeless effort. Strauss looks thoroughly bemused.

Contrary to public expectation, there isn't a massive party this evening. My most important mission after we leave the ground for the last time is to nip to a shop to buy some Ugg boots for my daughters. I will be leaving the hotel for the airport before the shops open in the morning, so my girls have the Australian batsmen and England's quick bowlers to thank for giving me the time to pick up the present each will receive on Monday.

My final work obligation is on the Radio 5 live breakfast programme with Mark Pougatch. We are on the pavement of a busy street in the Rocks, England fans are wandering about, catching a last glimpse of the iconic Harbour scene and we can clearly hear the Barmy Army celebrating in a hotel they have taken over on Circular Quay.

Over the last twenty years I have often dreamed about today – of England winning here. There have been many times I have questioned whether it is something I would ever see for myself. I wondered how we would celebrate and how it would feel. As it turns out, it isn't a wild and crazy night at all. Instead, when we pack up from the pavement, it is a quiet dinner with my BBC colleagues that brings the day, and the tour, to an end. It is a time to chat about everything we have seen and done, and to thank each other for the teamwork and camaraderie without which a successful and enjoyable tour is impossible.

Surrounded by friends toasting an England win, coupled with a sense of relief that it is all over and with the huge excitement of finally going home in the morning I can't help thinking that it doesn't get much better than this. The day has, indeed, been all I hoped for.

> *"I think that even in most of our wildest dreams, three innings victories was more than we could have expected."* Geoffrey Boycott, TMS

END OF MATCH REPORT

England's performance in Australia has been really awesome. They did not just win an Ashes series here for the first time in 24 years, they became the first team ever to consign Australia to three innings defeats in a home series. The celebrations in Melbourne were big – and there were more people there too – but the scenes in Sydney were unprecedented. It was an astonishing moment for all the England fans to witness when Andrew Strauss held up the little urn.

When you see the England captain jumping up and down on the podium with all the ticker-tape blowing around, what they have achieved out here finally sinks in. And they had to come back from two crisis moments to do it, on the third evening in Brisbane when it looked like they would lose the First Test, and then in Perth, where they were heavily beaten. It was a serious achievement.

For the last few days in Sydney, Australia have looked like a beaten side. They have gone. We have seen England be that way before, but this is a different England, who have played some ruthless cricket. There has been tremendous concentration in the batting, superb application in the field, with run-outs and catching that put them and Australia miles apart.

As for the bowling, the reverse swing in the last two games, led by James Anderson, has shown Australia how Test cricket has progressed. The Aussies will not thank me for saying this, but they needed a beating like this to look at their game from top to bottom, and put some plans in place to address their problems. England have had to do exactly the same in the past.

They must establish what the best role is for Greg Chappell [the National Talent Manager]. Decisions have to be made over whether coach Tim Nielsen and Chairman of Selectors Andrew Hilditch keep their roles, and there is the issue over the captaincy too.

It is a strange decision by Michael Clarke to resign from Twenty20s just when he has the opportunity to stake a claim for the captaincy across all three formats. Australia have been muddled from the start, in fact ever since I arrived on 1 November. All the focus was on the home team from start to finish. The debate about the make-up of the Australian side was never satisfactorily resolved.

Two England players have produced some remarkable statistics: Alastair Cook hit 766 runs, the second best aggregate by an Englishman in any series, and James Anderson's 24 wickets were the best haul achieved in Australia by an English bowler since Frank Tyson in the 1950s. Let's be clear – these are not passing stats that only interest geeks, these are massive performances.

With Anderson, we always wondered whether he would perform, whether he would get the ball to swing. The results were outstanding: orthodox swing in Adelaide, reverse swing in Melbourne and Sydney, all three of those Tests won by England. England prepare the ball for swing so well, getting it to reverse after just 10 overs, earlier than any other team.

Chris Tremlett and Tim Bresnan have been given opportunities and done well, but Anderson has always been the attack leader. He has been very hostile and aggressive and has got under the skin of the batsmen. When nothing is happening, the England bowlers are very good at building up pressure and containing the opposition batsmen with carefully set fields. It is something the Australians would do well to replicate.

Six months ago, Cook's technique was all wrong. The bat was coming down at the wrong angle, there was no footwork and his head was moving too far towards the off stump. Now he is a transformed player, standing up tall, driving through the covers, and cutting the ball so effectively. As the vice-captain it was important for him to lay to rest the ghosts and ghouls of last summer – and he is a delightful fellow to boot.

My prediction before the series was a 3-1 win to England, and I was pleased to get that right. The England players gave us all what we wanted to see, and it's been noticeable how incredibly relaxed, friendly and happy they have appeared from start to finish.

I promised to do the Sprinkler Dance on the SCG outfield if we won the Ashes, and it was a promise I had to keep. It wasn't at the end where the Barmy Army were located, it was in front of the members. Maybe that was more appropriate, in a way.

"I've just cast my eye over to the Australian team, shoulders slumped, slinking off. This is what England have had to cope with on all those tours over here." VIC MARKS, TMS

AUSTRALIA v ENGLAND

5th Test

Result: England won by an innings and 83 runs

Played at Sydney Cricket Ground, Sydney
on 3,4,5,6,7 January 2011

Toss: Australia
Referee: RS Madugalle

Umpires: Aleem Dar & BF Bowden (TV: AL Hill)
Debuts: Aus: MA Beer and Usman Khawaja

Man of Match/Series: AN Cook

Notes: Strauss scored his 50 off 49 balls
in England's 1st innings.

AUSTRALIA	Runs	Mins	Balls	4	6		Runs	Mins	Balls	4	6
SR Watson c Strauss b Bresnan	45	182	127	5	-	run out (Pietersen/Prior)	38	51	40	7	-
PJ Hughes c Collingwood b Tremlett	31	121	93	5	-	c Prior b Bresnan	13	74	58	1	-
Usman Khawaja c Trott b Swann	37	120	95	5	-	c Prior b Anderson	21	89	73	2	-
*MJ Clarke c Anderson b Bresnan	4	25	21	-	-	c Prior b Anderson	41	96	73	6	-
MEK Hussey b Collingwood	33	113	92	2	-	c Pietersen b Bresnan	12	66	49	1	-
†BJ Haddin c Prior b Anderson	6	15	13	-	-	c Prior b Tremlett	30	51	41	3	-
SPD Smith c Collingwood b Anderson	18	85	53	1	-	not out	54	132	90	6	-
MG Johnson b Bresnan	53	89	66	5	1	b Tremlett	0	1	1	-	-
PM Siddle c Strauss b Anderson	2	2	4	-	-	c Anderson b Swann	43	85	65	4	-
BW Hilfenhaus c Prior b Anderson	34	88	58	3	1	c Prior b Anderson	7	14	11	1	-
MA Beer not out	2	23	17	-	-	b Tremlett	2	9	9	-	-
Extras (b 5, lb 7, w 1, nb 2)	**15**					**Extras (b 11, lb 4, w 3, nb 2)**	**20**				
TOTAL (106.1 overs)	280					TOTAL (84.4 overs)	281				

ENGLAND	Runs	Mins	Balls	4	6
*AJ Strauss b Hilfenhaus	60	92	58	8	1
AN Cook c Hussey b Watson	189	488	342	16	-
IJL Trott b Johnson	0	6	6	-	-
KP Pietersen c Beer b Johnson	36	87	70	4	-
JM Anderson b Siddle	7	41	35	1	-
PD Collingwood c Hilfenhaus b Beer	13	68	41	-	-
IR Bell c Clarke b Johnson	115	296	232	13	-
†MJ Prior c Haddin b Hilfenhaus	118	237	130	11	1
TT Bresnan c Clarke b Johnson	35	116	103	5	-
GP Swann not out	36	47	26	3	1
CT Tremlett c Haddin b Hilfenhaus	12	31	28	1	-
Extras (b 3, lb 11, w 5, nb 4)	**23**				
TOTAL (177.5 overs)	644				

Eng	O	M	R	W		O	M	R	W	
Anderson	30.1	7	66	4		18	5	61	3	(1 w)
Tremlett	26	9	71	1	(2 nb)	20.4	4	79	3	(2 nb)
Bresnan	30	5	89	3	(1 w)	(4) 18	6	51	2	(2 w)
Swann	16	4	37	1		(3) 28	8	75	1	
Collingwood	4	2	5	1		-	-	-	-	

Aus	O	M	R	W	
Hilfenhaus	38.5	7	121	3	(1 w)
Johnson	36	5	168	4	(2 w)
Siddle	31	5	111	1	(1 nb, 1 w)
Watson	20	7	49	1	(2 nb, 1 w)
Beer	38	3	112	1	(1 nb)
Smith	13	0	67	0	
Hussey	1	0	2	0	

FALL OF WICKETS			
	Aus	Eng	Aus
1st	55 (2)	98 (1)	46 (1)
2nd	105 (1)	99 (3)	52 (2)
3rd	113 (4)	165 (4)	117 (3)
4th	134 (3)	181 (5)	124 (4)
5th	143 (6)	226 (6)	161 (5)
6th	171 (5)	380 (2)	171 (6)
7th	187 (7)	487 (7)	171 (8)
8th	189 (9)	589 (9)	257 (9)
9th	265 (8)	609 (8)	267 (10)
10th	280 (10)	644 (11)	281 (11)

SYDNEY MILESTONES

Ⓜ **Australia had scored 171/6 in 80 overs** when England took the new ball. This was their lowest total after 80 overs in a Test innings since 1997/98 when they had 164/4 against South Africa at Adelaide.

Ⓜ **Alastair Cook passed 5,000 Test runs** during his innings of 189. At the age of 26 years, 10 days he is the second youngest player to achieve this. Only Sachin Tendulkar, aged 25 years, 301 days, has reached 5,000 runs at a younger age. The previous youngest Englishman was David Gower, aged 28 years, 123 days.

Ⓜ **Cook's final series aggregate of 766** is the second most for England in a series:

Name	Series	Venue	Season	M	Inns	NO	Runs	HS	Avg	100	50
WR Hammond	v Australia	Australia	1928/29	5	9	1	905	251	113.12	4	0
AN Cook	v Australia	Australia	2010/11	5	7	1	766	235*	127.66	3	2
DCS Compton	v South Africa	England	1947	5	8	0	753	208	94.12	4	2
GA Gooch	v India	England	1990	3	6	0	752	333	125.33	3	2
H Sutcliffe	v Australia	Australia	1924/25	5	9	0	734	176	81.55	4	2

Ⓜ **It is also the third most by an opening batsman** for any country:

Name	Team	Series	Venue	Season	M	Inns	NO	Runs	HS	Avg	100	50
MA Taylor	Australia	v England	England	1989	6	11	1	839	219	83.90	2	5
SM Gavaskar	India	v West Indies	West Indies	1970/71	4	8	3	774	220	154.80	4	3
AN Cook	England	v Australia	Australia	2010/11	5	7	1	766	235*	127.66	3	2

Ⓜ **Cook batted a total of 2,151 minutes** in the series. This is a record for England for any series, passing the 2,006 that John Edrich batted in the 1970/71 series in Australia. The only recorded cases of any batsman batting longer than Cook in a series are Mark Taylor, who batted for 2,283 minutes for Australia against England in 1989 and Mudassar Nazar who batted 2,199 minutes for Pakistan in the home series against India in 1982/83.

Ⓜ **Cook completed 1,000 first-class runs** for the tour, a rare feat in the modern game with very few first-class matches on tours these days outside of Tests. He finished with 1,022 first-class runs on the tour at an average of 85.16. He was the first Englishman to score 1,000 first-class runs of a tour of Australia since Geoff Boycott and John Edrich did so in 1970/71.

Ⓜ **Ian Bell finally made his first Ashes century** in his 31st innings and his 18th match. He had previously scored 11 fifties against Australia. This is the most number of fifties before scoring a first Ashes century for either team, passing the previous record of eight by Mike Gatting.

Ⓜ **Matt Prior became the fifth wicketkeeper** and first Englishman to score a century and take 5 dismissals in an innings in the same Test:

Name	Batting	Dismissals	Team	Against	Venue	Season
DT Lindsay	69 & 182	6 cts & 2 cts	South Africa	Australia	Johannesburg	1966/67
IDS Smith	113*	4cts, 1 st	New Zealand	England	Auckland	1983/84
SAR Silva	111 & 11	3cts, 1 st & 5 cts	Sri Lanka	India	Colombo-PSS	1985/86
AC Gilchrist	133 & 37	4cts, 1 st & 1 ct	Australia	England	Sydney	2002/03
MJ Prior	118	2 cts & 5 cts	England	Australia	Sydney	2010/11

Ⓜ **His 118* was the third highest score** by a number eight batsman in a Test for England and the first century by a number eight batsman for England in an Ashes match. Centuries at number eight for England are:

Score	Name	Against	Venue	Season
134*	H Wood	South Africa	Cape Town	1891/92
128*	MC Cowdrey	New Zealand	Wellington	1962/63
118	MJ Prior	Australia	Sydney	2010/11
113	R Illingworth	West Indies	Lord's	1969
104	TG Evans	West Indies	Manchester	1950
101*	JM Parks	West Indies	Port-of-Spain	1959/60
100*	P Willey	West Indies	The Oval	1980

Ⓜ **Prior's 23 dismissals equaled the third most** in a Test series for England. It also equaled the second most in a series for England against Australia and is the most for England in a five-match Ashes series:

Name	Series	Venue	Season	M	Ct	St	Total
RC Russell	v South Africa	South Africa	1995/96	5	25	2	27
APE Knott	v Australia	Australia	1970/71	6	21	3	24
APE Knott	v Australia	Australia	1974/75	6	22	1	23
AJ Stewart	v Australia	England	1997	6	23	0	23
AJ Stewart	v South Africa	England	1998	5	23	0	23
MJ Prior	v Australia	Australia	2010/11	5	23	0	23

Ⓜ **Prior achieved the double of 250 runs and 20 dismissals** in a series. This is the fourth time that an England wicketkeeper has achieved this:

Name	Series	Venue	Season	M	Runs	Avg	Ct	St	Total
APE Knott	v Australia	Australia	1974/75	6	364	36.40	22	1	23
AJ Stewart	v Australia	England	1997	6	268	24.36	23	0	23
AJ Stewart	v South Africa	England	1998	5	465	51.66	23	0	23
MJ Prior	v Australia	Australia	2010/11	5	252	50.40	23	0	23

Ⓜ **Prior took 11 catches** off James Anderson's bowling in the series. This is the second most dismissals by a wicketkeeper/bowler combination in a series for England. The England record is 12 (9ct, 3 st) by Bert Strudwick of Sydney Barnes against South Africa in 1913/14.

Ⓜ **England added 418 runs** after the fall of their fifth wicket at 226. This is the fourth highest number of runs added after the fall of the fifth wicket in Test matches:

Runs	Total	Team	Against	Venue	Season
474	561	Pakistan	New Zealand	Lahore	1955/56
467	564	Australia	England	Melbourne	1936/37
435	668	Australia	West Indies	Bridgetown	1954/55
418	644	England	Australia	Sydney	2010/11
415	749-9*	West Indies	England	Bridgetown	2008/09

Ⓜ **England's previous best** after the loss of five wickets was 399 v Pakistan at Lord's in 2010. On that occasion England recovered from 47/5 to 446 all out.

Ⓜ **England set new partnership records** at Sydney for the sixth wicket: 154 between Cook and Bell, and the eighth wicket: 102 between Prior and Tim Bresnan. It was the first time in Test cricket that there were century partnerships for the sixth, seventh and eighth wickets in the same innings.

Ⓜ **England became the fourth team** to make four totals over 500 in the same series. Australia achieved this against West Indies in 1954/55 and 1968/69 and South Africa did it in 2003/04 also against West Indies. It was the second time that England had made two scores over 600 in the same series, having previously done this against Australia in 1938.

Ⓜ **Shane Watson** had a good consistent series with the bat, but he has failed to convert scores into centuries. He finished the series with two centuries and 16 fifties in his Test career. Of Australians with 15 scores over fifty in Tests only Monty Noble has a lower conversion rate than Watson's 11.76 per cent. Noble only converted one of his 17 scores over fifty into a century, a conversion rate of 5.88 per cent. On the other hand, Watson's consistency is reflected by the fact that he has reached 30 in 30 of his 49 Test innings, a percentage of 61.22. As at the end of the series only two batsmen in Test cricket history with 40 or more innings had a higher percentage of reaching 30: Don Bradman 66.25 per cent and Everton Weekes 61.72 per cent.

Ⓜ Having threatened his previous top score of 38 at Perth, **Peter Siddle** made a career best 40 at Melbourne and followed it up with another best of 43 at Sydney. His 154 runs in the series came at an average of 19.25. By comparison, Ricky Ponting and Michael Clarke combined for 306 runs at an average of 19.12 in the series.

Ⓜ **The innings defeat** was Australia's third in the series, the first time they had suffered this ignominy. The last time Australia suffered consecutive innings defeats in a series was against England in 1985. England became the second touring team to win three Tests by an innings in a series. The only previous occasion was Australia in South Africa in 1935/36.

Ⓜ Having also won in 2009, **Andrew Strauss** became the third England captain to win series at home and away against Australia. The others are Len Hutton (1953 and 1954/55) and Mike Brearley (1977, 1978/79 and 1981).

Ⓜ **The five spin bowlers Australia used** in the series took five wickets between them at an average of 135.80. Only twice have Australian spinners had a worse combined series return: at home to India in 1985/86 when they took four wickets at an average of 157.75 and again at home to India in 1991/92 when they took three wickets at an average of 160.00.

Ⓜ **No batsman in the top four of the order** made a century for Australia in the series. This was the first time in any five-match series that no top four batsmen made a century for them since the home series against West Indies in 2000/01. It was the first time that no top-four batsmen made a century in an Ashes series for Australia since 1956. In that particular series no Australian batsman scored a century.

Ⓜ **Ricky Ponting's** overall record as captain is quite impressive. However, it is not so good when he has played without Warne or McGrath in the team. This applies both to his captaincy results and his own batting:

	P	W	L	D	Runs	Avg	100	50
With both	24	19	0	5	2677	78.73	10	11
Warne only	10	8	2	0	847	47.05	3	4
McGrath only	1	0	1	0	23	11.50	0	0
With neither	42	21	13	8	2995	41.02	6	20
Totals	77	48	16	13	6542	51.51	19	35

AFTERWORD

DAY 68 **8 January 2011**

I am sitting in Singapore airport where I have about six hours to fill before I board my flight to the UK and home – at last. I have just logged on to Twitter on my phone and it is all about the IPL auction. I tweet words to the effect that as we have witnessed some truly terrific and memorable Test cricket over the last couple of months, you can keep your vulgar IPL auction. Unsurprisingly, I get a certain amount of feedback from a number of my Indian followers, who assume that I am in some way jealous about the 'success' of the IPL or that I must be miffed about the IPL auction's virtual disregard of any English players, while there are vast sums of money being laid out for players that I have never heard of from South Africa and so on. My correspondents totally miss the point.

I admit that I have never been a great fan of IPL, and cannot help but think the players are going to India for one reason only, the cash; in fact my tweet describes it as money for old rope. When compared with what we have just seen for the last six weeks, it seems to me to be very sad that cricket feels the need to dress itself up in this rather ostentatious way, and I am repulsed by the obscene amounts of money being thrown around. Cricket at its best doesn't need any of that at all, and I think this Ashes series has really proved it.

Unintentionally, my Twitter antagonists have, in making me think about proper Test cricket versus the IPL and Twenty20 in general, caused me to reflect more thoroughly on my 68-day Ashes journey. What made it such a momentous series? What was the difference between the sides and which players really delivered when it mattered? And what are the reasons for the decline in Australian Test cricket? So let's start with the England players, and who better than the successful captain, Andrew Strauss.

There have been questions about Strauss's on-the-field captaincy, but never questions about his conduct off it. Nor has there ever been any dispute about how good a man-manager he is. I would argue that he has earned a huge amount of respect as a captain. The players like him; they don't necessarily have to like a captain, but I think it's a bit of a bonus when they do. They admire him as well, but there has been some talk about whether tactically he is good enough. Personally, I have some sympathy for the modern Test cricketer aspiring to captain the team in that they really don't have much of a chance to learn the art of leading a side as they very rarely captain their counties these days. They are often lumbered with the Test captaincy and expected to be the next Ray Illingworth or Mike Brearley in a matter of a Test or two, something that simply isn't fair.

I thought Strauss had a really good series as captain. There was some thoughtful field placings, particularly the men catching at short extra-cover and short mid-wicket. For a while there, I thought I was back at prep school where we used to have a silly mid-on and a silly mid-off because no one hit the ball very hard. But Strauss had thought through these positions for full-swing bowling – either the orthodox swing or reverse swing. And sure enough these positions did produce wickets. It must also have helped to have fielders right in the Australian batsmen's faces. In other words they were quite intimidating field settings as well. When the pressure was on Australia's batting – as it was virtually throughout the series – those men standing there gave England a presence in the field undermining an already fragile Australian batting mentality.

The way that Strauss used Graeme Swann was excellent, and you could see Swann responded after, what was for him, a slow start. Any questions about Strauss's captaincy in Test cricket were answered on this tour. There are still one or two to be settled about his one-day captaincy, and we'll see more of that in the World Cup, but I think that his Test captaincy was spot on. The fact that he was able to bring his team back from the defeat in Perth says a lot about him and Andy Flower, the team director. Of course Andy had the most awful start to the series when he had to have potentially life-saving surgery to remove a cancerous growth from his face during the First Test match. In fact both men had poor starts, with Strauss out third ball of the series and Flower laid up in hospital. But they came through it, each the stronger in his own way, and as the series progressed, I think they showed a huge amount of character.

Andy Flower's decision to send his front-line bowlers early to Brisbane to acclimatise was entirely vindicated, despite receiving quite a critical response from some of the travelling media at the time. He took another controversial decision to give the players so much time off to spend with their families in Melbourne after losing so badly in Perth. Other coaches would have had them in the nets with hours of fielding drills – a sort of naughty-boy nets, but there was none of that. It was, as Ian Bell explained to me, preparation as usual, which ultimately proved to be exactly the right way to do it. And, of course, Flower's input into team selection had a huge impact. They chose Chris Tremlett when forced to replace Broad, which was the right decision, and they rested Steven Finn – itself a brave decision because Finn had contributed hugely to the series up to that point. So all the way down the line, at the critical moments when decisions had to be taken, things very much went England's way. Often they weren't easy decisions to make, but Strauss and Flower made the right ones.

James Anderson really came of age. What really impressed me about him on this tour was not so much his orthodox or reverse swing, but that he bowled so few bad balls. It has been a bit of a weakness of his in the past: he had his off days, really inexplicable bad days, which made him, in a way, rather unreliable. As a captain you would always want to pick him, expecting much of the time that he would be a terrific bowler, but you knew that there were going to be days just around the corner when he was going to be all over the place. In Australia he didn't have any of those days at all; he just bowled absolutely brilliantly throughout. He was very aggressive – which, on a personal level, is very unlike him. As an individual he is the one of the quietest people you will ever meet, a very shy chap really, particularly when dealing with the media. By all accounts he is a bit more of a character in the dressing room where he is what they call the bowling captain. He has been given authority and is relishing the responsibility. It always makes me chuckle to see him bristling and sledging because it is so unlike the quietly spoken lad from Burnley we see in press conferences. But it clearly gets him going. And it certainly got right up the Australians' noses, absolutely under their skin. They managed to get thoroughly wound up about it from Perth onwards. Anderson has emerged as one of the leading swing bowlers in the world. His challenge now is to keep going – particularly maintaining his newly-found accuracy, making him England's first-choice bowler. It is also worth noting that his fielding is outstanding – wherein lies a danger. It is tempting for Strauss to have him in key positions, but I really think it has got to the time now, particularly when he's bowling, when Anderson needs to have a rest – down at fine-leg or standing in the gully, rather than rushing around all over the place. I think England need to look after him a little bit. In conclusion, Anderson absolutely deserves his wings, as it were, after this tour.

Alastair Cook was an entirely transformed player, a complete revelation. I have seen him score all of his Test hundreds, and in none of them have I seen him bat anything like the way that he did in Australia. He became a completely different batsman, growing in confidence as the series went on. Cook has, like Anderson, a really steely centre and while he might give you a nice smile and friendly wave, he is actually a very driven and motivated individual. He had a horrible time against Pakistan in the summer and was an innings away from being dropped. I still think he would have opened with Strauss on this tour, but was coming into the series from a very shaky beginning and we in the media were still talking about his place at the top of the order in the practice games. To go on and bat as he did was remarkable and it says a lot for his self-effacing nature that he had really no idea, or apparent interest in, the records he had broken and the totality of his batting achievements. He just rather shrugged them off, but I suspect they will come to mean a great deal to him one day. What is clear is that Alastair needs to get hold of and keep a before-and-after video tape, because it is so easy to see what he was doing wrong last year. Geoffrey Boycott told us all about it during the Pakistan series: how he was planting his right foot in front of his off stump, getting stuck and having to bring his bat around his leg. In Australia, where he played so beautifully, his right foot was pushed forward, right down to the pitch of the ball, driving through mid-off, something he didn't do once last summer. That's all there is to it, simple footwork – and, of course, so much of batting is connected with how you place your feet. If that goes awry, you're going to struggle and, conversely, when the footwork is good and solid and it is absolutely in the right place, you're going to play well. That was the foundation of Cook's brilliant tour.

I suspect Alastair Cook is going to score more runs than anybody for English cricket – not only because he opens the batting, but also because of his age and the time he has ahead of him in his career. If he is not top of the tree by the time he finishes I will be absolutely staggered. He has an evident determination to carry on where he has left off in Australia, and will probably be Strauss's successor as captain. We don't know yet whether that will have an impact on the way he bats, but I would hope not. Every batsman goes through troubled times and that is why I suggest he gets hold of that video tape. He will have a constant reminder of why it all went so well for him in Australia. Cook has got the world at his feet right now, and wants to play one-day cricket; he really wants to be a regular in England's one-day team. If I were him, I wouldn't be too stressed about it – just carry on batting the way he has shown the cricketing world he can.

Jonathan Trott surprised everybody – well, he certainly surprised me. Again, I think he is one of those players with a core of steel, a very driven individual who can shut everything else out. His ability to focus entirely on the moment was obvious in his continued pawing at the ground – a sort of OCD he goes through. It was something he managed to control to a certain extent, but not entirely. The important thing about his at-the-crease ritual is that it did not prove to be the distraction I thought it might, and the Australians weren't able to get at him about it. I thought they would really give him a hard time, complaining about time wasting for example, but for some reason they didn't take that particular initiative.

Trott is not a naturally athletic fielder, in fact he is probably the worst in the team, but he took a brilliant one-handed catch in

Adelaide in the warm-up game, and I think something like that gives a player a confidence boost, especially if you are on that slight cusp of, am I going to play/am I not going to play? It would have given him the belief in himself that we saw at Brisbane where, of course, he cleaned up with Cook, and then in Melbourne where he was the man of the match.

He is not flamboyant, he's not pretty, nor is he necessarily an exciting batsman to watch, but he is thoroughly solid and an ideal number three, a place in the order he has made his own for the foreseeable future. Returning to key moments: his run-out of Simon Katich (who was yet to face a ball) in the fourth ball of the Adelaide Test consisted of a brilliant pick-up and throw. That sort of sublime moment helps a player feel he is really contributing. Nevertheless, there were mutterings about his and Pietersen's South African provenance, and there were moments when the Australians tried, in desperation, to use it to get at him. Even Allan Border waded in calling the England side a Commonwealth XI. The jibes proved entirely ineffectual, and while I would much rather have English players brought through the county system given precedence, something I think is important for the credibility of our selection process and our academies, it is difficult to argue against selecting people who are available to play for England.

Ian Bell was another great success story of the tour, even if batting at number six would have been frustrating for him. Paul Collingwood's departure from Test cricket will ease the way for him. Bell has had his chances at number three, but with Trott's excellent form will have lost that spot for now. He must, however, go up the order and I am sure that was part of Collingwood's thinking when he voluntarily ended his Test career. Bell is the most beautiful batsman in the England team – a glorious driver, rather like a Geoffrey Boycott with shots. I've never told Bell that, but with his lovely high elbow and with everything else in the right position, it is just like watching Geoffrey in his prime. Particularly his off-drive, it is pure Boycott. Bell has matured hugely as an individual and, ironically, if given the number three spot in the order right now, would probably make a very good job of it. But it is not so bad having him at number five. It was a big thing for him to get over the line and scores an Ashes century – a monkey he had to get off his back – and now he has it under his belt, there is no doubt the Australians accord him a great deal of respect.

Matt Prior was at the centre of everything. I can remember only two mistakes that he made behind the stumps in the entire series, and both of them were standing up to the wicket, which is never easy. What I liked about Prior was not just the way he kept wicket so efficiently, and the aggressive way he batted, but the hard work he put in during the time England were in the field. Always chirping, always encouraging the fielders – he was on the case all of the time. Wicketkeepers must fulfil that motivating role, but Prior has now matured from his early days of doing it in rather a silly juvenile way with lots of verbal stuff to the batsmen, to being a considerable part of the sheer presence that the England side have in the field. It will have frustrated him that he wasn't in the one-day side initially, but he is undoubtedly England's best wicketkeeper/batsman. He scores his runs quickly, which is so important when you are batting at number seven with the tail coming in around you. Prior has to bat positively and England couldn't have had a better batsman coming in to support Bell, and then take the game and scoring on in the latter stage of the innings, something Prior did so well throughout the series.

When I first landed in Australia, I encountered a sense of unease about the way the series would pan out coupled with a general feeling of gloom about Australian cricket, the like of which I had never known in the last twenty years of touring the continent. Although there was a lot of talk coming from the Australian camp about how everything was okay, the media knew that everything was certainly not okay – and that was how they were writing up their eve-of-series analyses. The journalists were, of course, absolutely right; in their hearts they knew there was trouble just around the corner. The administrators either felt they couldn't talk openly about how things truly were, or simply refused to see the truth for what it was. There were warning shots fired during that Sri Lanka one-day series being played (and lost by Australia) as we arrived, and talk about Ponting's future as captain was already rife. From my current vantage point, I suspect his captaincy after the World Cup is still very much in the balance. He had a rotten tour with the bat and as captain managed to lose his rag a few times, notably at Adelaide with umpire Dar and then in Melbourne over the Pietersen catch behind that never was, something that resulted in calls for Ponting to be suspended. It may well be that he is hanging on to his position by his fingernails, yet on the other hand with Ricky, you get a very professional, very business-like person who is quite excellent in press conferences – he can be both funny and thoughtful when answering at times difficult questions. In fact he is something of a split character. On the field, he tries to control everything, off the field he is entirely professional, but there are days when the red mist comes down and then he loses it. England seized on his evident disquiet and soon proved they knew how to undermine him. Although Paul Collingwood didn't contribute much with the bat during the series, he was Ponting's nemesis – playing a huge part in undermining the Australian captain's batting confidence with two vital catches, one off Swann in Adelaide and the other off Anderson in Perth.

Ponting will tell you that he didn't have much luck. Apart from Collingwood's two brilliant catches, Ponting was caught down the leg-side twice and managed to chop the ball on to his wicket on another occasion. From a batsman's perspective, they were soft dismissals. But nothing can disguise the fact that both he and Michael Clarke had an awful series. Their collective failure meant Australia's middle-order were exposed time and again, which was really the key battleground. Australia's batting was almost always up against it.

What an enigma Mitchell Johnson is. He came to England with a great reputation on the last Ashes tour but I must say I've never rated him. I don't understand why his low arm action hasn't been coachedcs out of him. Although the Australians have always been happy with slingers down the years, I don't see how he's ever going to bowl straight unless he takes advantage of the considerable level of coaching assistance available these days. Lasith Malinga is an absolute one-off in the way he can bowl in his bizarre way, almost like a discus thrower, but Johnson should have his arm higher, and until he does he will always be wayward. The frustrating thing from an Australian perspective is they can obviously see what happens when it all clicks, but Perth is the only time that I have seen everything come together for him – and I have watched him play about ten Tests now. He's got pace, but he is all over the shop, and I think Australia will have to make a decision about whether they send him away to a really good coaching clinic or they move on. Right now, they have not got the depth of resources to do that, but by the end, the Barmy Army had finished him anyway.

We were all anxious to have answered another key question, the answer to which would be critical in determining the outcome of the series. Who was going to bowl spin for Australia? It was part of this absurd hankering after the McGrath/Warne/Gilchrist/Langer/Hayden era that had well and truly gone. It would seem a lot of Australians didn't want to own up to the problems they would inevitably face once these great players retired from international cricket. There was an awful lot of nonsense spoken and written about how Shane Warne should come back into the side. Absolute rubbish of course, but it showed how desperate the Australians felt, and from what slim pickings they were trying to operate. It is very odd, really, because if you recall that Shane Warne's ball of the century was bowled in 1993 – getting on for twenty years ago – and if any 8- or 10-year-old impressionable Australian young spinner had been watching cricket then, and had been inspired to bowl spin like Warne, then that individual would be available for selection by now. I can remember everyone saying at the time, "Wow, Shane Warne is going to inspire a whole new generation of leg-spinners, and Australian spinners in particular." Well, somehow he hasn't. In Warne, of course, they had someone who could tie up an end and take wickets – a very rare asset that every team hankers after. Graeme Swann can do it for England, but until Australia locate a quality spinner, I'm afraid the Australian comeback is going to remain some way off. Some of the Australian selections were bewildering; the Nathan Hauritz saga, in particular, was just bizarre. I don't think anyone really got to the bottom of why Hauritz wasn't picked. Was there something going on behind the scenes that they managed to keep quiet? As the series went on, it seemed increasingly strange that he wasn't playing. He can bat, he has experience and would have been more respected by England's batsmen, who, frankly, got stuck into both Doherty and Beer – neither of whom came into the series with adequate experience. It all added up to Ponting lacking the control he needed when the Australians were in the field, when he had nobody to turn to when these young spinners failed him.

Another unlooked-for advantage that came England's way early on was the competence or otherwise of the team's respective selectors. Australia had Greg Chappell swanning around in a position that no one really understood – he is not the coach, he is not the chief selector, he floats somewhere between the two. While notionally head of Australian cricket, he is not in control of anything and it is something Cricket Australia are going to have to take a long hard look at. Even before the Tests got underway, the Australian squad announcement was a shambles. Instructed by the marketing men to launch the series with the squad announcement before the last round of Sheffield Shield matches were played, and with the threat of possible injury to key players, the selectors were forced to pick a cover-all-options squad of seventeen, more than the entire England touring squad. It gave out all the wrong signals, suggesting the selectors didn't know who they should be picking. Naturally, the media had a field day. I believe it also had the effect of undermining the senior Australian batsmen because it meant their replacements had already been named. That, I think, finished off Marcus North for a start, and if Hussey had not started off with that brilliant innings in Brisbane, I suspect he would have gone as well. In short, there was a lot of uncertainty and a lack of confidence in the Australian team created by this ridiculous situation of having to name an inflated squad.

Meanwhile, the England selectors had to make a number of key decisions, and, importantly, got them right. The first was about Alastair Cook and whether he should play. The faith they showed in him throughout last summer absolutely came good on this tour. I don't think England's selectors were challenged like the Australian selectors were because the selection of England's core team was known midway through last summer. Nevertheless, when they did have to make the big calls they got them right, including picking Tremlett in Perth, when they might have gone for the safer option of Bresnan, and then choosing Bresnan ahead of Finn in Melbourne, all of which really paid off. Two vital calls and they got them absolutely right.

There were times on this tour when it felt more like England were playing at home rather than in Australia. And that was down to the Barmy Army – they were loud, funny and their acerbic wit got under plenty of Australian skins (including Mitchell Johnson's). Realistically, I think, they contributed rather more than some of the old stagers might like, and the players certainly fed off the atmosphere generated by the ever-present and noisy Army. It is a shame in a way that the Barmy Army has a reputation of being too loud and intrusive, but in these big overseas grounds, which are often concrete jungles and where the Army is some distance away from other people, I think it works really well. As a team playing away from home, having a determined and passionate support behind you can make a huge difference. That day in Melbourne when Australia were in the field all day, getting slogged around and knowing they were going to lose, the Australian fielders were gradually picked off by the Barmy Army. There was nowhere for them to hide. From an Australian perspective, it was very intimidating. When several thousand England supporters stand up, sing at the tops of their voices and chant invective, believe me you don't want to be fielding in their vicinity.

I've always dreamt about being in Australia to see England win the Ashes and, if I am honest, there have been times over the last twenty years when I thought it might not happen in my lifetime. So in retrospect, was the experience all that I hoped it would be? The answer is a definitive yes. To tour Australia and experience a completely different atmosphere in the press and commentary boxes, to be among people who, on past tours, would somehow walk taller and unintentionally (or otherwise) look down their noses at me as the England correspondent, giving me the 'bad luck mate' smile as I walked past. Instead, this time, it couldn't have been more different. I often encountered an appreciative, respectful nod. The Channel Nine lot were very polite and Bill Lawry and Ian Chappell, who in the past had given me a good old friendly sledge, were entirely respectful of England. This is a team that has won over the Australian media (and many former Australian players) with their professionalism, fielding and the skill they showed with the ball. It was a brilliant experience to see this complete transformation in the attitude of the Australians including their supporters – evident from the contents of various phone-in programmes I heard. It is the first time that I've been in Australia and experienced such a reaction to an England performance. It made me proud to be English, which is a bit of a cliché, but all of the English journalists I spoke to who covered the tour said they did so with a great deal of pride. It helped enormously that the players and England management set-up are just such a decent bunch of people.

Just before the Tests began, I had said to Andrew Strauss that he and his team should make sure they enjoyed the series. On balance, by the end, I believe that they did. Of course poor old Strauss's tour had a rocky start with his third-ball dismissal in Brisbane, but as the tide turned and the match was saved, they began to love it. They have got a really strong support system within the team, a very good team spirit, and one that can involve Kevin Pietersen, who is clearly not an outsider. I still think Shane Warne was wrong in saying before the First Test that his friend Pietersen had been pushed outside the team. Pietersen is a bit different to everyone else, he exists without the team structure, but that doesn't mean you can't include such a strong individulalist in the team, and equally a strong team can include all sorts of characters, yet still make them feel part of the overall set-up. England achieved that. Right now, I think anyone can actually go and play in the current England set-up and be made to feel welcome – something that is both rare and important. Paul Collingwood's retirement from Test cricket was, from a timing point of view, about as good as it gets. He leaves a triumphant England side with the ability, temperament and organisation to go on and become the best Test-playing side in the world. Roll on 2013.

HOW THE ASHES WERE WON

Tom Fordyce | 7 January 2011

Three innings victories. The highest total ever scored on Australian soil. A 3-1 series win that left Australia on their knees. We all know the happy facts. But what were the key reasons behind England's remarkable Ashes triumph of 2010-11? Here is my top ten.

1. Proper preparation

Four years ago, England played almost no first-class cricket before the First Test at the Gabba. This time around, they played two three-day games and one four-day fixture and took them all extremely seriously. The Test batsman played all three; the first-choice bowlers played the first two and then travelled to Brisbane to acclimatise while the reserve bowlers, including Chris Tremlett and Tim Bresnan, honed their skills. When England arrived Down Under, Australia were doing things rather differently, playing one-day cricket against Sri Lanka. They began the Test series with several players unfit (Doug Bollinger, Ryan Harris) and were playing catch-up from then on.

2. Super selections

England's picks came off every time. Both Tremlett and Bresnan attracted criticism when originally selected for the touring party, but both played pivotal roles in the eventual triumph. Tremlett took 17 wickets in his three matches, Bresnan 11 in his two. Steven Finn had been England's leading wicket-taker when he was rested after Perth, but the decision to leave him out of the last two Tests proved to be correct. Australia's selectors on the other hand were an unmitigated disaster. Overly influenced by the marketing department, they named their initial squad ten days before the First Test and so had to name 17 players, more than England's entire touring party. Xavier Doherty bombed; Bollinger was picked when unfit and, in his captain's words "hit the wall"; Phillip Hughes got the nod despite woeful domestic form and continued in exactly the same vein; Steve Smith was never a Test number six; and the all-pace attack was found horribly wanting in Melbourne.

3. Contrasting captains

Once the nightmare of that first-over duck in Brisbane was out of the way, almost everything Andrew Strauss tried worked out. His field placings were solid, his bowling plans spot on; with the bat he averaged over 40. In stark contrast, Ricky Ponting had his worst series in memory, hapless with the bat, fidgety in the field and unable to arrest his side's alarming decline. "Ponting needed to score runs," says former England skipper Michael Vaughan. "You get to the stage as a captain when you're under pressure that you start looking at too many other areas: you start looking at your PR, how the media are treating you, when fundamentally you just need to score runs. Ponting didn't. If he had scored his usual runs and averaged, say, 50, Australia would have had something for their bowlers to aim at. Their bowlers have been criticised a lot, but it's their top six that just hasn't worked on pitches that have been good, and Ponting should have been their leading light."

4. Tactical triumphs

England bowled to carefully worked out plans devised by coach Andy Flower and bowling coach David Saker, based on hours of video footage and laptop analysis. They then had the skill to implement those plans. Australia seemed unable to identify English weaknesses; they targeted Jonathan Trott's body in Melbourne, allowing him to score 80 per cent of his runs through the leg side, and then fed Matt Prior outside off stump during his rapid-fire century in Sydney. "For Peter Siddle not to bowl one ball round the wicket at Alastair Cook in the Fifth Test, when he scored 189, was scandalous," says Michael Vaughan. "The result in Perth didn't actually help them. It made them produce a green wicket in Melbourne, and England's bowlers destroyed them. If they'd produced a normal wicket in Melbourne and given their batsmen a chance to get 400 in the first innings, they may have had a chance. That's an example of the sort of error England just didn't make."

5. Runs on the board

England decided before the series began that their best bet was to use scoreboard pressure to attack Australia. They delivered in no small measure. Cook scored more runs in a Test series than all but one man – Wally Hammond – in history. The team compiled two of their biggest ever innings scores, and a new series record of nine centuries were scored. Australia only scored 400 once in the series. Not one of their top four batsmen scored a century, the first time that has happened since 1956. They were simply outbatted.

6. Bowling brilliance

England's attack was supposed to struggle with the Kookaburra ball on Australian pitches. Instead, it dominated. With the invaluable inside knowledge of Victoria-born Saker, the fast bowlers found conventional swing early on and reverse-swing much earlier – and to a much greater extent – than any touring England team had ever done before. When the ball wasn't moving around, their relentless accuracy squeezed the life out the Australian top order. James Anderson's 24 wickets was the best haul achieved in Australia by an English bowler since Frank Tyson in the 1950s. Tremlett took 17 in three, Finn 16 from the same number and Bresnan 11 from two. With the exception of Perth, Australia's best just couldn't get close.

7. Perfect pairs

England's batsmen produced 11 century partnerships. Australia produced four. With the ball it was the same one-sided story. There was rarely a loose end when England were bowling, the bowlers hunting in pairs to leave the opposition no room to relax, but when Australia bowled, relief was always at hand. Never was this more obvious than in Adelaide, where Harris's hard work was wasted as Doherty and Bollinger were punished at the other end.

8. Catches win matches

This is undoubtedly the best England fielding side of all time, and specialist coach Richard Halsall deserves enormous praise. Collingwood took nine catches in the series, Strauss eight, Swann six, far more than managed by any Australian. It wasn't just the number of catches either, although those were remarkable; barely any went down, and the best (Collingwood off Ponting in Perth, Strauss off the same man in Adelaide) were outstanding. England pulled off four run-outs, two of them from a man – Trott – who no one would have had down as an ace fielder, and dived and chased relentlessly. Australia not only dropped catches (Johnson off Strauss in Brisbane being the most costly) but even failed to touch them (Haddin and Watson off Strauss in Perth). They missed at least four clear run-out chances and then ran between the wickets themselves like amateurs. In their past 11 Tests they have conceded ten run-outs and made just four. Once the world's premier fielding unit, they are now among the weakest.

9. Spin supremacy

Graeme Swann took 15 wickets on pitches that have broken lesser finger spinners. He did so with an economy rate of 2.72 runs an over. Australia's spinners (Doherty, Beer, North and Smith) between them took five wickets at a cost of 666 runs, beastly numbers indeed. "When Swann has had the conditions in his favour, he's taken wickets," says Vaughan. "When he hasn't, he has blocked up an end so the pace bowlers could have a rest. In Adelaide, without his wickets and with the weather coming in, England would have drawn that game. If they had then been 1-0 down after the Perth Test, having to win the last two matches to win the series, it would never have happened."

10. A team game

Every England player contributed in at least one match. They make up four of the five leading wicket-takers, have seven of the top nine individual scores and all three of the top catchers. "Cook got man of the series, but you could pick out three or four guys who played major roles," says Vaughan. "Anderson has been brilliant throughout; Tremlett came in and played a massive role; Trott had his best series to date; and Prior was exemplary behind the stumps and made valuable runs in the last two Tests. That's what happens in good teams, someone always sticks their hand up, but it's not always the same person."

The simple truth is that the best team won. England had better players from 1 through to 11. Only Hussey would have made a composite team. Whichever yardstick you choose – batsmen, bowlers, captain or backroom staff – England had the upper hand. For Australia, they are in for a serious period of rebuilding before the Ashes comes round again.

THE RECORDS

Series averages

England

Batting & Fielding

Name	M	Inns	NO	Runs	HS	Avg	SR	100	50	Mins	Balls	4s	6s	Ct	St
AN Cook	5	7	1	766	235*	127.66	53.26	3	2	2151	1438	81	1	5	0
IJL Trott	5	7	2	445	168*	89.00	50.39	2	1	1234	883	52	0	1	0
IR Bell	5	6	1	329	115	65.80	56.14	1	3	814	586	38	1	3	0
KP Pietersen	5	6	0	360	227	60.00	63.94	1	1	775	563	50	1	5	0
MJ Prior	5	6	1	252	118	50.40	78.26	1	1	545	322	25	2	23	0
AJ Strauss	5	7	0	307	110	43.85	51.85	1	3	761	592	39	1	8	0
GP Swann	5	5	1	88	36*	22.00	88.88	0	0	172	99	9	1	6	0
TT Bresnan	2	2	0	39	35	19.50	32.50	0	0	138	120	5	0	0	0
PD Collingwood	5	6	0	83	42	13.83	46.62	0	0	259	178	8	0	9	0
CT Tremlett	3	4	1	19	12	6.33	36.53	0	0	72	52	1	0	0	0
JM Anderson	5	5	0	22	11	4.40	26.50	0	0	113	83	3	0	4	0
ST Finn	3	3	2	3	2	3.00	37.50	0	0	9	8	0	0	2	0
SCJ Broad	2	1	0	0	0	0.00	0.00	0	0	1	1	0	0	0	0
Totals	55	65	9	2713	235*			9	11	7044	4925	311	7	66	0
			Extras	151										subs	0
			Total	2864		51.14								66	

Bowling

Name	Overs	Mdn	Runs	Wkts	Avg	RpO	SR	NB	Wd	BB	5I	10M
KP Pietersen	5	0	16	1	16.00	3.20	30.00	0	0	1/10	0	0
TT Bresnan	82.4	25	215	11	19.54	2.60	45.09	0	4	4/50	0	0
CT Tremlett	122.3	28	397	17	23.35	3.24	43.23	6	2	5/87	1	0
JM Anderson	213.1	50	625	24	26.04	2.93	53.29	0	4	4/44	0	0
ST Finn	107.4	9	464	14	33.14	4.30	46.14	2	2	6/125	1	0
PD Collingwood	31	6	73	2	36.50	2.35	93.00	0	3	1/3	0	0
GP Swann	219.1	43	597	15	39.80	2.72	87.66	0	0	5/91	1	0
SCJ Broad	69.5	17	161	2	80.50	2.30	209.50	1	2	1/18	0	0
Totals	851	178	2548	86				9	17	6/125	3	0
	b/lb/pen	83	4		run outs							
	Total	2631	90	29.23	3.09	56.73						

Australia

Batting & Fielding

Name	M	Inns	NO	Runs	HS	Avg	SR	100	50	Mins	Balls	4s	6s	Ct	St
MEK Hussey	5	9	0	570	195	63.33	52.53	2	3	1582	1085	67	3	5	0
SR Watson	5	10	1	435	95	48.33	48.17	0	4	1209	903	57	1	5	0
BJ Haddin	5	9	1	360	136	45.00	54.87	1	3	906	656	35	5	8	1
SPD Smith	3	6	1	159	54*	31.80	49.07	0	1	455	324	15	0	2	0
Usman Khawaja	1	2	0	58	37	29.00	34.52	0	0	209	168	7	0	0	0
SM Katich	2	4	0	97	50	24.25	46.85	0	1	291	207	11	0	1	0
MJ Clarke	5	9	0	193	80	21.44	44.16	0	1	578	437	24	0	3	0
PM Siddle	5	9	1	154	43	19.25	56.41	0	0	343	273	15	1	2	0
MG Johnson	4	7	0	122	62	17.42	58.37	0	2	275	209	13	2	0	0
MJ North	2	3	0	49	26	16.33	36.02	0	0	162	136	7	0	1	0
PJ Hughes	3	6	0	97	31	16.16	38.80	0	0	364	250	11	0	0	0
RT Ponting	4	8	1	113	51*	16.14	51.59	0	1	334	219	14	1	4	0
BW Hilfenhaus	4	7	2	55	34	11.00	50.92	0	0	166	108	7	1	1	0
XJ Doherty	2	3	0	27	16	9.00	46.55	0	0	85	58	4	0	0	0
MA Beer	1	2	1	4	2*	4.00	15.38	0	0	32	26	0	0	1	0
RJ Harris	3	5	1	14	10*	3.50	37.83	0	0	66	37	2	0	0	0
DE Bollinger	1	2	2	7	7*	–	36.84	0	0	21	19	1	0	0	0
Totals	**55**	**101**	**11**	**2514**	**195**			**3**	**16**	**7078**	**5115**	**290**	**14**	**33**	**1**
			Extras	117							subs				0
			Total	2631		29.23									33

Bowling

Name	Overs	Mdn	Runs	Wkts	Avg	RpO	SR	NB	Wd	BB	5I	10M
RJ Harris	83.4	19	281	11	25.54	3.35	45.63	0	2	6/47	1	0
PM Siddle	147.1	28	484	14	34.57	3.28	63.07	9	6	6/54	2	0
MG Johnson	136.3	22	554	15	36.93	4.05	54.60	2	5	6/38	1	0
BW Hilfenhaus	157.5	42	415	7	59.28	2.62	135.28	6	5	3/121	0	0
SR Watson	76	19	223	3	74.33	2.93	152.00	3	6	1/30	0	0
XJ Doherty	75.5	11	306	3	102.00	4.03	151.66	0	0	2/41	0	0
MJ North	38	3	110	1	110.00	2.89	228.00	0	0	1/47	0	0
MA Beer	38	3	112	1	112.00	2.94	228.00	1	0	1/112	0	0
DE Bollinger	29	1	130	1	130.00	4.48	174.00	0	2	1/130	0	0
MEK Hussey	1	0	2	0	–	2.00	–	0	0	–	0	0
MJ Clarke	3.2	0	13	0	–	3.90	–	0	0	–	0	0
SPD Smith	31	3	138	0	–	4.45	–	0	0	–	0	0
Totals	**817.2**	**151**	**2768**	**56**				**21**	**26**	**6-38**	**4**	**0**
		b/lb/pen	96	0	run outs							
		Total	2864	56	51.14	3.50	87.57					

Series summary

Centuries

England scored nine centuries to Australia's three. England's nine centuries is the most that they have scored in an Ashes series, having scored eight in each of the 1924/25, 1928/29, 1938 and 1985 series.

England

Score	Name	Venue
235*	AN Cook	Brisbane
227	KP Pietersen	Adelaide
189	AN Cook	Sydney
168*	IJL Trott	Melbourne
148	AN Cook	Adelaide
135*	IJL Trott	Brisbane
118	MJ Prior	Sydney
115	IR Bell	Sydney
110	AJ Strauss	Brisbane

Australia

Score	Name	Venue
195	MEK Hussey	Brisbane
136	BJ Haddin	Brisbane
116	MEK Hussey	Perth

Century partnerships

England made 11 century partnerships to Australia's four, including eight of the nine highest partnerships in the series.

England

Wkt	Part	Batsmen	Venue
2	329*	AN Cook and IJL Trott	Brisbane
1	188	AJ Strauss and AN Cook	Brisbane
3	175	AN Cook and KP Pietersen	Adelaide
2	173	AN Cook and IJL Trott	Adelaide
6	173	IJL Trott and MJ Prior	Melbourne
1	159	AJ Strauss and AN Cook	Melbourne
6	154	AN Cook and IR Bell	Sydney
5	116	KP Pietersen and IR Bell	Adelaide
7	107	IR Bell and MJ Prior	Sydney
8	102	MJ Prior and TT Bresnan	Sydney
4	101	KP Pietersen and PD Collingwood	Adelaide

Australia

Wkt	Part	Batsmen	Venue
6	307	MEK Hussey and BJ Haddin	Brisbane
4	113	SR Watson and MEK Hussey	Perth
4	104	MJ Clarke and MEK Hussey	Adelaide
2	102*	SR Watson and RT Ponting	Brisbane

Australia's top order struggled to get going in the first innings of each Test. The comparative scores at the fall of the fifth wicket in each Test tell a story:

Venue	Aus	Eng
Brisbane	143	197
Adelaide	156	568
Perth	69	98
Melbourne	66	286
Sydney	143	226
Average	115.40	275.00

England had the higher average partnership for all but the fourth, ninth and tenth wickets:

Average partnerships

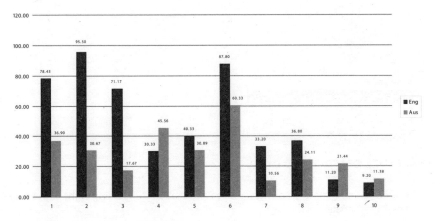

Five wickets in an innings

England

Score	Name	Venue
6/125	ST Finn	Brisbane
5/87	CT Tremlett	Perth
5/91	GP Swann	Adelaide

Australia

Score	Name	Venue
6/38	MG Johnson	Perth
6/47	RJ Harris	Perth
6/54	PM Siddle	Brisbane
6/75	PM Siddle	Melbourne

Test career records after the series

■ Career bests   ▲ Averages that have improved   ▼ Averages that have declined

Australia

Batting

Name	Debut	M	Inns	NO	Runs	HS	HSv	Avg	100	50
MA Beer	2010/11	1	2	1	4	2* ■	Eng (Sydney) 10/11 ■	4.00	0	0
DE Bollinger	2008/09	12	14	7	54	21	Pak (Lord's) 10	7.71 ▲	0	0
MJ Clarke	2004/05	69	114	12	4742	168	NZ (Wellington) 09/10	46.49 ▼	14	20
XJ Doherty	2010/11	2	3	0	27	16 ■	Eng (Brisbane) 10/11 ■	9.00	0	0
BJ Haddin	2007/08	32	54	6	1905	169	NZ (Adelaide) 08/09	39.68 ▲	3	8
RJ Harris	2009/10	5	7	2	42	18*	NZ (Hamilton) 09/10	8.40 ▼	0	0
BW Hilfenhaus	2008/09	17	26	10	242	56*	Pak (Lord's) 10	15.12 ▼	0	1
PJ Hughes	2008/09	10	19	1	712	160	SA (Durban) 08/09	39.55 ▼	2	2
MEK Hussey	2005/06	59	103	12	4650	195 ■	Eng (Brisbane) 10/11 ■	51.09 ▲	13	24
MG Johnson	2007/08	42	60	8	1152	123*	SA (Cape Town) 08/09	22.15 ▼	1	6
SM Katich	2001	56	99	6	4188	157	WI (Bridgetown) 07/08	45.03 ▼	10	25
MJ North	2008/09	21	35	2	1171	128	Ind (Bangalore) 10/11	35.48 ▲	5	4
RT Ponting	1995/96	152	259	28	12363	257	Ind (Melbourne) 03/04	53.51 ▼	39	56
PM Siddle	2008/09	22	31	7	410	43 ■	Eng (Sydney) 10/11 ■	17.08 ▲	0	0
SPD Smith	2010	5	10	1	259	77	Pak (Leeds) 10	28.77 ▲	0	2
Usman Khawaja	2010/11	1	2	0	58	37 ■	Eng (Sydney) 10/11 ■	29.00	0	0
SR Watson	2004/05	27	49	2	1953	126	Ind (Mohali) 10/11	41.55 ▲	2	15

Bowling & Fielding

Name	Balls	Runs	Wkts	Avg	RpO	BB	BBv	5I	10M	Ct	St
MA Beer	228	112	1	112.00	2.94	1/112	Eng (Sydney) 10/11 ■	0	0	1	0
DE Bollinger	2401	1296	50	25.92 ▼	3.23	5/28	NZ (Wellington) 09/10	2	0	2	0
MJ Clarke	1704	822	21	39.14 ▼	2.89	6/9	Ind (Mumbai) 04/05	1	0	69	0
XJ Doherty	455	306	3	102.00	4.03	2/41 ■	Eng (Brisbane) 10/11 ■	0	0	0	0
BJ Haddin	0	0	0	-	-	-	-	0	0	118	3
RJ Harris	925	488	20	24.40 ▼	3.16	6/47 ■	Eng (Perth) 10/11 ■	1	0	1	0
BW Hilfenhaus	3783	1906	55	34.65 ▼	3.02	4/57	Ind (Mohali) 10/11	0	0	5	0
PJ Hughes	0	0	0	-	-	-	-	0	0	3	0
MEK Hussey	186	105	2	52.50 ▼	3.38	1/3	WI (Brisbane) 09/10	0	0	57	0
MG Johnson	9689	5378	181	29.71 ▼	3.33	8/61	SA (Perth) 08/09	7	2	10	0
SM Katich	1039	635	21	30.23	3.66	6/65	Zim (Sydney) 03/04	1	0	39	0
MJ North	1258	591	14	42.21 ▼	2.81	6/55	Pak (Lord's) 10	1	0	17	0
RT Ponting	539	242	5	48.40	2.69	1/0	WI (Brisbane) 96/97	0	0	178	0
PM Siddle	4646	2376	74	32.10 ▼	3.06	6/54 ■	Eng (Brisbane) 10/11 ■	4	0	12	0
SPD Smith	372	220	3	73.33 ▼	3.54	3/51	Pak (Lord's) 10	0	0	3	0
Usman Khawaja	0	0	0	-	-	-	-	0	0	0	0
SR Watson	2601	1351	43	31.41 ▼	3.11	6/33	Pak (Leeds) 10	2	0	21	0

England

Batting

Name	Debut	M	Inns	NO	Runs	HS	HSv	Avg	100	50
JM Anderson	2003	57	76	31	524	34	SA (Leeds) 08	11.64 ▼	0	0
IR Bell	2004	62	106	11	4192	199	SA (Lord's) 08	44.12 ▲	12	26
TT Bresnan	2009	7	5	0	164	91	Ban (Mirpur) 09/10	32.80 ▼	0	1
SCJ Broad	2007/08	34	46	6	1096	169	Pak (Lord's) 10	27.40 ▼	1	5
PD Collingwood	2003/04	68	115	10	4259	206	Aus (Adelaide) 06/07	40.56 ▼	10	20
AN Cook	2005/06	65	115	7	5130	235* ■	Aus (Brisbane) 10/11 ■	47.50 ▲	16	24
ST Finn	2009/10	11	12	9	16	9*	Pak (Nottingham) 10	5.33 ▼	0	0
KP Pietersen	2005	71	123	6	5666	227 ■	Aus (Adelaide) 10/11 ■	48.42 ▲	17	21
MJ Prior	2007	40	61	11	2148	131*	WI (Port-of-Spain) 08/09	42.96 ▲	4	16
AJ Strauss	2004	82	147	6	6084	177	NZ (Napier) 07/08	43.14 ▲	19	24
GP Swann	2008/09	29	36	6	741	85	SA (Centurion) 09/10	24.70 ▼	0	4
CT Tremlett	2007	6	9	2	69	25*	Ind (The Oval) 07	9.85 ▼	0	0
IJL Trott	2009	18	30	4	1600	226	Ban (Lord's) 10	61.53 ▲	5	5

Bowling & Fielding

Name	Balls	Runs	Wkts	Avg	RpO	BB	BBv	5I	10M	Ct	St
JM Anderson	12056	6595	212	31.10 ▲	3.28	7/43	NZ (Nottingham) 08	10	1	25	0
IR Bell	108	76	1	76.00	4.22	1/33	Pak (Faisalabad) 05/06	0	0	53	0
TT Bresnan	1482	707	25	28.28 ▲	2.86	4/50 ■	Aus (Melbourne) 10/11 ■	0	0	3	0
SCJ Broad	6693	3489	99	35.24 ▼	3.12	6/91	Aus (Leeds) 09	3	0	9	0
PD Collingwood	1905	1018	17	59.88 ▲	3.20	3/23	NZ (Wellington) 07/08	0	0	96	0
AN Cook	6	1	0	-	1.00	-	-	0	0	57	0
ST Finn	1828	1207	46	26.23 ▼	3.96	6/125 ■	Aus (Brisbane) 10/11 ■	3	0	3	0
KP Pietersen	873	584	5	116.80 ▲	4.01	1/0	SA (Lord's) 08	0	0	44	0
MJ Prior	0	0	0	-	-	-	-	0	0	117	4
AJ Strauss	0	0	0	-	-	-	-	0	0	94	0
GP Swann	7431	3598	128	28.10 ▼	2.90	6/65	Pak (Birmingham) 10	10	1	25	0
CT Tremlett	1594	783	30	26.10 ▲	2.94	5/87 ■	Aus (Perth) 10/11 ■	1	0	1	0
IJL Trott	114	86	1	86.00	4.52	1/16	Ban (Lord's) 10	0	0	9	0

Paul Collingwood: Test career

Against	M	Inns	NO	Runs	HS	Avg	SR	100	50	Ct	Balls	Runs	Wkts	Avg	RPO	BB	5I
Australia	16	27	1	783	206	30.11	42.39	1	4	21	336	186	3	62.00	3.32	1/3	0
Bangladesh	2	3	0	148	145	49.33	73.26	1	0	4	6	8	0	-	8.00	-	0
India	8	15	2	597	134*	45.92	44.85	2	2	6	252	139	4	34.75	3.30	2/24	0
New Zealand	6	10	1	276	66	30.66	40.52	0	3	9	299	147	5	29.40	2.94	3/23	0
Pakistan	10	17	1	632	186	39.50	46.95	1	3	13	294	180	1	180.00	3.67	1/33	0
South Africa	7	12	2	576	135	57.60	48.52	1	4	12	222	118	0	-	3.18	-	0
Sri Lanka	8	15	1	390	57	27.85	36.24	0	2	13	275	116	3	38.66	2.53	2/25	0
West Indies	11	16	2	857	161	61.21	57.13	4	2	18	221	124	1	124.00	3.36	1/34	0
Totals	68	115	10	4259	206	40.56	46.44	10	20	96	1905	1018	17	59.88	3.20	3/23	0

Test centuries

Score	Against	Venue	Season	Mins	Balls	4s	6s
134*	India	Nagpur	2005/06	355	252	13	4
186	Pakistan	Lord's	2006	440	327	23	0
206	Australia	Adelaide	2006/07	515	392	16	0
111	West Indies	Lord's	2007	278	209	14	0
128	West Indies	Chester-le-Street	2007	264	188	17	0
135	South Africa	Birmingham	2008	288	195	19	1
108	India	Chennai	2008/09	373	250	9	0
113	West Indies	St John's	2008/09	302	202	14	0
161	West Indies	Port-of-Spain	2008/09	340	288	12	0
145	Bangladesh	Chittagong	2009/10	243	188	10	4

He was dismissed seven times in eight Tests by Sri Lanka's Muttiah Muralitharan and five times in seven Tests by Australia's Stuart Clark.

Renowned as a partnership breaker, the average partnership that he broke in Test cricket was just 42.58, well short of the record amongst bowlers with 15 or more Test wickets. England's Norman Yardley took 21 Test wickets with an average partnership broken of 92.19. The only batsman that Collingwood dismissed more than once was India's Sourav Ganguly who he dismissed twice.

Collingwood retired in sixth place amongst England's fielders:

Name	Years	M	Cts	Cts/M
IT Botham	1977-1992	102	120	1.17
MC Cowdrey	1954-1975	114	120	1.05
WR Hammond	1927-1947	85	110	1.29
GP Thorpe	1993-2005	100	105	1.05
GA Gooch	1975-1995	118	103	0.87
PD Collingwood	2003-2011	68	96	1.41

His ratio of 1.41 catches per match is second only for England to Tony Greig amongst fielders with 50 or more catches. Greig took 87 catches in 58 matches at 1.50 per match.